# Royal Families

# of

# Medieval Scandinavia,

# Flanders, and Kiev

\* \* \* \* \*

Rupert Alen

and

Anna Marie Dahlquist

Kings   River   Publications

ISBN 0-9641261-2-5
Library of Congress Catalog Card Number: 96-80004

Kings River Publications
1643 Winter Street
Kingsburg, CA 93631

# Preface

This book deals with the early royal families of Scandinavia, as well as those of Flanders and ancient Kiev and Novgorod. The latter are included in the narrative because in medieval times they were closely connected by blood and intermarriage with the royal houses of Norway, Denmark, and Sweden.

Many excellent books have been written about medieval times, and this book does not intend to duplicate the efforts of their authors. What makes this book somewhat unique is its emphasis, not upon the broad sweep of history, but upon the individual rulers within the context of their families. We have attempted to highlight their lives, and to show through genealogical charts how they were all related.

The charts are not intended to be comprehensive; not every descendant of every ruler is included in them. However, instead of merely showing how each royal line went from father to son, the charts aim to include daughters and thus to reveal how the various monarchies were related through marriages. Since the Scandinavian monarchs eventually intermarried with the continental nobility, by the end of the twelfth century virtually all of them were related to such important figures as Karl the Great (Charlemagne), king of the Franks, and Alfred the Great, king of England.

We hope the book will prove of value both to genealogists and to Scandinavians who are searching for their family roots. Many commoners of Scandinavian ancestry may find themselves descended from medieval royalty; the Svinhuvuds, the Boethius family, and many others are descended from Erik X of Sweden. If a person could trace his ancestry back twelve generations, he would find 4,096 ancestors on his family tree, and some of them just might be royalty!

It is the sincere wish of the authors that the book will be of interest, not only to genealogists, but to anyone who enjoys history and who wishes to view the medieval monarchs in the context of their family relationships.

A note about the spelling of names in this book: We have generally favored the Swedish spelling. Thus, for example, we speak of *Olof* rather than *Olav* (the Norwegian form of the name) or *Oluf* (the Danish form). The patronymic surnames also follow the Swedish pattern; so the reader will find such names as Erik Eriksson and Rikissa Boleslavsdotter mentioned in the text.

Charlemagne was born with a Teutonic name, Karl. Later, he became known to the Germans as *Karl der Grosse,* to the Spaniards as *Carlomagno,* and to the French as *Charlemagne.* To the Scandinavian people, who traditionally used the patronymic surname, he was *Karl Pepinsson* or *Karl den Store.* The more learned among them used his Latin name, *Carolus Magnus.* Some named their sons after him, and thus eventually the name Magnus became common in Scandinavia. We have chosen to call him Karl the Great in this book.

Many people have helped in the preparation of the manuscript. Special thanks is due to Mats Häger, a Swedish genealogist who provided helpful material; to Gösta Hallberg of Sweden who supplied articles from Swedish encyclopedias; and to Marjorie Hall of the Kingsburg Public Library, as well to as the staff of the main branch of the Fresno County Library, who cheerfully filled our requests for countless books on inter-library loan.

# Contents

# Chapter 1

## Scandinavian Roots and the Legendary Yngling Dynasty

Scandinavia, like most parts of the world, has been peopled by successive migrations, and in turn, the Scandinavians have migrated to the ends of the earth and have left their mark and their descendants in many different lands.

As early as 2000 B.C. tribes from Southern Europe began moving north to find a new life in what is now Scandinavia. These were primitive hunters and gatherers. As these tribes increased, the Stone Age gave way to the Bronze age and the settlers turned to farming.

About 600 B. C., the Bronze age gave place to the Iron Age with its improved tools and armor. The Iron Age also brought bands of invading Celts who were moving north and west from their original homelands in Central Europe. The Greeks called them *Keltoi*, while the Romans called them *Cimbri* and gave their name to the Jutland (or Cimbrian) peninsula of Denmark.

The Celtic tribes mixed with the Teutonic tribes and eventually adopted their culture and language.

The Teutonic languages of Denmark, Sweden and Norway were—and still are—very similar. These in turn were much like the Saxon tongue and the ancient Anglo-Saxon or Old English. Thus, in the early Middle Ages it was possible for the Swedes and Norwegians to travel to England or the European mainland and maintain a coherent conversation with people of other tribes.

The Germanic peoples worshiped the one-eyed Odin (Woden), as well as Tiw, Thor and Frey, legendary heroes who have given their names to our Wednesday, Tuesday, Thursday and Friday.

Odin was said to be the progenitor of the Yingling dynasty, and Scandinavian rulers claimed to be descended from him. The Swedish kings, Emund the Old and Anund Jakob, believed themselves descended from the Yinglings, and so did the Danish and Norwegian kings. Even the Saxon king Witikind, whom Karl the Great (Charlemagne) conquered and converted, claimed to be descended from Odin.

Thjodolf the Learned, court poet for Harold the Fairhaired and writer of the saga *Ynglingatal,* traced the ancestry of his patron back through thirty generations to Yngvi, the legendary ancestor of the kings of both Uppsala in Sweden and Vestfold in Norway. According to this poem, the kings were descended from the god Frey, who also bore the name of Yngvi. Thjodolf states, "And the name of Yngve was kept for a long while thereafter in his line as a royal name, and the men of his line were thereafter called Ynglings."

Even some modern genealogists are bold enough to list Yngvi Frey as one of the early ancestors of the Scandinavian kings. According to the old legends, Yngvi's grandfather was Sigge Fridulfsson (alias Odin), a resident in Åsgård in the first century A. D. The city of Åsgård was later (rightly or wrongly) connected in the minds of Scandinavians with Byzantium.

Sigge Fridulfsson is said to have traveled north, claiming to be the god Odin, in order to win the adulation and subservience of the Scandinavians whom he conquered. He is said to have passed through many realms—Russia, Saxony, and Denmark—passing himself off as Odin and making his sons kings of all the lands where he traveled. Leaving his son Skjold to be king over Denmark, Odin/Sigge proceeded to Lake Mälaren in Sweden, where he built himself both a palace and a temple, and reigned over all the land.

Odin/Sigge was succeeded in Sweden by his son Njord, and he in turn by his son Yngve Frey, in whose time there was peace over all the earth. We are told the following regarding Ynge Frey: "After his death he was worshiped as a god. The day Friday is named in his honor. His wife's name was Gärd."

We are told that Yngve Frey was buried at Uppsala in the tombs of the kings. A statue of him was erected at the Uppsala temple, along with the statues of Odin and Thor. The Swedish people gathered there three times a year to sacrifice to their gods and to hold their councils or *Things.* At these events, the king heard the complaints of his subjects, consulted his wise men, and, together with his people, made important decisions for his kingdom.

The modern historian has difficulty in separating mist-shrouded legends from truth. Who knows? There may have been a real king named Yngve Frey, who was later worshiped as a god. It would not be the first time a human being has been deified by descendants who wished to strengthen their claim to the throne by making their distant ancestors into gods. The pharaohs of ancient Egypt, the Inca rulers of South America, and the kings of many other countries subscribed to similar myths. Even the famous Virgil tells us that the Romans were descendants of Aeneas, a Trojan hero said to be the son of Venus.

In the twelfth century, Snorri Sturlusson of Iceland drew on Thjodulf's poem in recording the history of the early Scandinavian monarchs. The stories of the thirty generations following Odin are certainly as full of adventure, magic, intrigue, and sensationalism as any Greek or Roman myth, and the protagonists are anything but noble. Yngve's son Fjolnir drowned in a mead vat, Fjolnir's drunken son Sveigthir was lured into a rock by a dwarf, and there remained trapped forever. Sveigthir's son Vanlandi succeeded him as king at Uppsala, but was killed by a nightmare that an evil witch conjured up. Visbur, the son of Vanlandi, was murdered by his own sons who burned him one night in his hall. Domaldi succeeded Visbur, but he was sacrificed by the nobles in order to end a famine brought about by his treachery.

The remarkable stories go on and on for thirty generations. King Dag, who understood the speech of birds, perished in battle while seeking to avenge the death of his slain pet sparrow. King Agni was hanged, while in a drunken stupor, by the revengeful Finnish princess he had captured and married against her will.

King Aun sacrificed one of his sons to Odin every ten years in order to prolong his life. After he had sacrificed nine sons and attained to the age of one hundred and ninety, his subjects forbade him to sacrifice his tenth son, and he died of old age, so weak that he had to suck nourishment from a horn like a baby. While his life was ignobly prolonged, he missed out on the greatest glory a Viking could imagine—that of dying nobly in battle.

The old sagas, of course, cannot be trusted genealogically, but they do give the modern reader a great deal of insight into the fighting, revenge, and even incest that marked the unhappy family life of the early Scandinavian kings. The twentieth king of the Yngling dynasty in Sweden was said to be Adil. This legendary monarch was married to Yrsa, the daughter of King Helge of Denmark. Yrsa, although Helge's daughter, had also been his lover and had born him a son named Rolf, who later became king of Denmark.

There was, predictably, a great deal of jealousy and fighting between Adil of Sweden and Helge of Denmark. In the end, Helge was treacherously murdered by Adil.

Adil did not live long after this. While at a great sacrifice in Uppsala, he died by falling from a horse, a death which was considered shameful. Yrsa's son Rolf, on the other hand, died in battle, which was considered glorious. Rolf's praises were then sung over all of Scandinavia.

Another Yngling king in Sweden was Ingjald Illråde. From his saga, we learn something about how kings were chosen. When a king died, his successor was supposed to attend the funeral feast and there sit at the foot of the throne.

A huge horn beaker was brought in. The heir had to pledge to do some mighty deed of valor, and then drain the beaker to the bottom. After this ceremony, he was led to the throne and proclaimed king.

When Ingjald planned the funeral of his father Anund the Cultivator, he invited all the petty kings and *jarls* (earls) of the neighboring areas to attend the feast. There he stood up, made a vow to increase his kingdom by the half on every side, and drained the beaker. He then allowed his guests to drink until they became intoxicated. At this point, he left the hall, surrounded it with his men, set it on fire, and thus killed all his potential rivals. The people hated him for his treachery, and named him Ingjald Illråde, or Ill-ruler.

King Ingjald is said to have been the last king of the Yngling dynasty to rule in Sweden. According to the old sagas, he died about 600 A. D. by setting fire to his palace on Lake Mälaren and thus destroying both himself and his daughter. It was a fitting end for a man who had murdered his vassals by that very method.

In Sweden, Ingjald Illråde was succeeded by Ivar Vidfamne (Wide-Reacher). Ivar started a new dynasty, called *Ivarska* after himself.

The line of the ill-ruling Ingjald, however, did not die out. His son Olof Tretelgia escaped to Norway, where he became the progenitor of the Norwegian Yngling kings.

The records finally come down to the historical Halfdan the Black who lived in the ninth century A. D. We shall trace his story in the next chapter.

# Chapter 2

## The Kings of Norway to 1093

### Early Legendary Kings of Norway

Medieval Norway, like most European countries in the Dark Ages, was not a united nation, but rather a conglomerate of petty kingdoms. By the eighth century A. D., there were nearly thirty small realms within Norway.

The medieval Norwegians were very class conscious. They believed that each person's place in society was determined by the gods, and that children should not try to rise above the class of their parents.

At the bottom of the social ladder were the thralls, or servants. Above them were the *bonders,* or peasant landowners. Still farther up the ladder were the *jarls* (earls) who ruled as vassals of the kings. Some of the jarls wielded a great deal of authority, but none of them dared to assume the title of king. For the top of the ladder belonged only to a king descended from a king.

The kings were not always chosen on the basis of primogeniture, but rather were elected by an assembly of landowners called the *Thing.* The *Thing* would ideally choose among the descendants of a deceased monarch, not necessarily the male heir with the most "right of succession" to the throne, but rather the most able. A similar form of government existed in Sweden, Iceland, and even England. The idea that *the oldest son* had the most right to succeed the father did not gain in popularity until much later.

Sometimes two or more sons (whether they were legitimate or illegitimate didn't seem to matter) would govern Norway jointly. For example, Harald Hårdråde's sons Olof III Kyrre and Magnus II ruled jointly until Magnus died in 1069.

In the earlier days, many of the petty kings found their land too narrow and perhaps too cold for them. So back to Europe, home of their Celtic and Germanic ancestors, they came to plunder, ravage and finally to settle. The raiders came to be known as Northmen, Norsemen, or *Vikings* (which means "fjord men," "estuary men," or "bay men" in the Scandinavian tongues). They sailed the high seas, but often moored their long ships in creeks or bays, hence the term.

In 793 the Viking marauders attacked the monastery of Lindisfarne on the coast of England. Holding no regard for either Christianity or learning, they sacked the site, killing the monks and destroying many valuable manuscripts. They also made numerous raids upon France, plundering, murdering, and extorting money from the helpless Carolingians until at last the weak king Charles the Simple ceded Normandy to the Norse chieftain Rollo in 911.

In the ninth century, while the Swedes were colonizing Russia to the east, the Norwegians were sailing west and colonizing Iceland and the Faeroes. Towards the end of the tenth century, under Eric the Red, they discovered Greenland. Leif Eriksson, inheriting his father's adventuresome spirit, reached the shores of North America about the year 1000, just at the time when to the east Olof Skötkonung was becoming Sweden's first Christian king and another King Olof—Olof Tryggvesson of Norway—was being converted to Christianity by a hermit in the Scilly Islands.

In keeping with the purpose of this book, however, we will skip over most of the adventurers who left Norway, and look instead at the kings who remained there. We learn of these early kings through the writer and historian Snorri Sturlusson, who lived at the close of the twelfth and the beginning of the thirteenth century. He, no doubt, based his stories on ancient sagas and oral tradition. Although much of what he recorded, especially as regards the dim past of Norway, is certainly fanciful, there is also much which is factual. Snorri tried hard to make his record complete and accurate. He included a great deal of genealogical information about the kings of his day, making it possible for modern genealogists to construct detailed family trees.

The kingly line which Snorri traces claimed descent from the ancient Yngling kings who ruled at Uppsala in Sweden. Their legendary Yngling ancestor was Olof Tretelgia Ingjaldsson, who had escaped the aftermath of his father's conflagration by fleeing to Norway.

Here King Olof earned his nickname, which means "the Woodcutter," by clearing the forest and cultivating the land. He named his new domain Värmland and such a large group of Swedes followed him there "that the land could not give them sustenance."

After a season of bad harvests, the woodcutting king was sacrificed to Odin so that his people might have good crops. He was succeeded by his son Halfdan Whiteleg, who is said to have extended his rule over much of southern Norway. Halfdan died at a ripe old age, was duly placed in a burial mound, and his deeds were sung by the bards.

After Halfdan Whiteleg's death, according to the sagas, his son Eystein ruled Vestfold until a rival king named Skjold used his magic powers to have Eystein knocked overboard during a sailing expedition. Eystein's body was recovered from the sea and buried with great ceremony.

Eystein, we are told, was succeeded by his son Halfdan the Generous and the Stingy of Food. Halfdan gained this title by paying his men generously in coin but poorly in food. He died of a malady, was duly buried in a mound beside his father Eystein, and was succeeded by his son Gudröd. Gudröd is considered to be a historical personage, although the tales that are told about him are no doubt at least partly legendary.

### Gudröd Halfdansson — ruled during early 800's.

*"If Harald Redbeard won't give me his daughter Åsa, I shall kill him and get her by force!"*

Gudröd Halfdansson ruled over the petty kingdoms of Vestfold and Hedemark in southeastern Norway, as well as over the lesser known regions of Toten and Jylland. His reign extended to Hadaland on Norway's western shores, but not as far north as Sogn or Trondheim.

Gudröd ("Good Ruler") was married first of all to Ålfhild, daughter of King Ålfar of Ålfheim. They had a son named Olof.

When Ålfhild died, Gudröd desired to marry Åsa, daughter of Harald Redbeard, king of Agthir in the extreme south of Norway. Harald refused his permission, so Gudröd killed Harald, got Åsa by force, took her home and married her. Åsa bore him three sons—Erik, an unnamed second son, and Halfdan—but she was not happy about being kidnapped by her father's murderer. When her baby Halfdan was but one year old, Åsa got her revenge. One dark night she sent her page to stab Gudröd in his drunken stupor.

The throne then went to Olof, Halfdan's half brother, who was twenty years his senior. When Olof succumbed to a leg disease, Halfdan became king in Vestfold at the age of eighteen. In English he has become known as Halfdan the Black. His chief claim to fame is that he was the father of Harald the Fairhaired.

**Halfdan Svarte ("the Black")—ruled from about 839 to 860.**

*"Go after Haki, and bring me Ragnhild, Sigurd Hart's daughter!"* Snorri tells us that Halfdan, the son of a kidnapped princess, spoke in this manner when he planned to do some kidnapping of his own.

Halfdan's first wife was Ragnhild, the daughter of Harald Goldenbeard, king of Sogn in western Norway. Since Harald Goldenbeard had no sons, he gave Sogn to Halfdan the Black, his son-in-law. This dowry greatly increased Halfdan's domains, so that by the time he died, his kingdom was larger and better organized than any other in the whole of Norway. He forced his people to pay taxes, something they had never had to do under previous rulers. Yet the people regarded him as a wise and fair ruler.

Halfdan the Black's second wife was also named Ragnhild. Scandinavians call her Ragnhild Sigurdsdotter, but in English her patronymic surname could be spelled *Sigurd's daughter*. Snorri relates how she was the orphaned daughter of Sigurd Hart, who had been killed by the berserker Haki of Hadeland. Haki intended to marry Ragnhild Sigurdsdotter. But while the berserker was still recovering from battle wounds, Halfdan the Black told his retainer, "Go after Haki, and bring me Ragnhild."

Halfdan's men surrounded Haki's hall, kidnapped the bride and her young brother Gudorm, collected all the booty they could find, then set fire to the hall and fled. Haki followed them, vowing to take vengeance, but died along the way. King Halfdan married Ragnhild that very day, she became a powerful queen, and bore to Halfdan a son named Harald. He is known to history as Harald the Fairhaired.

About the year 860, when he was forty years old, Halfdan the Black made a trip over thin ice, fell into a lake and was drowned. His ten-year-old son Harald succeeded him as king.

**Harald I Hårfager ("the Fairhaired")—from about 860 to 933.**

*"I have no use for petty kings, Harald. But if you'll conquer all of Norway, I'll gladly marry you."* As Snorri tells it, this was the challenge that a woman named Gyda threw out to Harald. And he rose to meet it, becoming the first truly national ruler of Norway.

Harald's Teutonic name, like its English equivalent "Harold," means "mighty in battle," and he certainly lived up to it. At first Harald the Fairhaired ruled only his father's realm, a small area of southern Norway. In his boyhood, his uncle Gudorm acted as regent.

From childhood, Harald must have felt that he was destined to rule a great kingdom. His mother had dreamed that her children would flourish like a great tree with blood-red roots, green trunk, and snow-white branches which would cover the whole of Norway. His father dreamed that he had the longest hair of any man on earth, and that it hung down in many ringlets, symbolizing his many descendants.

Yet, according to the old sagas, Harald's rise to power was due more than anything else to the ambition of the woman to whom he felt attracted. Gyda told her suitor that she had no use for "little kings." But if he would conquer all of Norway, she would gladly become his queen.

Harald was so anxious to win Gyda's hand that he vowed he would not cut his fair hair until he had proven his worth to her. Although the story of Gyda is thought by most historians to be mostly myth, Harald's unification of Norway is fact.

After eight years of warring against other petty kings, Harald won a decisive victory at Hafrs Fjord. The poet Thorbjörn describes the battle in alliterative verse reminiscent of the style of *Beowulf:*

*They carried a host of warriors with white shields*
*And spears from the Westlands,*
*And Welsh-wrought swords.*
*The berserkers were roaring ...*
*The wolf-coated warriors howling,*
*And the irons clattering.*

The traditionally accepted date for the battle is 872, although some historians feel it probably took place closer to the year 900. After the battle, Harald was recognized as the undisputed king of all Norway. He then is said to have married Gyda. His reign, which lasted for more than sixty years, is remarkable for its longevity even by today's standards.

Harald the Fairhaired thus accomplished in Norway what Karl the Great did on the Continent and what Alfred the Great did in England. The fractured jarldoms and petty kingdoms were melded together under one great sovereign, and Norway became a unified nation for the first time.

Harald had many wives besides Gyda, and he fathered many children. Some sources say he had twenty sons, some say he had sixteen, and the most conservative sagas name nine. One of them, Håkan, was raised in England as the foster son of King Athelstan.

We are told that Gyda's children were Ålof, Hroerek, Sigtrygg, Fröthi, and Thorgils. Another wife, Svanhild, bore Olof, Björn, and Ragnar to Harald. There was also Åshild, who bore him four children.

Still another of Harald's wives was Ragnhild the Powerful, a daughter of King Erik of Jutland. Snorri says that when Harald married Ragnhild he let eleven of his other wives go. Their son, named for his maternal grandfather, was later called Erik Bloodaxe.

In his old age, we are told that Harald fell in love with a maiden named Sanefrid. Among the sons she bore to Harald was Sigurd—often called Sigurd Rese or Hrisi, meaning "the bastard."

It was during Harald's reign that Rollo (called Ganger-Hrolf by Snorri) came to Normandy. The reason Rollo left Norway for France was probably because Harald the Fairhaired chased him—along with many other petty kings or chieftains—away from their lands. When Rollo got to Normandy, he conquered it and left there a line of Vikings that became ancestors of William the Conqueror and the modern rulers of England.

Harald kept adding the lands of the exiled chieftains to his domains. He divided his growing kingdom into districts, placing a *jarl* or earl in charge of each one. The jarl was allowed to keep one third of the taxes he collected for the king, but he was also required to maintain a standing army that would be at the king's beck and call.

Harald greatly enlarged the Norwegian navy, fighting many sea battles and eventually conquering the Hebrides Islands.

In 912 Harald assembled a *Thing* and there publicly gave his multitudinous sons the royal title and divided his kingdom among them. Generally speaking, each was sent to rule the part of Norway from which his mother had come. The result was that Norway, which had been united under Harald, was destined to become once again a fractured federation of small kingdoms. However, Harald's many sons were required to submit to Erik—the favorite son, and the most royal since his mother was a genuine princess—as their overlord.

At last Harald died of old age and was duly buried with great ceremony in a royal mound at Haugar, in southwestern Norway. Upon his death, his fifteen-year-old son Håkan left England and returned to Norway hoping to rule. The other sons also had high hopes, and refused to submit to Erik. Harald united Norway under his rule, but unfortunately he did not manage to maintain unity within his family. His son Erik had to fight to maintain the position of high king.

### Erik I Haraldsson "Bloodaxe"—ruled from about 933 to 935.

*"Prepare to meet your death, my brother!"* Erik may have muttered to himself. *"You will kiss the lips of my bloody axe!"*

Erik, son of Harald and Ragnhild, was his father's favorite. His name, oft repeated among Scandinavian royalty, means "ever king." (The Teutonic root *rik,* meaning king or ruler, is easily discernible in this and many other Scandinavian names.)

Upon Harald's death about 933 Erik assumed the role of high king, but he earned the epithet Bloodaxe because of his violent deeds. He burned his brother Ragnvald in his hall, slew his brother Björn for failing to pay tribute, and killed two more brothers, Olof and Sigröth, in battle. In all, he is said to have killed seven of his brothers.

Unhappy with this state of affairs, the remaining brothers ousted him about 935. Sigurd, jarl of Lade, joined in the effort to force Erik into exile. The high throne then went to Erik's younger half brother, Håkan the Good, while the exiled Erik ravaged foreign shores.

Erik (who was half Danish himself, through his mother) was married to Gunnhild, a daughter of King Gorm the Old of Denmark. Their sons—all of them warriors to the core—were Gamle, Harald, Ragnfröd, Gudröd, and Sigurd Sleva.

Erik was everything that the word "Viking" calls to mind. He wielded his bloody axe in many lands, including England. His family went with him to York, and so his sons were raised there. For two brief periods, Erik was king of York, but the first time he was expelled, and the second time, in 954, he was killed in a bloody battle at Stainmore in Northumberland. His widow Gunnhild fled with her five sons to her brother Harald Bluetooth in Denmark.

### Sigurd Rese—ruled in Ringerike during the tenth century

One of Erik's vassal half brothers was Sigurd Rese. The root "Sig" in his name means "victorious" and is found in many Teutonic names.

Sigurd the Bastard, as he was known, was the son of Sanefrid of Ringerike—a district northeast of modern Oslo. As a young man, Sigurd was sent to his mother's people in Ringerike. There he grew up to be "well trained in all accomplishments," according to Snorri. Upon his father's death, Sigurd became the kinglet of Ringerike. Sigurd's son was Halfdan Sigurdsson, another small-time king.

Halfdan Sigurdsson's heir, named for his grandfather, was Sigurd Syr. Although Sigurd Syr was never more than a petty king himself, he became the father of the famous Harald Hårdråde, who traveled to the ends of the known world and who ruled Norway from 1047 to 1066. These family ties may be noted on Chart 1, *The Family of Harald the Fairhaired.*

**Håkan I Haraldsson "the Good" —ruled from about 935 to 961.**

*"Go ahead. Offer sacrifices to Thor and Odin. I'd rather keep the peace than force all of you to become Christians."* This was the policy of Håkan the Good.

Håkan had been brought up in England by the Anglo-Saxon king Athelstan. There he received Christian training. When he became king of Norway, he tried at first to convert his people to Christianity, but he found the task to be impossible. Jarl Sigurd insisted on maintaining the old ways, and the people threatened to rise against their king if he insisted on their conversion. So in the end, Håkan not only let the Norwegians practice the old heathen rituals, but he also reverted to paganism himself.

Håkan's reign is remembered for its fairness, peace and prosperity. He left the rule of the northern Trondheim area in the hands of the great Jarl Sigurd of Lade who had helped him come to power. And he allowed two nephews—Tryggve Olofsson and Gudröd Björnsson—who had been orphaned by his brother Erik's bloody axe, to rule in the eastern part of Norway.

In 955 Håkan fought against his encroaching nephews, the five sons of his half brother Erik Bloodaxe. These men, who had fled to Denmark upon their father's death, had made an alliance with their Danish uncle Harald Bluetooth. Håkan defeated them in the great naval battle near the island of Frei, and one nephew—Gamle—perished. The other four fled back to Denmark, vowing revenge.

In 961 they returned, landing on the island of Stord, where King Håkan was staying. Although the sons of Erik Bloodaxe were defeated a second time, Håkan received a mortal wound and died soon after the battle. Once again medieval inter-family warfare had claimed a life. Håkan's loyal subjects, believing that they were sending him on a speedy journey to Valhalla, buried him with full pagan rites.

Håkan was only forty-six years old, and he left no heirs. His court poet, alluding to the myth that the wolf Fenrir would be loosed at the end of the world, wrote:

*The wolf Frenrir shall be freed from his fetters*
*Before another such king*
*Shall follow in Håkans's footsteps.*

### Harald II Eriksson Gråfell ("Graycloak")—961 to 970.

*"I really like this gray sheepskin! Let me wear it as a cloak, and all my subjects will want one, too,"* Harald told the merchants. Forever after, he was known as Harald Graycloak.

Harald, the oldest son of Erik Bloodaxe, replaced his uncle, Håkan the Good, as Norway's chief king. His brothers helped him extend his domains, and ruled under him as sub-kings. Amazingly—for that time and that family—they didn't seem to want the high throne for themselves. And Harald, unlike his father, seemed disinclined to fratricide. With the help of his brothers he killed off two rival kings— Tryggve Olofsson and Gudröd Björnson—and took their lands. They were, of course, his first cousins, grandsons of Harald the Fairhaired like himself. But that fact didn't deter him in the least. After all, his father had killed off their fathers.

The old sagas tell how Harald got his surname. Some seafaring traders from Iceland arrived in Norway one summer with a cargo of sheepskins, but nobody wanted to buy any. King Harald persuaded the skipper to give him one. The king draped his sheepskin over his shoulders, and upon seeing him, all his subjects promptly decided they simply *must* own one, too! Soon the sheepskins were completely sold out.

Harald, along with his brothers, had been baptized as Christians in England. He is said to have tried to convert his people, but all he did was destroy their temples and break up their sacrifices. This method of "evangelism" made him very unpopular, to say the least. His subjects were also unhappy with the fact that he had killed leaders like Tryggve Olofsson and Gudröd Björnson.

Harald's reign was also marked by strife between his followers in southern Norway, and the men of Trondheim, in northern Norway, who opposed his leadership.

Harald eventually dispatched Sigurd, Jarl of Lade. This leader had always sided with Håkan the Good, and had never submitted either to Erik Bloodaxe or his son Harald. Sigurd had ruled the Trondheim province practically independently.

Harald, therefore, considered Sigurd a dangerous rival. Following the example of his legendary ancestors, Harald destroyed Jarl Sigurd by burning him to death within his own house. Sigurd's son Håkan was exiled to Denmark, but revenge against his father's murderer was burning in the young man's heart. It was not long before Håkan Sigurdsson obtained the aid of his enemy's uncle, King Harold Bluetooth of Denmark.

Civil war broke out, King Harald Graycloak's Danish relatives turned against him, and about 970 he was killed off the coast of Jutland in a battle against the men of Denmark and Trondheim.

His mother Gunnhild and her two surviving sons fled to the Orkney Islands; from there the brothers engaged in Viking raids, but at last they, too, passed away.

### Jarl Håkan and Harald Bluetooth—ruled from about 970 to 995.

After the death of Harald Graycloak, the rule of Norway passed to the foes who had vanquished him. Håkan, Jarl of Lade, ruled seven western provinces under the Danish overlordship of Harald Bluetooth. The eastern provinces went directly to the Danish monarch.

Jarl Håkan Sigurdsson was an ardent heathen. He restored the temples which Harald II Graycloak had plundered and kept up the pagan sacrifices.

Jarl Håkan, holding to the belief that a man must never rise above the station alloted him in life, never took the title of king. That honor went to the foreigner Harald Bluetooth. Håkan paid him tribute and for a while was his military ally; but in the end the two rulers turned against each other and fought some mighty battles at sea. At last the great jarl beat off the Danish king and took possession of the whole of Norway.

Jarl Håkan's subjects, however, soon tired of his greed, his arrogance and his ways with women. He had a reputation for seducing them, tiring of them, and then rejecting them after two or three weeks.

The Norwegians longed for "the good old days" and wished to be under the rule of a descendant of Harald the Fairhaired—a genuine Yngling—once more. Such a person was available: his name was Olof Tryggveson; a son of the Tryggve whom Harald Greycloak had vanquished.

A peasant named Kark murdered Jarl Håkan in his sleep, then cut off his head and took it to Olof Tryggveson. Olof, instead of rewarding the murderer, had him beheaded as well.

Jarl Håkan did not die without heirs. His descendants, the jarls of Lade, were rivals of the Yngling dynasty for many years to come.

### Olof I Tryggvesson — ruled from 995 to 1000.

*"You will become a famous king and work famous deeds. You will bring many to the true faith, and in so doing benefit both yourself and others. This will be a sign to you. You will soon encounter a traitor band, and receive a mortal wound. But within seven days you will be healed and be baptized soon after."* So prophesied the hermit whom Olof met in the Scilly Islands. And, according to the old sagas, the hermit's words all came true.

Olof Tryggvesson was a legitimate great-grandson of Harald the Fairhaired. He was brought up at the court of the Grand Prince Vladimir in Novgorod, where his mother Astrid had found refuge after her husband Tryggve's assassination. But young Olof, an adventurer at heart, was not content to remain in Russia. He set out for foreign shores and led many a successful Viking raid in England and on the mainland of northern Europe. Here his travels brought him into contact with foreign princesses. One of these was Geira, said by Snorri to be a daughter of Boleslav I of Poland. In reality, however, she was more likely Boleslav's sister — a daughter of Mieszko I.

According to Snorri (who more than most historians, enjoyed reporting royal romances), Olof and Geira took a great liking to each other and were married. Olof lived at the Polish court for three years, until Geira took sick and died. The brokenhearted Olof did not wish to stay in Poland, so he went again on Viking expeditions to Frisia, Saxony, Scotland, England, and Wales.

The Old English poem, "The Battle of Maldon," tells how, in 991, Olof Tryggvesson led a fleet of ninety-three Viking ships up the Thames, where the Norsemen plundered Kent and Suffolk before defeating the English at the bloody battle of Maldon. King Ethelred the Unready was forced to pay the Vikings 10,000 pounds of silver in order to achieve peace.

Shortly after this, while in the Scilly Islands Olof met the hermit who prophesied that he would become a famous king, explained to him the Christian faith, and persuaded him to be baptized.

After some time, Olof Tryggvesson sailed from the Scilly Islands to the British mainland. There he met a queen named Gyda, the widow of an English earl. Her brother was Olof Kvåran, a Norwegian king who ruled in Dublin, Ireland, from 938 to 980. (The Norwegians ruled Dublin, Waterford and Limerick until 1014.) Olof won the hand of the fair Gyda, who chose him over her many other suitors.

Olof made one more attempt to take London. In the fall of 994, in alliance with Sven Forkbeard of Denmark, Olof sailed up the Thames with ninety-four ships. King Ethelred once again was forced to buy the Vikings off, paying them 16,000 pounds of silver in return for their promise of peace. In the presence of the bishop of Winchester, Olof and Ethelred made a treaty in which Olof promised never again to invade England. He faithfully kept his part of the bargain, and never again participated in Sven's invasions of the British Isles.

When he returned to Norway and was made king, Olof began in a systematic way to try to convert his people. He even sent missionaries to Greenland and to Iceland, where the new religion was adopted by the Icelandic *Thing*.

The missionaries were mostly British monks and priests; the English can take plenty of credit for the evangelization of Norway. It took several generations, however, before the Norwegians were ready to accept the new religion, learn to live by the Scriptures and church rule, and to develop an ecclesiastical organization.

The Norwegians, on the whole, resisted Christianity because they did not want to give up their many wives, their heathen sacrifices and feasts, or the eating of horse meat. (The church forbade this Viking delicacy.) They also felt that such customs as penance, tithing, and fasting were too onerous. And, of course, many of them were unwilling to stop raiding and pillaging.

Olof I had many setbacks in trying to convert his own subjects. We are told that he called a meeting where he preached Christianity to the farmers at Trondheim, but they would have none of it. "Stop!" they cried. "We refused to let Håkan, the foster child of Athelstan, convert us, and we do not value you more highly than him."

Olof then spoke more gently to the farmers, and even agreed to attend their midsummer sacrifice. When he arrived, he said, "If I am to sacrifice with you, then I will order the greatest possible sacrifice— the noblest of your men." He began naming those whom he intended to sacrifice. The farmers quickly changed their mind, cried out for peace, and agreed to be baptized. In this way, many of Olof's subjects became at least nominal Christians.

Olof, say the sagas, was at times merciless in his efforts to impose Christianity on his subjects. When a farmer named Rand persisted in his pagan beliefs, Olof had him bound, and then forced a serpent to slither down his throat. Rand, as might be expected, did not survive.

Olof also destroyed many idols. When his subjects saw that the statues of Thor and the other gods could not defend themselves, many people left off their idol worship and were baptized.

If we are to believe Snorri, Olof was not so successful in his efforts to convert Sigrid the Haughty, the widowed Swedish queen to whom he felt attracted. He offered to marry her if she would renounce her pagan faith and be baptized as a Christian.

Knowing how many suitors had been rejected by Sigrid the Haughty, Olof Tryggvesson should have stayed away from her. But he proposed to her anyway, hoping to add her dominions to his own.

Snorri states that Sigrid at first agreed to his proposal, but when Olof of Norway insisted that she accept Christianity as part of the marriage agreement, she haughtily broke the engagement rather than abandon the beliefs of her forefathers. "I don't intend to abandon the faith I have had, and my kinsmen before me," she said. "But I won't object to *your* believing in the god you prefer."

Most historians doubt the veracity of Snorri's romantic tale (some even go so far as to doubt that Sigrid existed at all), but the story certainly makes interesting reading. We are told that Olof Tryggvesson, furious at being rejected, slapped Sigrid on the face with his glove. "Why should I want to marry a heathen dog like you?" he shouted.

"This will be your death," Sigrid is reported to have replied in fury, and her words were prophetic.

Later, we are told, Sigrid married King Sven Forkbeard of Denmark, a man who shared her pagan beliefs. To get revenge against Olof Tryggvesson for striking her in the face and calling her a dog, Sigrid inspired an alliance between her new husband (Sven, king of Denmark) and her son (Olof Skötkonung, king of Sweden). Sven Forkbeard and Olof Trygvesson had previously been related by marriage (both had been wed to daughters of Mieszko of Poland), but now they were enemies. Sven and the Swedish Olof were joined in their anti-Tryggvesson alliance by the Norwegian Jarl Erik, the banished son of the Jarl Håkan whom Kark had murdered.

It wasn't long before the jilted Olof Tryggvesson found a new consort. We are told by Snorri that about 998 he married Sven Forkbeard's sister Tyra, who had run away from her previous husband, King Boleslav of Poland. Tyra tearfully begged her new husband to restore her lost lands on the island of Rügen, and Olof promised her, "Never shall I stand in fear of King Sven, your brother; and if ever we meet, he shall have to give way!"

Probably the rupture between Olof of Norway and Sven of Denmark was due to the political and economic situation of the times, rather than to the schemes of Queen Sigrid the Haughty or the tears of Queen Tyra. But whatever the reason, the rift between Olof and his enemies kept growing.

Olof Tryggvesson may have bragged about how he would beat the Danes, but he was not counting on the strength of Sven Forkbeard and his allies. As King Olof sailed to Rügen, he was met by Jarl Erik, Sven Forkbeard, and Olof Skötkonung. These had agreed that if they could vanquish their foe, they would divide Norway three ways, and each man would keep whatever ships he captured in battle.

The deciding battle took place at Svölder, off the coast of the island of Rügen, in the year 1000. Olof Tryggvesson had crowded two hundred soldiers into a ship that was meant to hold only thirty-four men. It is no surprise that the *Long Serpent* capsized under these conditions. Olof Tryggvesson, clad in his scarlet cloak and holding his shield above him, tried to protect himself from the showers of lances and arrows which the forces of Jarl Erik, Sven Forkbeard, and Olof Skötkonung aimed directly at him. After many of his brave warriors fell, and the Norwegian king saw that all hope was lost, he threw himself overboard. His few remaining men, including his brother Torkel Nefia, followed his example, and the triumvirate won the day. The defeat of the *Long Serpent* was mourned by the bard Hallfröd:

*Many sank down from the Serpent,*
*Sorely wounded in spear-fight . . .*
*Never will the Serpent have another such crew*
*Though a stalwart,*
*Stout-souled king might steer it hereafter.*

According to their previous agreement, the victors divided Norway into three parts. Olof Skötkonung received part of Trondheim and the region now called Bohüslan, which had formerly belonged to Norway. These lands the Swedish king gave to his son-in-law Jarl Sven (a brother of his ally Jarl Erik) as a dowery for his daughter Holmfrid. Jarl Sven then became regent over the section of Norway that was handed over to the Swedish throne.

If Sigrid was truly a historical person, and as dedicated a pagan as Snorri paints her, she must have gloated over the results of the battle. Norway was again plunged into paganism, and the nation that had been united under Harald the Fairhaired a century before was once again torn apart.

### Danish and Swedish Kings—ruled from 1000 to 1015.

For several years Norway was ruled by these conquerors. Sven Forkbeard of Denmark was the titular head of state, and Olof Skötkonung of Sweden probably ruled Ringerike on the east coast of the Oslo Fjord as well as Bohuslän and the eastern Trondelag.

Jarl Erik ruled at Lade, and his brother Jarl Sven lived at the head of the Trondheim fjord. The town of Nidaros (Trondheim) which Olof Tryggvesson had founded fell into ruins.

The people of Norway seemed happy to have the great *jarls* ruling over them, with the "real kings" far away in Sweden or Denmark. The *jarls* let the people return to paganism, and so, as the sagas report, "they were popular men and good rulers."

### Olof II Haraldsson (St. Olof)—ruled from 1015 to 1030.

*"I would rather have you become supreme king of Norway, even though you lived to rule no longer than Olof Tryggvesson, than be a petty king like your stepfather and die of old age."* This was Åsta's ambition for her son Olof, and her words proved to be prophetic.

Olof was born to Åsta and her first husband, Harald Gränske (he was a descendant of Harold the Fairhaired, and he ruled as a vassal king in Vestfold). But Olof was brought up by his stepfather, the *jarl* Sigurd Syr of Ringerike, a fertile inland district in Norway. Sigurd Syr was also a descendant of Harald the Fairhaired, as one can see on Chart 1, *The Family of Harald the Fairhaired.*

Olof grew up with a half brother, a son of Sigurd Syr named Harald. This younger brother was destined to go down in history as the famous Harald Hårdråde.

The sagas state that when Olof was only three years old, King Olof Tryggvesson made a missionary journey to Ringerike. Little Olof and his entire family were baptized, and it is possible that young Olof was given his name at that time in honor of the visiting monarch.

For many years, Olof Haraldsson conducted Viking expeditions, ravaging the coasts of Denmark, Sweden, Finland and Frisia, going as far south as France and Spain.

Olof even got to England, helping King Ethelred regain his throne after he had been exiled by the Danes. Olof and his mighty men, according to Snorri, rowed up the Thames and broke down London Bridge. The local people were then "seized with terror of the ships, gave up the town to Ethelred, and acknowledged him as king."

About 1015, Olof and his men returned to Norway. They overturned the ships of a new Jarl Håkan, who ruled as a puppet under the Danish conquerors. (This Jarl Håkan was a grandson of the Jarl Håkan whom Kark murdered, and a son of the mighty Jarl Erik who had helped to vanquish Olof Tryggvesson.) The terrified Jarl Håkan promptly fled to the court of King Canute of England.

Olof next visited his mother Åsta and his stepfather Sigurd Syr. Here he was given a royal welcome. Snorri liked to paint his medieval queens as strong and ambitious—witness Gyda's imperious challenge to Harald the Fairhaired— and Åsta is no exception to this rule.

Snorri reports her as saying: "I shall spare nothing I have to further your progress, though I can help little with my counsels. But if I had the choice, I would rather have you become supreme king of Norway, even though you lived to rule no longer than Olof Tryggvesson, than be no more of a king than Sigurd Syr and die of old age."

Åsta's ambition for her son was realized. The local kinglets called an assembly and elected the youth as Olof II, King over all Norway.

Although Olof I Tryggvesson had tried to convert Norway to Christianity, it is Olof II Haraldsson who is credited with accomplishing Norway's conversion. In 1024, he called a regional *Thing* in order to draw up a church code, which included severe punishments for worship of the old Norse gods. However, Olof incorporated some of the old ways, such as beer feasts, into the new liturgy. Another sign of the syncretism of the old and new religions can be seen in Norway's unique stave churches with their dragon carvings.

Snorri describes Olof's character and habits. He would rise in the morning, go to church for matins, then go to meetings and reconcile people or solve their problems. He brought wise men to his court to help him revise the laws of the land when needed. He was, according to Snorri, a man of few words, yet well-mannered. However, he had a few vices. He was "greedy of money" and said to be overly fond of concubines.

Olof II Haraldsson was married to the Swedish princess Astrid, a daughter of King Olof Skötkonung, who ruled Sweden at that same time. (The story of Olof Skötkonung's trickery in this marriage will be told later on in this book.)

Olof of Norway and his wife Astrid had a daughter named Ulfhild, who married Ordulf of Saxony. From this line came Adela of Flanders, who married St. Knut, King of Denmark. And St. Knut's daughters married into the Folkung nobility of Sweden. In this rather round-about way, the later kings of Sweden were descended from St. Olof of Norway.

Around 1024, a beautiful serving girl named Ålfhild gave birth to a son at Olof's court. Everyone at the palace assumed that King Olof was the father. Only a few people were present at the birth. Snorri relates how one of them, the bard Sigvat, named the boy Magnus.

Later the king asked, "Why did you have the baby baptized as Magnus? That name does not run in our kin."

"I named him after King Karl Magnus, for he was the greatest man in the world," the bard replied. This interesting story sheds some light on why the name "Magnus" has been borne by no less than seven kings of Norway and two kings of Sweden, as well as by many peasant folks of Scandinavia.

In 1028 Olof was forced to flee the country when Canute the Great of England sailed to Norway with a fleet of 1,400 ships. Winning the hearts of the people with grand promises, Canute took over the country without bloodshed. He installed Jarl Håkan as viceroy. When Håkan died shortly afterward, Canute put his Anglo-Saxon mistress Alfgifu and their son Sven on Norway's throne.

Olof was now an exile, a king without a throne. He sought asylum first in Sweden, his wife's home. Later he went still further east to hide with Prince Yaroslav the Wise of Kiev. This was a natural refuge, since Olof's wife Astrid was a sister to Yaroslav's wife Ingegerd.

In the spring of 1030, Olof returned to Norway, leaving his illegitimate son Magnus at the Russian court. He gathered a few hundred followers who rallied to his side, among them his fifteen-year-old half brother Harald.

Olof was determined to regain Norway, but the odds were against him. On July 29, he was killed by his fellow countrymen in a terrible battle on the green meadows of Stiklestad, near the Trondheim Fjord. Olof's enemies outnumbered him two to one. From noon until three the midsummer sky was darkened by an eclipse, a terrible portent to the medieval mind. As his mother had wished, Olof did not die of old age as a petty king, but rather in a battle as king of all Norway.

Amazing miracles were reported after the battle; blood from Olof's corpse was said to heal a soldier's fingers and restore a blind man's vision. The bard Sigvat composed many verses honoring his master, and before long Olof began to be worshiped as a saint. Although he is sometimes called Olof the Stout, he is better known to English history as St. Olof, and to the Scandinavians as *Olof den Helige*. He was buried in the Nidaros cathedral at Trondheim (where his remains were eventually lost), and in 1164 he was officially declared to be Norway's patron saint.

**Various foreigners under Canute—ruled from 1030 to 1035.**

Canute the Great was now king of Norway as well as Denmark and England. He made his illegitimate son Sven, who was about fourteen years old, viceroy of Norway. The youth's English mother Alfgifu, although given the mere title of "advisor," was the real power behind the throne while Sven ruled. Sven and Alfgifu established Danish laws and began to oppress the people. The property of all convicted murderers and outlaws was immediately taken into Canute's treasury, and people were taxed for fishing, for boating, for building, and even for "Christmas gifts." The Norwegians were not happy with the foreign rulers, and they let their unhappiness be known. Sven and his mother, fearing an uprising of the peasants, left the country. St. Olof's young son Magnus, who had been in Russia since 1028, was brought home about 1035.

**Magnus I Olofsson "the Good"—ruled from about 1035 to 1047.**

*"Here is the son of Holy King Olof, whose name is Magnus. He is coming to Norway to take his father's place. I will support him in this endeavor, for he is my stepson, as everyone knows."* These were the words of Astrid, the widowed queen of Norway, to the assembly which had been called to elect Olof's successor. Everyone must have marveled at her generosity toward Magnus, who was merely her husband's illegitimate son by his maid.

When he was only a boy of four, Magnus had gone to Russia with his father, who had been exiled by Canute. But in 1035 the Norwegian nobles rebelled against Canute and his son Sven, and set Magnus up as king instead. He was received cordially by the people, who were glad to have a son of "the Holy Olof" ruling them.

That same fall King Canute died in England, after having ruled Norway from afar for more than five years. Canute's son Sven died in Denmark a year later. And although Canute's son Hardecanute laid claim to the Norwegian throne for a brief period, he later surrendered his place to Magnus. The two kings agreed that if one of them died, the other would rule both Denmark and Norway and would try to make a united kingdom out of Denmark, Norway and England.

Magnus' place on the throne was now uncontested. Sigvat, the bard who had named him, became a trusted advisor, and the kingdom thrived. The people loved Magnus, calling him "Magnus the Good."

Under Magnus the Good, the laws of Norway were copied onto a special parchment. This parchment, which still survives, is called "the Gray Goose" because of its color. The laws gave a standard for weights and measures, listed rules for patrolling the market places, and required the rulers to meet the needs of the sick and the poor.

Hardecanute died in 1042; and Magnus, according to his agreement, became king of Denmark as well as Norway. The Danes were not happy with this arrangement, and Sven Estridsson of Denmark (Canute's nephew) fought many battles for the throne against Magnus. Some of the Danes followed Magnus, and others followed Sven Estridsson. Magnus was often victorious in these clashes.

With the help of the Danish troops who were loyal to him, Magnus also fought many battles against the Slavic Wends in southern Jutland.

Magnus, according to his agreement with the deceased Hardecanute, even laid claim to England. But Hardecanute's successor—the Anglo-Saxon king Edward the Confessor—refused to give up his domain. He sent the following message to Magnus: "I have been consecrated king of this country with as complete authority as my father before me. And I shall not give up this title while I live. If King Magnus comes here with his army, I shall gather no army against him, and he may then take possession of England after depriving me of my life."

Magnus did not want to claim England without a fair battle. Slowly, he gave his reply to the messengers: "I consider it most fitting to let King Edward have his kingdom in peace, so far as I am concerned, and to hold on to the one which God has permitted me to possess."

In 1047 Magnus found himself in Denmark with his uncle Harald Hårdråde, once more attempting to conquer Sven Estridsson. While in Seeland, according to both Saxo Grammaticus and Adam of Bremen, Magnus was thrown from his horse. His injuries were so great that he died shortly afterward on board his ship.

Since Magnus left no heirs, Sven Estridsson became the uncontested king of Denmark, while Magnus' uncle—Harald Sigurdsson Hårdråde—became king of Norway. Magnus' remains were taken to Trondheim, and it is said he was buried in the Nidaros cathedral beside his father, St. Olof.

**Harald III Sigurdsson Hårdråde—ruled from 1047 to 1066.**
Harald Hårdråde was one of Norway's most colorful rulers, and Snorri's sagas made the most of his adventuresome exploits.

Since there are so many King Haralds in Norwegian history, it is a good thing that posterity has accorded them surnames. Harald I was called the Fairhaired; Harald II was called Graycloak, and Harald III is known as Hårdråde, which means Hard Ruler. Since his father was Sigurd Syr, he was also called Harald Sigurdsson.

Harald III grew up with his half brother St. Olof. Both had the same mother—Åsta Gudbrandsdotter—and both were descended from Harald I the Fairhaired through their fathers. Olof's father Harald Gränske was a great-grandson of Harald I through Björn, and Harald III's father Sigurd was also a great-grandson of Harald I, through Sigurd Rese. (The interested reader can check this out on Chart 1.)

The half brothers were devoted to each other, and Harald fought loyally beside Olof in the Battle of Stiklestad in 1030. When Olof was killed, Harald, still in his teens, fled abroad.

During the next fourteen years Harald traveled widely. His first stop was in Sweden. He gathered some of Olof's men who had escaped from the battle, and together they traveled to the court of Yaroslav the Wise. Harald was made captain of the Russian royal guard and distinguished himself in the Polish campaign of 1031.

After three years, Harald and 500 of his warriors sailed down the Dnieper to Constantinople. There they enlisted in the service of the Empress Zoe, who ruled from 1028 to 1052. Zoe is a fascinating subject in her own right for the student of medieval history.

Harald got such high marks in the service of the Empress that he was soon made leader of the whole Varangian guard (the Scandinavian mercenaries of Byzantium).

Harald is credited with leading the Varangians to many victories throughout the Mediterranean. If we are to believe Snorri, Harald conquered eighty Saracen cities in North Africa and also vanquished Sicily and Jerusalem. He bathed in the Jordan, made great gifts to the Church of the Holy Sepulchre, and rid Palestine of robbers.

When he returned to Byzantium, it was rumored that he wished to marry the Empress. Her husband at the time (she had a succession of husbands) was Constantine Monamach. This man, we are told, became insanely jealous and had Harald put into a dungeon. The Norwegian managed to escape, sailed north across the Black Sea, and returned up the Dnieper to Kiev, where he once again was welcomed at Yaroslav's court. That winter (1045) Yaroslav gave his daughter Elizabeth in marriage to Harald. Elizabeth's mother—a daughter of King Olof Skötkonung—was Swedish, so the young couple shared a common Scandinavian heritage.

Retracing his steps, Harald came back to Sweden. From there, he made raids upon Denmark and added more gold to the treasures he had heaped up in North Africa and elsewhere in the Mediterranean.

By 1046, Harald was ready to return home to Norway. He had left as a fifteen-year-old youth, but he was returning as a seasoned warrior, already past thirty.

Harald's nephew, Magnus the Good, offered him half the kingdom in return for half the treasure he had amassed while abroad. With the blowing of trumpets, a great banquet, and much pomp and ceremony, Harald was given his royal title. In the presence of a great assembly, he then poured out his gold upon a large ox hide, weighed it carefully, and divided it with Magnus.

A year later, as we have seen, while Magnus and Harald were both in Denmark, Magnus fell from his horse and died. Harald was then made king over all Norway.

Harald and his wife, Elizabeth of Kiev, had two daughters: Maria and Ingegerd.

In 1048 Harald took a second wife. According to Snorri, he did this without repudiating Elizabeth. Some modern historians doubt that the clergy of Norway would have allowed their king to live in open bigamy, so they assume that Snorri was wrong. They surmise that Elizabeth must have died in Russia before Harald left there.

On the other hand, it seems to us that Snorri could easily be right. Norway had been "Christian" for only a few decades, and it is possible that the people and even their clergy would not have frowned upon a king's having more than one wife. Furthermore, most Scandinavian kings of Harald's time had their share of concubines or *frillas,* and these enjoyed many wifely privileges, including the right of succession for their sons.

Harald's new wife was Tora, the daughter of Torberg Arnasson. They had two sons—Magnus and Olof—and we may assume that Tora patiently played second fiddle to Elizabeth who continued to bear the title of queen.

Harald's long reign (nearly twenty years) was marked by endless and seemingly pointless strife against the Danish king Sven Estridsson, a grandson of Sven Forkbeard. Harald fought him on both land and sea. When on land, he not only wielded his mighty battle ax, but also burned Danish towns to the ground. Even the great city of Hedeby, with all its wooden houses, was consigned to flames. In a great sea battle at Nissa, Harald is said to have emptied seventy Danish ships into the sea.

By 1064, it seemed that everyone, including Harald, was tired of the Danish-Norwegian conflict. Harald and Sven arranged a truce. Harald would have Norway and Sven would have Denmark, and the ancient boundaries would be respected. They agreed never again to fight each other during their lifetimes. The former enemies became such friends that later Harald's son Olof Kyrre was married to Sven's daughter Ingegerd. And after Harald died, his daughter Ingegerd was married to Sven's son Olof.

Harald certainly earned the epithet *Hårdråde*, or "Hard Ruler." Although this nickname may have referred to his cruelty, it is more likely that "hard" carried the connotation of "powerful." Although no parent today names a son Hårdråde, many people name a son Richard, which means essentially the same thing: *Ric* (meaning "ruler" in both Tuetonic and Celtic speech) plus *hard*.

In 1066 Harald III of Norway sailed to England in order to help Tostig, earl of Northumbria, in his combat against Tostig's brother, King Harald II Godwinsson of England. Although Godwinsson and Tostig were technically English, plenty of Scandinavian blood coursed in their veins, so again it was almost brother fighting brother.

Before leaving Norway, Harald had his son Magnus proclaimed king. Harald's second wife Tora remained in Norway with young Magnus, but her other son (Olof) accompanied Harald to England. According to Snorri, Harald's queen Elizabeth and her daughters Maria and Ingegerd sailed with him, but he left them in the Orkneys.

Harald spent some time ravaging the coast of Scotland and England. He is said to have burned Scarborough to the ground and to have besieged York until it surrendered to him.

On September 25, 1066, Harald joined his ally Tostig in the fateful battle of Stamford Bridge. In the terrible fray, he grew almost mad, running out to the front of the battle line and slashing his enemies with both his hands. Before long, an arrow pierced his throat, and he fell on English soil at the age of 50. His court poet wrote:

*Upon evil days has all the host now fallen.*
*Needless and for nought from Norway*

*Did Harald bring us ...*
*Ended is the life of him who*
*Boldly bade us battle here in England*

Harald's son Olof returned to Norway by way of the Orkneys. There, we are told, he learned that his half sister Maria had died suddenly at the same day and the same hour as her father. Ingegerd, together with her mother Elizabeth, sailed back to Norway with Olof III. Ingegerd was later married to Olof Svensson of Denmark, son of her father's former enemy.

Harald Hårdråde is remembered for his far-ranging travels, his adventures, his long years of strife against Sven Estridsson, and his political achievements. Among the latter was his founding of the city of Oslo about 1050. He was succeeded jointly by his sons Olof and Magnus.

### Olof III Haraldsson Kyrre ("the Quiet") — 1066 to 1093.

*"Let us eat by candlelight, and drink from engraved goblets."*

Olof III was with his father Harald II Hårdråde on the ill-fated expedition to England. After his father's death Olof and his brother Magnus II were made joint rulers of Norway. Magnus was to rule the north and Olof was to reign in the south.

When his brother Magnus died in 1069, Olof became sole ruler. His reign was one of the longest, most prosperous, and least eventful in Norwegian history.

Olof was given the name *Kyrre* ("the Gentle" or "the Quiet") in contrast to his hard-ruling father whom Adam of Bremen called "the Thunderbolt of the North." He was said to be a man of few words, but one who enjoyed the finer things of life. Harald, his father, had been content to drink from ox horns, pouring his own ale. But Olof Kyrre had cup-bearers stand at his table, pouring the drinks into elegant goblets. He also had candle-bearers stand near the royal table, holding tapers so that the guests could better enjoy the meal.

Olof built many churches and founded a number of towns, including Bergen. Norwegian power over several islands — the Faeroes, the Orkneys, the Isle of Man and the Hebrides — was strengthened, but Olof did not seem interested in roving far afield to conquer distant shores as his father had done.

Olof Kyrre was a great friend to Knut IV (St. Knut) of Denmark. King Knut, hoping to reconquer England for the Danes, asked Olof to join him in an invasion, but Olof declined. However, as a good friend, he provided Knut with sixty fully manned Norwegian warships for the venture. Fortunately for the peace-loving Olof, the invasion never actually took place, as we shall see later on in this book.

Olof the Quiet was married to Ingegerd, the daughter of Sven Estridsson of Denmark. It is of interest that Olof's father Harald Hårdråde had fought against this very Sven for over ten years, burning Danish towns, looting Danish treasures, and kidnapping Danish maidens. But now under Olof Kyrre the two nations were at peace.

Like his father, Olof had a mistress or second wife, as well as a queen. His mistress, like his mother, was named Tora, and she bore him a son named Magnus who according to Snorri "was very handsome" and "grew up at the king's court."

In 1093, while at Ranrike on one of his many country estates, Olof III Kyrre became ill and died. He was buried in Christ Church, which he had erected, and all his people mourned the passing of their benevolent and popular monarch.

## CHART 1 - The Family of Harald the Fairhaired

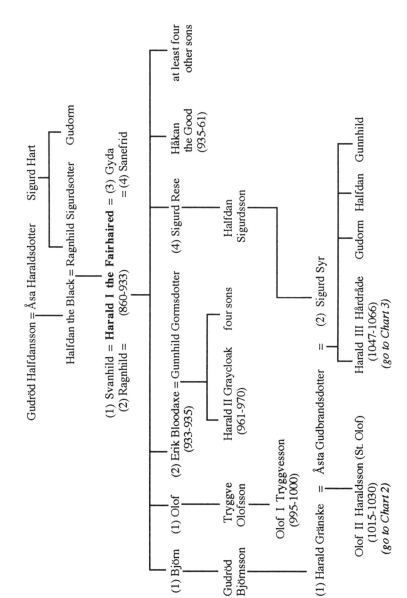

## CHART 2 - The Family of St. Olof

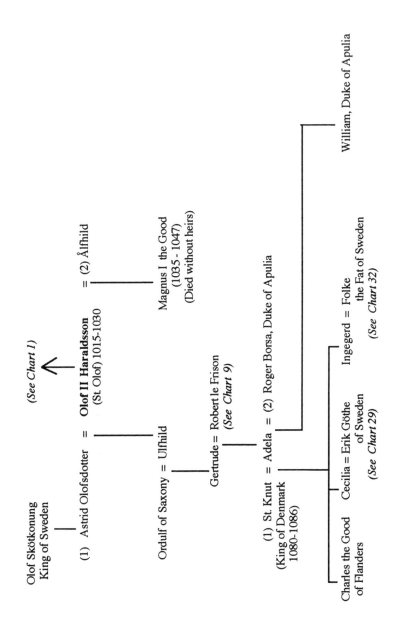

# CHART 3 - The Family of Harald Hårdråde

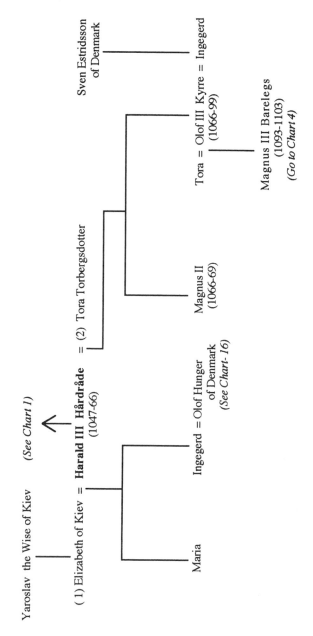

Yaroslav the Wise of Kiev    *(See Chart 1)*

(1) Elizabeth of Kiev = **Harald III Hårdråde** = (2) Tora Torbergsdotter
                        (1047-66)

Sven Estridsson
of Denmark

Maria

Ingegerd = Olof Hunger
           of Denmark
           *(See Chart-16)*

Magnus II
(1066-69)

Tora = Olof III Kyrre = Ingegerd
       (1066-99)

Magnus III Barelegs
(1093-1103)
*(Go to Chart 4)*

## Chapter 3

### The Kings of Norway from 1093 to 1202

**Magnus III Olofsson "Barelegs"—ruled from 1093 to 1103.**
*"Kings are made for honor, not for long life,"* said Magnus. His words proved to be prophetic, and he lived to be only about thirty.

When Olof Kyrre died, his son Magnus and his nephew Håkan were proclaimed joint kings, one ruling in the south and one in the north. This was the same arrangement that had been made in the time of Magnus I the Good and Harald Hårdråde, and also in the time of Olof Kyrre and his brother Magnus II. But as in the former cases, this joint rule did not last long. Some sources state that Håkan ruled for two years, while others relate that he ruled for only one winter. In any case, Håkan's rule was cut short when he died by falling from a horse. Magnus was then left to rule alone.

Snorri says, "King Magnus ... was a vigorous man, warlike and active, and in every respect more like his grandfather Harald [Hårdråde] ... than like his father [Olof the Quiet]."

Whereas his father Olof ruled for over a quarter of a century without being involved in a war, Magnus Barelegs is remembered for his warring raids upon the islands near Scotland. He made three expeditions to establish control over the Orkneys, the Hebrides, the Isle of Man, and parts of Ireland. At times, he was also in conflict with his fellow Scandinavians: Erik Svensson Ejegod, King of Denmark;

and King Inge Stenkilsson of Sweden. At one time Magnus invaded the Swedish province of Dalarna and even set up a fort—with 360 men to guard it—in Kåland Island in Lake Venern.

Like his grandfather, however, Magnus eventually made peace with these other kings. The three met at a town called Kongahälle (King's Hall) and agreed to respect the established boundaries and to make amends to each other for any booty taken in battle.

To cement the alliance, King Inge of Sweden gave his daughter Margaret in marriage to Magnus. She was later called *Fridkulla* ("Peace Woman"). Apparently she never bore any children to her royal husband.

Magnus already had a number of children by his Norwegian and Irish concubines. One was a Norwegian girl whom Snorri doesn't even mention by name; he merely states disparagingly that she was "of low birth." Magnus must have been devoted to her, for she bore him two daughters: Ragnhild and Tora, and two sons: Eystein and Magnus. Ragnhild later became the wife of Prince Harald Keisias of Denmark.

Eystein was King Magnus' oldest son. The king's second son, a year younger than Eystein, was Sigurd (later known as Sigurd I or Sigurd Jerusalem-farer). Sigurd's mother was a Norwegian girl named Tora.

The family situation of the young Magnus Barelegs must have been complicated indeed. Not only did he have a daughter named Tora, but apparently he also had two concubines by that name. Of course, the name Tora (sometimes spelled Thora) was very common in medieval Norway. No doubt parents sought to honor the god Thor by naming their daughters in this way.

What complicates Magnus' family line even more is that each concubine Tora apparently bore him a son named Sigurd. The first Tora's Sigurd (Sigurd Jerusalem-farer) was acknowledged by his royal father from the very beginning. He must have grown up knowing that some day he would inherit the throne.

The second Tora was the daughter of a man named Saxe, who lived in Trondheim. She was married to a priest, and when her son Sigurd was born, he was accepted by his stepfather and brought up by him. It wasn't until later that this second Sigurd (nicknamed Slembi) got the notion that he was of royal blood. Whether Sigurd Slembi was really a son of King Magnus is anyone's guess.

Saxe had another daughter, whose name was Sigrid. She also became Magnus' concubine and bore him a son named Olof (later Olof IV).

Still another girl, an Irish maid, claimed to have been a concubine of Magnus. Her son, named Harald, later became known as Harald Gille and ruled Norway from 1130 to 1136. His paternity has never been conclusively proven; and Magnus certainly never acknowledged him as a son.

Magnus maintained commercial ties with England, and an English merchant in Lincoln supplied him on a regular basis with arms, ornaments, and new costumes. While raiding Scotland, Magnus decided he liked the Scottish clothing styles. He began wearing short kilts, and therefore became known as *Barfot,* which translates to "Barelegs". Since he was one of the tallest of men, other folks preferred to call him "Magnus the Tall".

Snorri describes Magnus' appearance at his last battle against the Irish in 1103. "King Magnus had a helmet on his head and a red shield before him on which a lion was embossed in gold. He was girt with his sword, which was called Leg-Biter, whose hilt was carved of walrus-tooth and whose haft was wound with gold. Over his kirtle he wore a red silken jacket with a lion sewed on front and back with yellow silk." Magnus' war band was quickly overcome by the Irish, who were tired of the Norse raiders and anxious to defend their homeland. Many men were felled by Irish arrows, and an Irish battle-axe gave King Magnus a death-blow on the neck. According to the Irish chronicles, Magnus was buried at St. Patrick's church at Down.

Although he couldn't vanquish the Irish, Magnus is remembered for establishing firm control over the Scottish islands. This control was to last for many generations; the Orkney earls ruled as vassals of the Norwegian kings until 1468.

### Sigurd I Magnusson "Jerusalem-farer"—ruled from 1103 to 1130.

*"Here is a splinter from the Holy Cross. Guard it well and take it with you back to Norway,"* King Baldwin of Jerusalem told Sigurd.

Sigurd was very young when his father, Magnus Barelegs, perished. (Some authorities say he was about nine, and others say he was about fourteen years old.) He had already been named king of the Hebrides and the Orkneys before his father died.

King Magnus had not one single legitimate son, so at his death, his kingdom was divided among his acknowledged illegitimate sons. The northern portion went to Eystein I, who was about fifteen. Sigurd was given the south. The two youths were made regents for their five-year-old brother Olof, who was supposed to get his share when he was a bit older.

While Sigurd was still a boy, his father Magnus had arranged for him to be married to Bjadmynja, the daughter of Muirketach, the Irish king who ruled Munster from 1086 to 1119. This arrangement, no doubt political in its intent, was made during one of Magnus' many trips to Ireland, and Sigurd no doubt was with him at the time. Sigurd apparently remained in Ireland until his father's death. At that time, he seems to have abandoned both his wife and his father-in-law, for he saw that the Irish Muirketach had no real love for the family of Magnus the invader.

Later, Sigurd Jerusalem-farer was married to Malmfrith. Malmfrith's mother was Kristina, a daughter of King Inge I Stenkilsson of Sweden. Malmfrith's father was Mstislav I, Prince of Kiev. Although thoroughly Russian in culture, Mstislav had plenty of Scandinavian blood in his veins.

Sigurd Jerusalem-farer and Malmfrith had a daughter named Kristina, of whom we shall hear more later.

Besides his legitimate wives, Sigurd Jerusalem-farer had a concubine named Borghild, who bore him a son named Magnus after his grandfather. This boy, known as Magnus IV or Magnus the Blind, ruled Norway briefly and so he will figure later on in our narrative.

Sigurd Jerusalem-farer seems to have inherited the wanderlust of his great-grandfather Harald Hårdråde. In 1107, he launched sixty ships and sailed southward on a great crusade, leaving his brother Eystein to rule Norway by himself.

Sigurd sailed to England, to France, and then to Galicia in Spain, where he ravaged the land and killed a great many Saracens. Sailing still farther afield, he attacked the Balearic Islands and the Barbary Coast of North Africa.

He also reached Sicily, where the Norman duke, Roger II, welcomed him and spread a seven-day banquet before him. The Normans in Italy still considered themselves kinsmen of the Norwegians, and Roger of Sicily was married to Adela, the widow of St. Knut of Denmark.

At Jerusalem, Sigurd was welcomed by King Baldwin. (This King Baldwin, it may be remembered, was of Frankish ancestry. He left Europe on the First Crusade, and was with the Crusaders when they conquered Jerusalem in 1099. The following year, when his brother Godfrey of Buillon died, Baldwin succeeded him as ruler of Jerusalem, and reigned there until his own death in 1118.)

It was probably in 1110 that Sigurd and his Norwegian troops arrived in Jerusalem. Here Sigurd and his war band helped Baldwin conquer the Lebanese port of Sidon on the Mediterranean. Baldwin was grateful for Sigurd's help in extending his domain and gave him a splinter that supposedly came from Christ's original cross. Sigurd, on his part, promised to preserve the splinter at the Nidaros Cathedral in Trondheim, to collect tithes for the church, and to seek the establishment of Nidaros as an archbishopric.

Sigurd was also entertained royally in Byzantium. He told his men to ride into the city with a proud bearing, and not to show any astonishment at the marvels they might behold. A tapestry picturing the entrance of the Norsemen into Byzantium is still preserved in Norway.

The emperor, Alexius I, offered Sigurd the choice of a large sum of gold, or a seat at the Hippodrome to watch the games. Sigurd chose the games, and it was said that they cost the emperor as much as the gold he had offered.

Sigurd, desiring to give Alexius a gift in return, left his troops and his entire fleet of ships with the emperor. He then returned overland to Norway.

While Sigurd was away on his expeditions, his older half brother Eystein was building up monasteries and churches in Norway, and acting as regent for their younger brother Olof. Olof, who became ill and died in 1115 at age seventeen, is technically listed as Olof IV in the annals of the kings of Norway, but his "reign" was short and unimportant.

After ruling Norway for twenty years, Eystein became violently ill following a banquet. He died on August 29, 1122, and was buried along with his grandfather Olof Kyrre, at Christ Church. He left no male heirs—only a daughter named Maria.

Sigurd had governed Norway jointly for many years, although during much of the time he had been away from the country. He had returned from his voyages in 1111, shared the throne with Eystein and with his baby brother Olof until 1115, and ruled jointly with Eystein for another seven years after Olof died. But after 1122, Norway belonged to Sigurd alone.

Sigurd also looked greedily at Sweden. Much of Småland was still pagan, and Sigurd took it upon himself to carry out a "crusade" against the heathen Swedes. He converted the inhabitants by the edge of the sword, and demanded fifteen hundred head of cattle. Then he returned to Norway, satisfied that his Swedish crusade had been as successful as his Sidon endeavor. His raid on Småland can be accurately dated at 1122, since it occurred a year before an eclipse which astronomers have dated at 1123.

When he returned to Norway, Sigurd sensed that his traveling days were over. He then devoted himself to building. He ordered the construction of forts, a royal palace, and churches. His subjects were put to forced labor, each male nine years or more of age being required to carry to the fortification either five stones or five stakes. He also organized the Norwegian church, imposing tithes upon his subjects and incorporating the Scottish clergy of the Orkneys and the Hebrides Islands into the church of Norway.

Sigurd's pride and joy was the Church of the Holy Cross in Kongahälle. He ordered it to be built with the utmost care. In it he placed an altar-piece from Greece, set with enamel and jewels. There was also a missal, written in golden letters, which the Patriarch of Constantinople had bestowed upon him. Another gift to the church was an expensive chest donated by King Erik Emune of Denmark. And of course there was the splinter from the cross, which Sigurd had obtained in Jerusalem. Although he had promised to place it in the Nidaros Cathedral, it appears that he couldn't resist putting it in the church that he himself had built.

Sigurd could not have known that Norway was about to be plunged into a period of terrible civil war, where rival claimants to the throne would fight, murder, and perish violently.

Part of the problem was that there were no specific rules for determining succession to the throne. All male descendants of a king apparently had an equal right; it didn't matter whether they were first-born, last-born, legitimate, or illegitimate. Such a situation understandably could lead to a proliferation of impostors claiming to be of royal descent.

And this is exactly what happened. Shortly before Sigurd Jerusalem-farer's death, a young man from Ireland appeared in Norway, claiming to be the son of Magnus Barelegs by an Irish concubine. He called himself Harald Gillchrist, meaning "the servant of Christ," a surname which was shortened to Gille.

His claim seemed plausible enough. After all, Magnus Barelegs had many concubines, and he had even left a poem proclaiming his love for a maid from Dublin. But no one was ready to receive Harald into the royal family until there was some proof of his bloodline.

To prove his paternity, Harald submitted to a trial by fire. According to this ancient custom, he was required to walk over hot plowshares. After the test, he was to wrap up his feet. If, after three days, he unwrapped them and found no infection, he was considered to have passed the test.

Harald successfully walked barefoot over nine red-hot iron plowshares. After three days, his feet were found to be unburned.

By undergoing this ordeal, Harald convinced King Sigurd of his ancestry, and Sigurd accepted him as a half brother. Harald, in turn, promised Sigurd that he would not try to take the crown away from him or his son Magnus.

In his later years, King Sigurd suffered from violent fits of mental illness. He accused his queen, Malmfrith, of horrible things, and claimed that she had a goat's horn growing out of her forehead. At last he repudiated her, and sought to take as his new bride a young girl named Cecilia. The Bishop of Bergen refused to marry Sigurd to Cecilia, but Sigurd bribed another bishop to perform the ceremony. As for the repudiated Malmfrith, we do not need to feel sorry for her. She found another royal husband in King Erik Emune of Denmark.

In the spring of 1130, three years after dedicating the Holy Cross Church, Sigurd fell sick and died. He was only forty years old, but he had been king for twenty-seven adventure-packed years and had seen more of the world than many modern people, with our jet-age transportation, have seen in a much longer lifetime.

He was buried in Saint Halvard's Church in Oslo, behind the choir on the south side.

### Magnus IV Sigurdsson "the Blind"—ruled from 1130 to 1135.

*"Fight hard! We go to battle against Harald Gille, but we shall win, for the splinter from the Holy Cross goes before us!"*

At the death of Sigurd I, his illegitimate son was immediately crowned as Magnus IV. While Magnus set up his court in Oslo, Harald Gille made himself king in nearby Tønsberg, thus breaking his promise to his supposed half brother Sigurd. Some of the Norwegians favored Magnus Sigurdsson, and others favored Harald Gille, who claimed to be the young man's uncle.

Snorri tells us that Magnus was "much given to drinking...unfriendly, and hard to get along with." In fact, he couldn't even get along with his wife Kristina, a daughter of Prince Knut Lavard of Denmark. He repudiated her and sent her packing back to Denmark.

Harald Gille, on the other hand, although power-hungry and a womanizer, was "an affable man ... so generous that he begrudged his friends nothing." Not surprisingly, Harald began to win the hearts of the people away from the ill-tempered Magnus.

At first the two men agreed to share the realm, but eventually a predictable civil war ensued.

In the beginning, Magnus seemed to have the upper hand. In the famous battle in which Magnus had the Holy Cross borne before him,

Harald Gille was defeated and forced to flee. He took refuge in Denmark, where he found plenty of anti-Magnus feeling already brewing due to the fact that the Norwegian king had repudiated his Danish bride.

Because of this, it was not hard for Harald to charm the Danish king Erik Emune into giving him military and naval aid against Magnus.

Harald and his Danish forces arrived at Bergen, Norway, in December, 1135, the day before Christmas. In deference to the observance of the Holy Season, he waited until Twelfth Night to sound the trumpets for his men to leave the harbor.

It didn't take Harald's forces long to take the town from the unpopular king. Magnus was taken prisoner, blinded, mutilated and cruelly castrated. Finally in great humiliation he entered the cloister and was thereafter known as Magnus the Blind.

### Harald IV Gille—ruled from 1135 to 1136.

*"I shall kill, maim, or blind as many of Magnus' followers as I can find! Then no one will oppose my rule."*

Harald Gille's rule was short and cruel. He killed or blinded as many of Magnus' followers as he could find, first demanding their treasures. He hanged the bishop of Stavanger because the prelate could not pay the twelve gold pieces which Harald Gille demanded of him. To hang a bishop as though he were a common thief was considered one of the most heinous crimes possible.

Harald Gille, cruel in demanding treasure, was also prodigal in spending it. He entertained lavishly but neglected his subjects and their needs.

Although Harald Gille as a person did little for Norway, he left important descendants who were destined to rule long and become famous.

Harald was married to Ingegerd Ragvaldsdotter. She was a granddaughter of King Inge I of Sweden, who ruled there from 1080 to 1110. King Harald Gille and Queen Ingegerd had a daughter, Birgitta, and then a son, Ingi, who may have been named for his Swedish great-grandfather. Harald also had a son named Sigurd by one of his concubines, an illegitimate son Magnus, and another son named Eystein by the concubine Bjadok.

Poetic justice was soon to be dealt out to Harald, the usurper. Only one year after he deposed his supposed nephew Magnus the Blind, he was slain by yet another pretender to the throne, Sigurd Slembi. This Sigurd claimed he was an illegitimate son of Magnus Barelegs by the concubine Tora Saxesdotter. Actually, Magnus III Barelegs had never recognized the boy as his son.

Sigurd Slembi had an interesting life. Although he claimed to be the son of Magnus Barelegs, he was brought up by his stepfather, the priest Athalbrikt, who had married his mother Tora. (At this time the clergy were not necessarily celibate.) Sigurd was sent to the church to follow in his stepfather's footprints and study for the priesthood. He was even consecrated as a deacon. His full nickname is *Slembidiakon*, or "Gadabout-Deacon."

As soon as he was of age, he abandoned the ministry for a career more to his liking. He traveled far and wide as a merchant and an adventurer, visiting Jerusalem, the Orkneys, and Denmark, and making a great name for himself in the court of David, King of Scotland.

In 1136 he decided to return to Norway and get his supposed half-brother Harald Gille out of the way. It is said that Sigurd and his men went to the king's lodgings, broke down the door, and attacked him while he slept in a drunken stupor.

In the morning, Sigurd Slembi rowed out into the bay and loudly proclaimed himself king. Harald Gille's men, listening on the shore, refused to accept Sigurd because he had murdered his brother in cold blood.

### Ingi I Haraldsson "the Hunchback" and brothers—1136 to 1161.

*"Gregorius was my best friend. But we shall not long be parted. I will avenge his death!"* Thus spoke Ingi I shortly before his death. Let us now trace the story of his life.

When Sigurd Slembi was forced to flee, Ingegerd (Harald Gille's widowed queen) hurried to assemble the *Thing*, where her one-year-old son Ingi —Harald's only legitimate son— was proclaimed as king. He is known as Ingi I, and he ruled, at least in name, from 1136 to 1161.

Snorri informs us that Queen Ingegerd was later married to Ottar Birting, a staunch supporter of her infant son. Ottar, as we shall see, soon met a violent death, and Ingegerd once again found herself a widow. She later married Ivar Sneis, giving him a son called Orm. Her fourth marriage was to a man named Arni. Their children were another Ingi, Nikolas, Philip, and Margaret. Arni was apparently a good stepfather to young king Ingi.

While the infant Ingi Haraldsson was king over southern Norway, another *Thing* had proclaimed three-year-old Sigurd II, Harald Gille's illegitimate son, as king in the north. He is sometimes called *Sigurd Mund,* or Sigurd Mouth, because of his ugly mouth.

For three years the country was ravaged by a terrible civil war. On the one side were those who backed the joint rule of the child kings (the half brothers Ingi and Sigurd Mouth), and on the opposing side were those who backed Sigurd Slembi.

Meanwhile, Sigurd Slembi returned to Norway and brought the blind Magnus out of the monastery. Since Sigurd could not gain the people's favor by himself because he was a murderer, he thought he could gain some authority through his supposed nephew Magnus.

Magnus had the allegiance of many of the Norwegian people, but his forces were twice defeated by the supporters of his supposed cousins Ingi I and Sigurd Mouth. In 1139 Magnus and Sigurd Slembi began another attack on the forces of Ingi and Sigurd Mouth. In this battle, Magnus the Blind was slain, and Sigurd Slembi was captured. He was subsequently tortured to death in a most cruel manner. His captors first broke his leg and arm bones with the hammers of their axes. Next, they scalped and flogged him, broke his backbone, and dragged him to a tree where they hanged him. Finally, they cut off his head.

For a few years, the country was at peace. Able leaders ruled as regents for the boy kings, and all was well. Ingi was easily led and followed the advice of his statesmen. Sigurd Mouth, on the other hand, had a mind of his own and didn't want to listen to the nobles.

As a child, Sigurd Mouth was a "spoiled brat." As a youth, he was dissolute and prone to violence. By the time he became a man, he was not an admirable person in any sense of the word. His first act when he became of age was to order the assassination of Ottar Birting, the Queen Mother Ingegerd's new husband. No doubt he considered Ottar a rival, since Ottar was a staunch supporter of Sigurd Mouth's half brother Ingi.

There were other rivals. In 1142 a man named Eystein came east from Scotland, claiming to be an older son of Harald Gille by the concubine Bjadok. Since Harald had actually acknowledged the young man, the nobles had no choice but to give him a third of the kingdom. Yet Eystein was never very popular.

A fourth son of Harald Gille, named Magnus, also claimed a share of the kingdom. So Norway had four kings ruling simultaneously! Magnus, however, had never enjoyed good health, and he did not live long enough to do much actual ruling.

The king who had the strongest support during all this time was the youngest and only legitimate son of Harald Gille—Ingi. When he was very small, he was carried through a battle by one of his loyal supporters, and so badly wounded that he was crippled for life. Because of this, he was called Ingi the Hunchback.

During the reign of Harald Gille's sons, important events were occurring in the Norwegian church. In 1152 the Englishman Nicholas Breakspeare (later Pope Adrian IV) arrived in Norway as a legate from the pope. Snorri says of him that "no foreigner ever came to Norway whom all men respected so highly and who could so influence people." An archbishop, Jon Birgersson, was installed at Nidaros, at the cathedral which housed the remains of St. Olof.

In 1155 Ingi's half brothers—Sigurd Mouth and Eystein—formed a plot to depose him, claiming that a cripple was not worthy to be a king. Ingi's supporters attacked Sigurd in a fierce battle. According to Snorri, so many weapons flew against Sigurd's golden shield that it seemed as though one were looking into a snowstorm. Sigurd Mouth cried out for mercy, but there was none. Thus he perished, at only twenty-two years of age. But he did not die without heirs. He left a wife (Kristina, the daughter of Sigurd Jerusalem-farer) as well as three children which she had born to him: a daughter named Cecilia and two sons, Harald and Erik. Sigurd Mouth had also fathered a number of children by his concubines, and we shall hear more about his illegitimate sons as our story unfolds.

Now there were only two kings left. In 1156 Ingi and Eystein gathered their armies and dragon ships and prepared to engage in battle. Through mediation, they were able to make a peace agreement before the war broke out.

The peace agreement did not last long and harsh words were soon exchanged again between the brothers. Before long, Eystein, who had only forty-five ships, discovered that Ingi had followed him with a larger fleet of eighty ships. Terrified, Eystein and his men fled into a forest. There, some time later, Eystein was captured and killed.

Now Ingi was the only son of Harald Gille left to claim the throne. But his enemies, who had supported the slain Eystein, elected his nephew Håkan (the ten-year-old illegitimate son of Sigurd Mouth) as a rival king.

Håkan's mother (yet another Tora) was a humble serving woman on the estate of a farmer named Simon. Sigurd Mouth, according to the sagas, once heard her singing as he rode past Simon's estate. Her voice so charmed him that he spent the night with her. Later, she gave birth to Håkan, and Simon and his wife raised the prince along with their own children. Snorri says of Håkan that he "was cheerful and friendly in conversation, playful and boyish in his ways, and loved by the people."

For four long years, there was bitter civil war between Håkan and his uncle Ingi.

While the grandsons and great-grandsons of Magnus Barelegs were quarreling over the Norwegian throne, others among his descendants were proliferating throughout Scandinavia. The interested genealogist can find them on Chart 4, *The Family of Magnus III Barelegs.*

Magnus' daughter Ragnhild was married to Harald Keisias, Prince of Denmark. They had a son Björn whose daughter Kristina became the wife of Erik IX (St. Erik), King of Sweden.

Harald Gille's daughter Birgitta was married to another Swedish ruler named Magnus Henriksson. Later, she was married to the famous statesman Birger Brosa, who ruled Sweden from behind the throne during the time of King Knut Eriksson.

Because of his wife's Norwegian connections, Birger is said to have had a part in the choosing of the kings of Norway.

In early 1161 the conflict between Håkan and Ingi came to an end. Ingi's chief supporter, a statesman named Gregorius, was leading an attack against Håkan's supporters. When he came to an ice-covered river, he hesitated to cross, thinking it unsafe. His men challenged him to prove his bravery by trying it.

Unfortunately for Gregorius, Håkan and his men had chopped holes in the ice, and then covered them with snow.

Gregorius fell into the trap, sinking through the ice. He and twenty of his men were then slain by the enemy. Ingi mourned Gregorious, and then prophetically stated that he would soon follow his departed friend to the grave.

That same winter, Ingi traveled to Oslo to attend the wedding of Orm (his half brother on his mother's side). Orm was to be married to Ragina Nicolasdotter, the widow of King Eystein (Ingi's half brother on his father's side).

Hearing of Ingi's plans, Håkan decided to march into Oslo at the very same time. A battle was fought on the ice-covered fjord, and Ingi, vowing to avenge the death of Gregorius, rushed into the fray and was killed almost immediately. He was only twenty-six years of age. His death is dated at February 1, 1161.

### Håkan II Sigurdsson "the Broad-Shouldered" — 1161 to 1162.

*"My foes Ingi and Gregorius are out of the way. But now I must deal with Jarl Erling!"*

Håkan, surnamed *Herdebreid* (the Broad-Shouldered), became sole king of Norway upon his Uncle Ingi's death. But the crown did not rest easily upon the teenager's head. Ingi's followers were most unhappy with young Håkan and decided to choose a new king.

The most influential man among the deceased Ingi's supporters was a *jarl* known as Erling the Crooked Neck (or Wryneck). He had his own ideas about who should succeed Ingi to the throne.

Erling had taken as his wife Kristina, the daughter of Sigurd Jerusalem-farer, and the widow of Sigurd Mouth. A son named Magnus was born to this marriage. Since the boy was of royal blood through his mother, Erling coveted the throne for him. Erling's step-sons (the children of Kristina and Sigurd Mouth), however, stood in little Magnus' way.

Erling promptly had his stepson Harald beheaded. (One can scarcely imagine the grief Kristina must have felt when her husband did away with her son.) The second stepson (Erik) apparently did not pose as great a threat to Erling, and he lived until 1190. Cecilia, the daughter born to Kristina's first marriage, also escaped; she became the wife of Baard Guttormsson, and their son Ingi later became Ingi II of Norway.

With his stepson Harald out of the way, Erling persuaded the nobles to depose Håkon and put young Magnus on the throne.

In his conflict against Håkan, Jarl Erling obtained help from King Valdemar the Great of Denmark, promising him Norwegian lands in return for the aid. Their agreement was confirmed by solemn oaths.

In 1162, Håkan and Erling met in a great naval battle. Disorder soon broke out on Håkan's ship. As some of his men fell dead and others leaped overboard, Håkan jumped into a nearby ship. Only too late he realized that he had taken refuge on Erling's own ship! There he was vanquished and slain. He was only fifteen years old. Later his body was entombed in Christ Church.

### Magnus V Erlingsson — ruled from 1162 to 1179.

*"I am the Lord's anointed, for I have been crowned king by the grace of God."*

Upon Håkan's death, there was no one to challenge the rule of Jarl Erling's son Magnus. Because Magnus did not come from a direct male line of kings, Erling decided that an appropriate ceremony was needed to convince the people to accept the child as their king.

In 1163 Erling made a deal with Norway's Archbishop Eystein Erlendsson. Erling promised to support the Roman church, and even be Rome's vassal, if the archbishop would anoint and crown his son. The unction and coronation was carried out with great pomp in the presence of six bishops, a papal legate and "a multitude of clerics." No previous king of Norway had been crowned nor anointed by a churchman. Magnus was called "the Lord's anointed" and "king by the grace of God."

Snorri tells us that Magnus was only eight years old at the time of his coronation. His father Erling was named regent and remained the real power behind the throne until his death at the hand of Sverre's forces in 1179.

The boy king faced difficult times. It was said of him that he would rather "have played with other boys than sit among chieftains," but he had to face life seriously, for several other candidates for the throne were only too eager to depose him. One of these was Olof Ugava, the son of King Eystein I's daughter Maria. He certainly had as much right to the throne as Magnus, for both were descended from kings through their princess mothers.

Olof Ugava asked King Valdemar I of Denmark for help against Magnus, knowing that Valdemar was angry with Erling, who had failed to give him the lands he had promised the Danish king in return for naval aid against Håkan the Broad-Shouldered. For a while, there were actual hostilities between Valdemar and Erling, but in 1170 a peace treaty was confirmed and Valdemar was given some Norwegian land. Erling's wife Kristina, a cousin to King Valdemar, is said to have had a hand in the peace agreement.

Another candidate for the throne was Eystein Eysteinsson Meyla ("the maiden") so nicknamed because of his fair features. He was a grandson of Harald Gille. Yet chief among Magnus' rivals was Sverre Sigurdsson, who also claimed direct descent from Harald Gille.

Magnus' foes, a loose band of malcontents, often had to hide in the woods and mountains, where they had nothing but birch bark to wrap around their legs. Thus they came to be known as the Birchlegs.

A long war dragged on between Magnus and the Birchlegs. In 1177, Magnus, who was then twenty-one, soundly defeated the Birchlegs at Re near Tønsberg. Two years later, King Magnus' forces were overcome by the pretender Sverre and his followers. Magnus Erlingsson was forced to flee for his life, and his father was slain in the battle. We shall now trace the story of Sverre.

### Sverre Sigurdsson—ruled from 1179 to 1202.

*"No one knows anything about my parentage, except what I can relate."* These words of Sverre summarize the enigma which genealogists have never been able to solve. Sverre claimed to be the son of Sigurd Mouth, and he certainly believed firmly that he was of royal blood, but he was never able to prove his paternity.

Sverre was born about 1149 in Bergen and raised in the cold, wind-swept Faeroe Islands. His mother, a Norwegian woman named Gunnhild, was married to a Faeroe Islander called Unas the Comb Maker. Sverre was ordained as a priest at a young age, but after his mother told him that he was really the son of the former king Sigurd II Mouth, Sverre set out for Norway to claim the throne that he felt was rightfully his.

Interestingly, Sverre was doing almost exactly the same thing that his supposed grandfather, Harald Gille, had done years before.

He arrived in Norway about 1174 and before long he joined the Birchlegs, that ragged rebel band which opposed Magnus V. These men lived in the forest, robbing the farms of the gentry when they needed food, and getting their name from the birch bark which they tied around their legs when their clothing wore out.

On December 22, 1176, Sverre visited Birger Brosa in Sweden. Birger's wife, Birgitta, was the daughter of Harald Gille, and thus Sverre claimed her as his aunt. Sverre no doubt hoped to gain support for his efforts to obtain the Norwegian throne, but he was disappointed. Birger Brosa was backing another nephew of his wife's, Eystein Meyla. Birger had even given Eystein Meyla some money, so he told Sverre that he could not support him while Eystein was living.

Interestingly, both Sverre and his rival (and supposed first cousin) Eystein Meyla were leaders in the anti-Magnus band called the Birchlegs. In fact, the Birchlegs had crowned Eystein as their "king."

In the battle of Re in 1177, the Birchlegs were soundly defeated by Magnus; and Eystein Meyla was slain. When Sverre heard the news, he hurried to Sweden to see Birger Brosa, although he knew very well that Birger's four sons—through their mother Birgitta—had as good a right to the throne of Norway as did Magnus Erlingsson.

Birger Brosa conceded that his own sons were too young to rule Norway, and that in any case the Norwegians would not tolerate a Swedish king. So he gave his full support to Sverre on the condition that Filip (Birger Brosa's eldest son) would be the Norse *jarl*. By this time, the office of *jarl* was very similar to that of prime minister.

On June 19, 1179, as we have seen, Sverre soundly defeated the forces of Magnus and his father Erling the Crooked Neck. It is said that before the battle Sverre knelt in prayer, and then spoke to his men, assuring them of victory and promising that each man should be given the rank of the warrior he would kill. "He who slays a thane shall become a thane."

In the battle Erling received a death wound. His son Magnus bent over him, kissing him and promising him, "We shall meet on the day of joy, father." Magnus was forced to flee to Denmark, and Sverre became ruler over much of Norway.

On June 15, 1184, Magnus Erlingsson returned to Norway, having received military aid from the Danish king Knut VI Valdemarsson. Magnus' hopes for regaining the entire country were dashed to pieces. Almost his whole army perished with him in a naval battle at Fimreite.

Sverre was now king of the entire country of Norway. At least partly, his victory may have been aided by the support of his supposed uncle, Birger Brosa of Sweden.

Being a good politician, Sverre commanded that Magnus should be given a royal burial in Christ Church in Bergen, where he had been crowned some nineteen years before. The chroniclers state that at the funeral Sverre "spoke many fair words, for he did not lack words nor the skill to turn his speech wherever he wished."

Sverre's skill in diplomacy and oratory stood him in good stead. He was able to win many people to his side, and he strengthened his connections to the royal families of Scandinavia by marrying Margaret, a daughter of the Swedish King St. Erik. Birger Brosa may have had a hand in arranging this marriage. Birger also made sure that Sverre kept his promise, taking Filip Birgersson as his jarl.

Margaret of Sweden bore a son named Erling to Sverre, but the boy was not destined to reign over Norway. Sverre already had other children by his first wife Astrid. These included Sigurd Lavard (Lord Sigurd), Håkan (later Håkan III of Norway), and Ingeborg, who married a Swedish prince named Karl.

Sverre is remembered not only for his marvellous oratory but also for his conflicts with the church. He believed strongly that the king should have control over the church, a rather unpopular view in the Middle Ages. Archbishop Eystein, who had anointed Magnus, had to flee to England. Erik Ivarsson, the next archbishop, refused to crown Sverre and was forced to flee to Denmark in 1190. Other bishops, who supported the church rather than the crown, soon followed. The remaining bishops crowned Sverre in 1194, but were later excommunicated, along with their king, by Pope Innocent III. Sverre responded by publishing a polemical pamphlet against the bishops, defending the supremacy of the kingship by quotations from Scripture and Canon Law.

Norway was placed under a papal interdict, which was not lifted until after Sverre's death. The deposed bishops, along with other enemies of the king, formed an opposition party in Denmark, where they had been exiled. For a while, this opposition party won control of the area around Oslo.

Sverre, like most of his predecessors, had to contend with rival kings. One of these, a pretender named Inge (not to be confused with Ingi the Hunchback), proclaimed himself king in southern Norway in 1196. Two years later, he was proclaimed king in the north. Sverre defeated him in a battle near Trondheim on June 18, 1199. The defeated Inge fled from Sverre, but was murdered by peasants along the road as he fled.

Sverre died in 1202, and was succeeded by his son Håkan III. A period of terrible anarchy followed, in which the descendants of the previous kings fought one another for the throne. Håkan III was murdered in 1204, only two years after his succession to the throne. He was followed by Ingi II Baardson, the son of Sigurd Mouth's daughter Cecilia.

Many families in Sweden and America today can trace their ancestry to the kings of Norway. This includes those Swedes and Swedish-Americans who are descended from Birger Brosa. Through Birger's Norwegian wife Birgitta, they can trace their line to Harald Gille. And through Birger's ancestor Adela (the wife of St. Knut of Denmark) they can trace their ancestry all the way back to Norway's St. Olof and Harald I the Fairhaired.

In the next chapter, we will trace the story of the counts of Flanders—important in the royal Scandinavian genealogies as a link with Karl the Great and the nobility of the Continent. And then we will come back to Denmark, and see how the Danish royal line fits into the medieval picture.

CHART 4 - The Family of Magnus III Barelegs

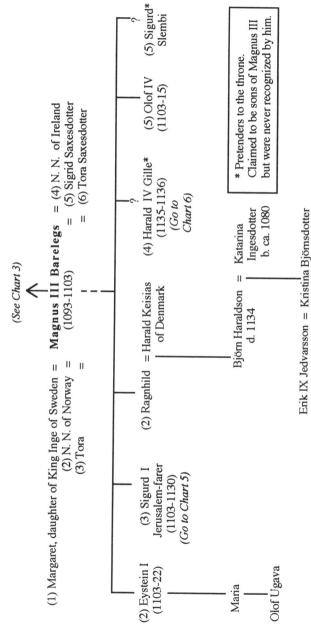

(See Chart 3)

(1) Margaret, daughter of King Inge of Sweden = **Magnus III Barelegs** = (4) N. N. of Ireland
(2) N. N. of Norway = (1093-1103) = (5) Sigrid Saxesdotter
(3) Tora = = (6) Tora Saxesdotter

(2) Eystein I (1103-22)

(3) Sigurd I Jerusalem-farer (1103-1130) *(Go to Chart 5)*

(2) Ragnhild = Harald Keisias of Denmark

(4) Harald IV Gille* (1135-1136) *(Go to Chart 6)*

(5) Olof IV (1103-15)

(5) Sigurd* Slembi

Maria

Olof Ugava

Björn Haraldson d. 1134 = Katarina Ingesdotter b. ca. 1080

Erik IX Jedvarsson = Kristina Björnsdotter
(St Erik, King of Sweden 1156-60)

* Pretenders to the throne. Claimed to be sons of Magnus III but were never recognized by him.

# CHART 5 - The Family of Sigurd Jerusalem-Farer

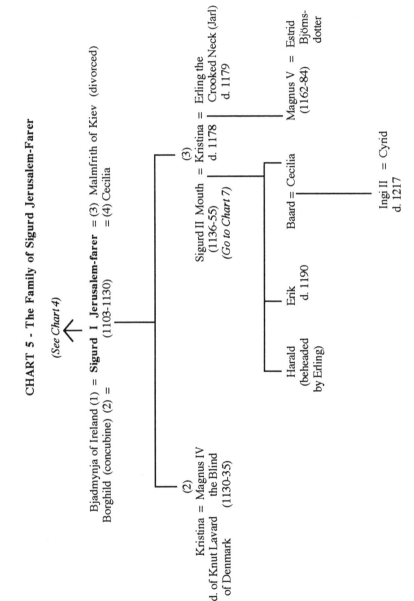

*(See Chart 4)*

Bjadmynja of Ireland (1) = **Sigurd I Jerusalem-farer** = (3) Malmfrith of Kiev (divorced)
Borghild (concubine) (2) =                (1103-1130)           = (4) Cecilia

(2)
Kristina = Magnus IV
d. of Knut Lavard   the Blind
of Denmark          (1130-35)

(3)
Sigurd II Mouth = Kristina = Erling the
(1136-55)         d. 1178    Crooked Neck (Jarl)
*(Go to Chart 7)*         d. 1179

Harald            Erik        Baard = Cecilia        Magnus V = Estrid
(beheaded         d. 1190                            (1162-84)   Björns-
by Erling)                                                       dotter

Ingi II = Cynid
d. 1217

## CHART 6 - The Family of Harald Gille

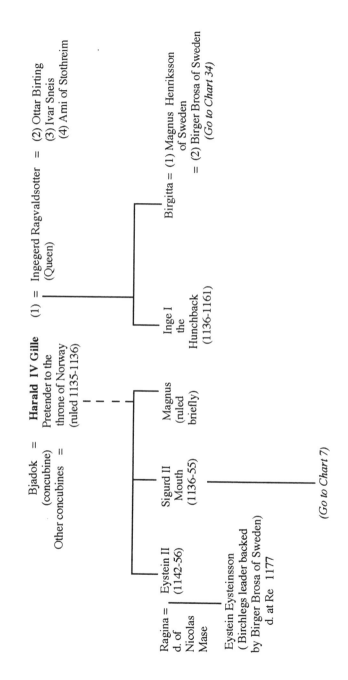

Bjadok =    **Harald IV Gille**    (1) =    Ingegerd Ragvaldsotter    =    (2) Ottar Birting
(concubine)    Pretender to the           (Queen)                   (3) Ivar Sneis
Other concubines =    throne of Norway                                      (4) Ami of Stothreim
(ruled 1135-1136)

Ragina =    Eystein II        Sigurd II        Magnus           Inge I           Birgitta = (1) Magnus Henriksson
d. of       (1142-56)     Mouth        (ruled         the                      of Sweden
Nicolas               (1136-55)   briefly)     Hunchback           = (2) Birger Brosa of Sweden
Mase                                          (1136-1161)            *(Go to Chart 34)*

Eystein Eysteinsson
(Birchlegs leader backed
by Birger Brosa of Sweden)
d. at Re 1177

*(Go to Chart 7)*

*(Note that at times Norway was governed by joint rulers or rival kings.)*

# CHART 7 - The Family of Sigurd Mouth

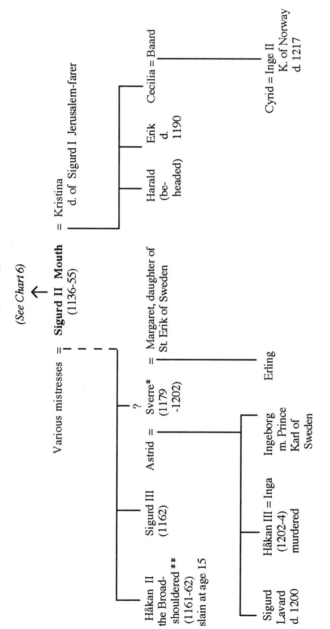

(See Chart 6)

Sigurd II Mouth (1136-55)

= Kristina
d. of Sigurd I Jerusalem-farer

= Margaret, daughter of
St Erik of Sweden

Various mistresses =

Håkan II
the Broad-
shouldered **
(1161-62)
slain at age 15

Sigurd III
(1162)

?
Astrid = Sverre*
(1179
-1202)

Erling

Sigurd
Lavard
d. 1200

Håkan III = Inga
(1202-4)
murdered

Ingeborg
m. Prince
Karl of
Sweden

Harald
(be-
headed)

Erik
d.
1190

Cecilia = Baard

Cyrid = Inge II
K. of Norway
d. 1217

* Claimed to be the son of Sigurd Mouth by Gunnhild
** Son of Sigurd Mouth by Tora

## Chapter 4

### The Counts of Flanders from 862 to 1068

Historic Flanders is basically modern Belgium, although part of Northern France and the Dutch province of Zeeland formerly belonged to Flanders. In medieval times, Flanders was a powerful county and after the twelfth century it became the industrial and commercial center of northern Europe.

The population of Flanders included both the Flemish people, who spoke a Germanic tongue similar to the ancient Frankish language, and the French-speaking Walloons. In addition, many Germans, Danes, Slavs, and even Anglo-Saxons from England found a home in Flanders. The county had a truly international flavor.

The name Flanders was used for this region as early as the eighth century, and probably means "flooded land."

The Baldwins of Flanders were a dynasty founded by the Carolingian Charles the Bald when he set his son-in-law up as the first count of that land. Judith, who married the first Baldwin, was a great-granddaughter of Karl the Great (Charlemagne). Through her, all the subsequent counts of Flanders were Carolingians. And that's precisely why we've included Flanders in our book on the genealogy of the Scandinavian monarchs; Flanders is the link which brought Carolingian genes into the royal houses of Denmark and Sweden.

**Baldwin I *"Bras de Fer"* (Iron Arm)—Count from 862-869.**

*"Judith, darling. If your father won't agree to our marriage, we'll run away to Rome and get it sanctioned by the pope."*

Baldwin I seems to have come from a noble family in Lorraine; we know little about his parentage or his early life except for the fact that his father was named Audacer. Baldwin's Teutonic name, which means *Bold Friend,* was passed down to many of his descendants.

Baldwin I had a daughter who was a nun at Laon; she seems to have been born either to a first wife or to a concubine. Later, Baldwin married Judith, a daughter of Charles the Bald.

Judith, who was born around 843, was first of all given in marriage to King Ethelwulf of England, in about 856. No doubt Charles the Bald hoped to cement the friendship between England and France with this alliance. History, unfortunately, never tells us how Princess Judith felt about being married at about age thirteen to a foreign king. Since she was so young, it is possible that the marriage was never actually consummated. Certainly no children were born to the union.

Ethelwulf died in 858, and Judith was almost immediately married to her stepson Ethelbald, who outlived his father by only two years. For the second time, she became a teen-aged widow.

Judith returned to France, and Baldwin fell in love with this "young and ardent widow of two English kings," who was still only about nineteen years old. The old stories tell how, with the help of Judith's brother (the future Louis II the Stammerer), Baldwin successfully abducted her much against her father's wishes.

Charles the Bald started out in hot pursuit of the couple, but was deterred by the threat of the Norsemen who were terrorizing France. Hearing that Baldwin and Judith were about to go to Rome to implore the protection of Pope Nicholas I, Charles decided that Baldwin would serve him better as a son-in-law and vassal than as a foe. He therefore sent word to the couple that he would accept their marriage and give Baldwin the land of Flanders. Thus the county was established in 862.

Flanders became a very important territory under Baldwin and his successors. For the descendants of Karl the Great, it became a strategic buffer against the heathen tribes to the east, and the raiding Scandinavians from the north.

Baldwin I and Judith had at least two sons: Baldwin II and Raoul, who died in 896.

Baldwin I died in 879. He was so famous that a thousand years later he would be celebrated by the American poet, Henry W. Longfellow, in *The Belfry of Bruges.* Longfellow wrote:

*Visions of the days departed, shadowy phantoms filled my brain;*
*They who live in history only seemed to walk the earth again;*
*All the foresters of Flanders, mighty Baldwin Bras de Fer ....*

Upon his death, his son Baldwin II succeeded him as count.

## Baldwin II "the Bald"—Count from 879 to 918.
*"The Northmen are making more and more raids into our country! We must ally ourselves with King Alfred of England in order to withstand them!"*
Baldwin II was born about 865. He governed Flanders from 879 until his death on January 2, 918.

In 882, Baldwin II made the city of Bruges the seat of his government, and it remained the center of the county's political administration for the succeeding centuries. The fact that Bruges was near the seacoast no doubt helped Baldwin and his successors to develop important relations with the Anglo-Saxon kings across the English Channel.

During all this time northern France (including the county of Flanders) was suffering from the raids of the Vikings. Some historians have surmised that the Danes whom Alfred the Great chased out of England went across the channel to wreak havoc in Flanders. They ravaged the country so thoroughly that a chronicler of the times wrote, "Flanders is left a widow."

Baldwin II was married in 884 to Efltrude (also called Alftrude, Iltrude, Alfthryth, Alfritha or Ethelsvida), a daughter of Alfred the Great of England. No doubt the marriage, in part, was arranged to cement the alliance of England and Flanders against their mutual foes—the raiding Danes. It is interesting that Alfred deemed Baldwin II worthy of his daughter, although he was a mere count, not a king. Because of this marriage, all the subsequent counts of Flanders were descended from Alfred the Great of England as well as from Karl the Great and the Carolingians. And in time, the genes of the royal house of Wessex, which had merged with those of Flanders, were passed on to the royalty of Scandinavia.

During the time of Baldwin II, the royal power in France was passing from the Carolingians to the Capetians. Although Baldwin II's mother Judith was a Carolingian, he did homage to Eudes, Count of Paris (a son of the Capetian forebear Robert the Strong) in 888. At the same time, Baldwin II also continued to serve as a vassal of the Carolingian king Charles the Simple.

In 911, Baldwin II gained a new neighbor to the southwest when Normandy was ceded to Rollo, the Viking pirate. Now at last, after many years of Scandinavian raids, there was peace between the Normans and Flanders.

Baldwin and Elftrude had two sons: Arnulf (whose name means *Eagle/Wolf*) and Adolf or Adelulf, whose name means *Noble Wolf*. (The Anglo-Saxon equivalent is *Ethelwulf,* the German is *Adolf,* and in French histories this Teutonic name is transposed to *Adalolphe.)*

When Baldwin II died in 918, his lands were divided. Arnulf was made count and marquis of Flanders, and Adolf was made count of Ternois and Boulonnais. A third brother Albert (who was illegitimate) was made provost of Drongen.

### Arnulf I "the Great" —Count from 918 to 965.

*"Go and kill my enemy, William Longspear of Normandy, just as you have already killed my nephew."* Thus Arnulf the Great commanded his servants to get his rivals out of the way.

Arnulf, who was able to count both Karl the Great and Alfred the Great as ancestors, became the third count of Flanders upon the death of his father Baldwin II. He was called both count and marquis, because he governed a march or mark (a border land).

In 933 Arnulf's brother Adolf took ill very suddenly and died. Arnulf then appropriated the lands of Ternois and Boulonnais, once more uniting what had originally been Flanders. To keep Adolf's heirs from trying to regain their father's lands, Arnulf ordered the execution of Adolf's oldest son. Another son of Adolf (whose name happened to be Arnulf) survived and was restored to Ternois and Boulonnais after 962.

Arnulf I governed Flanders for more than forty years—from 918 to 965. We are not given the name of his first wife, but we are told that he took as his second wife Adela of Vermandois, a county which lay between Flanders and Normandy. She is sometimes called Alisa, Alix or other variants of Adela. In some of her descendants—in Flanders, Denmark and Sweden—the name evolved into Edel or Edela. In all these names we can see the Teutonic root which means *noble,* and which is akin to the Anglo-Saxon *Ethel.*

Adela was the daughter of Heribert II of Vermandois, and like her husband Arnulf, she was of Carolingian descent. (The counts of Vermandois were descended from Pepin, a son of Karl the Great.) Adela and Arnulf named their son Baldwin in honor of his paternal grandfather. They also had a daughter (her name is lost to history) who married Thierry II, a count of West Frisia in what is now the Netherlands.

Arnulf I lived in one of France's most troubled periods. The conflict between the house of Robert the Strong and that of the Carolingians, which had been budding in the time of Baldwin II, now reached greater proportions.

In 923, Charles the Simple was defeated at Soissons by Robert I, son of Robert the Strong. Robert I ruled France briefly and his son-in-law Raoul reigned from 923 to 936. Arnulf I submitted to both Robert and Raoul as a vassal.

In 936, the Capetian Hugh the Great, who had no ambitions to achieve kingly status for himself, brought the Carolingian Louis IV d'Outremer back from England to France and had him crowned. Count Arnulf I, along with a number of other vassal counts, did homage to the teen-age king, although perhaps without full sincerity. Arnulf was eager to please whatever king was in power, as long as he could gain political advantage from the alliance.

Arnulf I enlarged the territory of Flanders, appropriating many lands to his south by conquest or by occupying them when their respective rulers passed away. He became celebrated in the ballads of his time as one of the richest men in France. For this reason, history has accorded him the name of *Arnoul Le Grand,* or Arnulf the Great.

Arnulf and his successors continued to expand their territory into German lands and south into Hainaut. Always, they were vassals of the French king for some of their lands. For other fiefs, they did homage to the Holy Roman Emperor.

Arnulf had a redoubtable foe in the person of William Longspear of Normandy, who wished to extend his eastern border into Flanders. As a result of this dispute, Arnulf in 942 ordered his servants to murder William. They apparently were used to obeying such orders; after all, Arnulf had ordered them to assassinate his own nephew some years before.

By getting William out of the way, Arnulf was able keep his own territories intact. He also fulfilled his goal of adding Montreuil and Pontheiu to Flanders by 948. By the time he died in 965, Flanders was a real power to be reckoned with.

### Baldwin III "the Young"—Joint count from 959 to 962.
*"Let's name our baby Arnulf. It will really please my father to have a namesake."* We can imagine Baldwin III saying something like this when a son was born to him.

Baldwin III was married in 959 or 960 to Matilda, a daughter of Hermann Billung, Duke of Saxony. About this time, he was made joint ruler of Flanders with his father Arnulf I. He apparently was given some jurisdiction over southern Flanders.

Neither his rule nor his marriage was destined to endure. The young Baldwin died quite suddenly in 962, leaving an infant son who had been named Arnulf after his illustrious old grandfather.

Having lost his son, Arnulf the Great wanted to make sure that his tiny grandson would succeed him to the countship. Arnulf the Great was afraid that his surviving nephew (also named Arnulf) would try to usurp the power. Therefore the old count appealed to Lothar, his Carolingian overlord, who ruled France from 954 to 986. Count Arnulf begged the king to promise that the baby would be given all of Flanders upon reaching his majority.

Lothar responded by dividing Flanders up again. Boulonnais and Ternois were given to Arnulf the Great's surviving nephew (Arnulf, the son of Adolf), and the rest of Flanders was promised to the baby who would become Arnulf II.

### Arnulf II "the Young"—Count from 965 to 988.
*"My wife may be the daughter of a deposed king. But she is a true Carolingian, just like me!"*

When Arnulf I died in 965, his grandson Arnulf II was still a small child, perhaps about four years old. The Carolingian king, Lothar, took over the government of Flanders while the boy was small. Some of the lands that Arnulf I had added to Flanders were given away by Lothar to other nobles.

By 976, Arnulf II was deemed to be old enough to govern the county, and at this time he did homage to Lothar. But his territory was not as large as his grandfather's. Ternois and Boulonnais to the south were governed by his father's first cousin Arnulf. And his aunt's husband, Thierry II, ruled as count in West Frisia.

When he reached marriagable age, Arnulf II was married to Suzanne Rozalle, a daughter of King Berengar of Italy. Berengar, of Carolingian descent, had been deposed by Otto I of Germany, but

Berengar's daughter was nonetheless a true princess. This was a politically arranged marriage, designed to benefit Flanders with some Burgundian dowery lands which Suzanne had inherited. Arnulf II was then given the grandiose title of "Count of Flanders and Burgundy."

Like his father, Arnulf II died very young; he was not yet thirty in 988 when he passed away. Suzanne was left alone with a tiny baby, who would later become Baldwin IV the Bearded.

After Arnulf II's death, his widow Suzanne remarried. Hugh Capet, wishing to extend his influence and prestige in Flanders, arranged for Suzanne's new husband to be his sixteen-year-old son Robert (later known as Robert the Pious). The marriage probably took place about 990, but it did not prove to be a happy one. Robert soon tired of Suzanne and repudiated her although he kept Montreuil, which had been part of her dowery.

### Baldwin IV "the Bearded" — Count from 988 to 1035.
*"Don't call me a mere count. I am monarch of the Flemings!"*

Upon the death of Arnulf II, Flanders was left once more in the hands of a child count. As Baldwin IV grew up, however, he proved to be an able ruler. He built a wall around Lille about 1030. Although his predecessors had assumed no title greater than that of count or marquis, Baldwin IV expanded the power of Flanders and called himself "Monarch of the Flemings." Like the counts of Barcelona in Spain, the counts of Flanders from this time on were almost as powerful as though they had been independent sovereigns.

In 1030 Baldwin issued a decree that all within his territories must keep the peace. This was the first such order to be issued within the Holy Roman Empire. Baldwin also deprived his feudal vassals of judicial powers and gave these powers to judges of his own choosing. Other rulers of western Europe soon followed his example in similar reforms.

Baldwin IV was married the first time to Otgiva (also spelled Ogive) of Luxemburg, a daughter of Frederick I of Lorraine. This was a politically arranged marriage, and Otgiva brought him some valuable lands as a dowery. Otgiva gave her husband a son, who would later be known as Baldwin V. Baldwin IV no doubt rejoiced in the birth of an heir, little realizing what trouble the boy would cause him later on.

Baldwin's second wife was Eleanor, a sister of Robert I, the duke of Normandy. From this marriage came Judith, who was married first to Tostig, earl of Northumbria, and later to Welf IV, duke of Bavaria.

Baldwin IV remained, at least on the surface, a vassal of the Capetian king Robert the Pious (who had briefly been his stepfather). When Robert the Pious died in 1031, Baldwin proved to be equally faithful to his overlord's son, King Henry I of France. Baldwin gave military support to Henry I in his campaigns against the rebellious counts of Chartres, Blois, Tours and Troyes. It is interesting to note that Robert, duke of Normandy (father of William the Conqueror and brother-in-law to Baldwin) also supported Henry I of France at this time.

Baldwin IV, while loyal to the Capetians, caused a great deal of trouble for the Germans, continually threatening the borders of the German king, Henry the Saint.

The age-old story of Absalom's treachery against his old father David was repeated far too often in the middle ages. Baldwin V rebelled against his father, but Baldwin IV was able to quell the insurrection with the aid of his brother-in-law, Robert I, duke of Normandy.

Baldwin the Bearded was a hospitable sovereign whose court was always open to refugees and exiles from other lands, especially those exiled from England by Canute the Great.

Like Canute, Baldwin the Bearded died in 1035. His subjects quickly forgave his son Baldwin V for his earlier rebellion, and accepted him as their new count.

## Baldwin V "of Lille"—Count from 1035 to 1067.

*"Welcome, you pirates, to my court. And welcome, Queen Emma of England! Here in Flanders exiles may find a safe haven."*

Baldwin V governed Flanders from 1035 to 1067, extending its territory and power. He added Hainaut (which is now part of western Belgium), Valenciennes (presently part of France), Brabant (the territory around modern Brussels) and Ghent to his possessions.

Baldwin V made his residence in Lille (which now belongs to France). For this reason he is sometimes called *Baudouin de Lille.* Still other French historians have called him *Baudouin Le Débonnaire.*

In 1055 Baldwin V built the church of St. Pierre. He also enlarged the city walls which his father had built, so that the church would be included within Lille's city limits. Perhaps because of this construction project, he is also sometimes called Baldwin the Pious.

Baldwin was unpopular with some of his neighbors because he gave asylum to politically undesirable refugees and because he let pirates sell their stolen goods on the open market in his county. He also fought against his neighbors upon occasion.

Some of the outcasts who found refuge at the court of Baldwin were from England. One of these was the queen of England herself— Emma of Normandy. She had been married to both King Ethelred and King Canute and was twice widowed. In 1037, when Harald I Harefoot was made king of England, Emma (his stepmother) fled to Flanders rather than to her girlhood home in Normandy. It was no surprise that she should go to Flanders, for her niece Eleanor was Baldwin V's stepmother.

Emma's son Hardecanute followed her, taking ten ships to Bruges. He apparently stayed there until 1040, consulting with his mother and plotting to regain the English throne by force. When Harald Harefoot fell ill and died on March 17 of that year, Hardecanute returned to England, where he reigned unworthily for two brief years.

Let us return to that refuge for exiles, Baldwin V, and talk about his family. Baldwin was married to Adela, a daughter of Robert II King of France. (Like the wife of Arnulf I, Baldwin's wife had a name with many variants. She is sometimes called Alisa, Adele, Aelis, or Alix.)

To the union of Baldwin V and Adela were born two sons: Baldwin VI—who succeeded his father as count of Flanders from 1067 to 1070—and Robert le Frison (the Frisian) who ruled Flanders after the deaths of his brother and nephew.

Baldwin V and Adela also had a daughter, Maud or Matilda of Flanders, who is famous in British history books as the wife of William the Conqueror.

Early in his government, Baldwin of Flanders sent his oldest son— the future Baldwin VI—to be educated at the court of the Holy Roman Emperor Henry III. In 1045 the young prince was placed in charge of the march, or borderland, of Anvers (now part of modern France).

The good relations between Baldwin V and Henry III were not destined to last. Baldwin joined Thierry IV, count of Holland, and Godfrey the Bearded, duke of Lorraine, in a campaign against the Holy Roman Emperor. Although their warfare was largely unsuccessful, they did manage to burn to emperor's palace at Nymegen in 1047.

Henry III, quite naturally, retaliated. *The Anglo-Saxon Chronicle* reports that in 1049 "the emperor collected an immense force against Baldwin of Bruges [Flanders] because he had stormed the place of Nymegen and because of many other injuries done by Baldwin. The force which the emperor had collected was beyond counting."

Among Henry III's allies against Baldwin were Pope Leo IX, King Edward the Confessor of England, and Sven Estridsson of Denmark. (Denmark and England were natural allies of Germany at this time. After all, Henry III's first wife Gunnhild was Danish/English—a daughter of Canute, King of England, Denmark and Sweden.)

The Germans, Danes and English sent a great fleet of ships to blockade the coast of Flanders. Upon seeing that he was opposed by such a large combined naval force, Baldwin was forced to surrender to Henry III without a fight. *The Anglo-Saxon Chronicle* continues, "The King [Edward the Confessor] therefore went to Sandwich and stayed there with a large naval force until the emperor obtained from Baldwin all he wanted."

Having made peace with the emperor, Baldwin V kept his county open as a safe haven for many refugees. *The Anglo-Saxon Chronicle* tells us of the conflict between King Edward the Confessor and his wife's brothers. It relates that in 1049 Sven Godwinsson (Edward's brother-in-law) "went east to Baldwin's country and stayed there all winter at Bruges under Baldwin's full protection." We also know that Tostig Godwinsson (another of Edward's brothers-in-law) fled to Flanders and there married Baldwin V's half sister Judith.

Since he had lost some lands in his ill-fated war against the German emperor, Baldwin was eager to gain new territories by more peaceful means. In 1051, Baldwin V arranged the marriage of his eldest son, Baldwin VI, to Richilda, the widow of Hermann I, count of Hainaut. Thus Hainaut was added to Flanders and Baldwin's eldest son was given the title of Baldwin I, count of Hainaut.

The emperor Henry III became angry because this arrangement was made without his approval. The old war between Baldwin VI and Henry III broke out anew. It went on intermittently until 1056, when Henry III died. At that time the emperor's widow Agnes of Poitou, regent for her young son Henry IV, was able to make peace with Baldwin. The boundaries of Flanders were agreed upon, and Baldwin did homage to the German monarch.

In 1051, the year that Baldwin V added Hainaut to his domains, another important event was occurring in England. There King Edward called a solemn council meeting and publicly outlawed his father-in-law Godwin and his sons. The exiled Godwin, with his sons Sven, Tostig, and Gyrth, sailed "to Bruges, to Baldwin's country, in one ship with as much treasure for each person as they could stow away" according to the writer of *The Anglo-Saxon Chronicle*. There they spent the winter in safety with the family of Tostig's wife Judith.

Tostig was not content to stay there, however. From Flanders he sailed to Great Britain and made an attack on his former earldom of Northumbria. After suffering defeat at the mouth of the Humber, Tostig sought refuge with Malcolm III of Scotland, and made plans with Harald Hårdråde of Norway to make a new invasion of England.

On September 25, 1066, Tostig and his ally Harald Hårdråde were defeated and killed at Stamford Bridge by the forces of Tostig's brother Harald of England. True to medieval form, brother had done violence to brother. That same year, Tostig's brother Harald was defeated by William the Conqueror at Hastings. William, of course, was related to Tostig in a round-about way, for William's wife Matilda of Flanders was a niece to Tostig's wife Judith of Flanders.

As the father-in-law of William the Conqueror, Baldwin V did not oppose William's invasion of England. In fact, he supported and accompanied the conqueror. After all, William was backed by the pope himself!

Baldwin V was far more than a mere count and marquis of Flanders. From 1060 to 1067, he was considered regent of all France, because the heir to the Capetian throne, fourteen-year-old Philip, was so young that it was thought necessary to place him under a guardian. Baldwin V must have been considered wise indeed to have been entrusted with this responsibility.

Baldwin V may have foreseen that having two sons might lead to succession problems. Perhaps it was because of this that he arranged for both sons to be married to rich widows who brought them so much valuable land that they would see no real need to fight each other over territory. His first son, Baldwin VI, had married the widow Richilda and thus gained Hainaut, as we have seen. Baldwin V was determined that his second son, Robert, should be no less fortunate.

Robert, like many an adventuresome knight of his times, had sought fame and glory in Spanish Galicia and Byzantium, but he was not successful in carving out a kingdom for himself in any of those exotic lands. When he returned from his expeditions, his father Baldwin V arranged for him to be married to Gertrude, the widow of Count Florent I of West Frisia (Holland). The marriage took place in 1063. According to the arrangement, Robert was made regent for his young stepson, Thierry V. In this way, he gained the name of *Robert le Frison,* or the Frisian. Robert, eager to prove his worth as a strong leader, ably defended his stepson against the attacks of the neighboring barons who coveted the youth's lands.

Meanwhile, in Flanders, the strong hand of Baldwin V kept Normandy and France at peace during the minority of Philip I. Baldwin V's rule ended with his death on September 1, 1067. He was buried in the St. Pierre Church which he had built at Lille. His wife Adela followed him to the grave in 1071.

Baldwin was eulogized profusely by his contemporaries. In a flight of poetic fancy, Galbert of Bruges wrote that like a great winged bird, Baldwin conquered all the lands over which he flew. William of Poitiers (chaplain and biographer of William the Conqueror) stated that Baldwin was not just a vassal of the Holy Roman Empire, but that "in reality he adorned the Empire, and in the midst of difficult circumstances, he was its most glorious counsellor." And the biographer of Edward the Confessor wrote that Baldwin was a great prince, superior to all the other vassals of France.

### Baldwin VI—Count from 1067 to 1070.

*"I know I shall not live much longer. Before I die, I must name able guardians for my young sons."*

In 1067, for the first time in more than a century, a count of Flanders died leaving more than one son. (In 918 Flanders had been divided between Arnulf I and his brother Adolf, but for the rest of the tenth century and the first half of the eleventh Flanders was blessedly free from brotherly struggles for the rulership.)

Baldwin V's first son— Baldwin VI— became Count of Flanders. (He had already ruled Hainaut for sixteen years.) The second son, Robert, still had the lands in West Frisia that he had acquired through marriage.

Baldwin VI ruled Flanders only for three years. During this time he maintained good relations with Normandy and his brother-in-law, William the Conqueror. Weakened by a terminal illness, Baldwin VI before his death named William fitz Osbern (a great vassal of William the Conqueror) as one of two joint guardians for his young sons. The other guardian was King Philip of France, who was sort of a foster brother to Baldwin VI.

Baldwin VI's prolonged illness resulted in his death in 1070. He was survived by his widow Richilda and his two sons: Arnulf and Baldwin. Arnulf inherited Flanders as Arnulf III, and Baldwin was given the title of Baldwin II of Hainaut.

**Arnulf III—Count from 1070 to 1071.**

*"I go to battle against my usurping uncle. And if I perish, I perish."*

When Baldwin VI died, Arnulf III was still an inexperienced youth. His mother Richilda, feeling that her son needed a guiding hand, made his decisions for him and thus alienated her subjects. In particular, she alienated her brother-in-law Robert, who felt *he* should have been young Arnulf's protector.

It wasn't long before a revolt broke out. Naturally, it was headed by Robert le Frison, who quickly won all of Flanders to his side.

A terrible struggle ensued between Robert and his sister-in-law, the Countess Richilda. Making the most of her situation as a medieval damsel in distress, she called on the Bishop of Liege and the Holy Roman Emperor for aid. She also appealed to her sons' guardians — William fitz Osbern and King Philip I of France. Fitz Osbern hurried to her side, for he hoped not only to win honor and glory in the battle, but also to marry the wealthy countess.

In spite of the aid sent by King Philip and others, the battle went badly for Richilda. Her son Arnulf III perished in the battle of Cassel on February 22, 1071, and so did her suitor William fitz Osbern.

With Richilda's son out of the way, Robert le Frison was now in charge of Flanders. In a sense, the story of Arnulf I and his murdered nephew was repeated, for once again, a medieval nephew had died at the hands of a power-hungry uncle.

**Robert I le Frison—Count from 1071 to 1093.**

*"I couldn't carve out a kingdom for myself abroad. But now I am ruler of all Flanders!"*

After the battle of Cassel, King Philip was forced to accept Robert as count of Flanders. Richilda retired to Hainaut with her second son, who became Count Baldwin II of Hainaut, and the ancestor of the Flemish dynasty of that county. There Richilda continued her unsuccessful struggle against Robert for many years.

As soon as Robert became count of Flanders he did homage to King Philip of France. Philip, who had at first fought against Robert, was now eager to be his friend. The alliance was confirmed by the marriage of Philip to Robert's stepdaughter Bertha of Holland. Philip also acquired Corbie from this treaty. But perhaps the main reason

Philip wanted Robert le Frison on his side was to gain another ally against Normandy, for he hoped to prevent William the Conqueror from seizing Brittany and other parts of his kingdom.

Although Robert's sister Matilda was married to William, the new count of Flanders pledged his loyalty to William's enemy Philip. William, angry because of the death of his loyal vassal fitz Osbern, refused to recognize his brother-in-law Robert. The tenuous good will between Normandy and Flanders was now ended.

Flanders prospered under Count Robert. In his time, towns began to develop, and the woollen industry became important. This industry greatly boosted the economy of Flanders in the Middle Ages.

As we have seen, Robert le Frison was married to Gertrude of Saxony. Her father was Ordulf, a duke of Saxony who came from line of Hermann Billung; and her mother was Ulfhild, a daughter to St. Olof of Norway.

Robert and Gertrude were the parents of Robert II, Adela, and Gertrude. Robert's daughter Adela was first married, in 1082, to Knut Svensson (later called St. Knut or *Knut den Helige*) of Denmark.

The marriage of his daughter to King Knut helped Robert strengthen his ties to Denmark, that ancient enemy of England. Robert was still feeling hostile toward his brother-in-law, William the Conqueror, and so in 1085 Robert and his son-in-law Knut Svensson outfitted an expedition against England. The campaign, however, was aborted due to Knut's death the following year; he was mobbed and killed at the altar of St. Albans church by angry peasants. Adela, his widow, had been queen of Denmark for a mere four years, but she had borne him two daughters and a son. The daughters were later married to Swedish nobles, and the son—Charles the Good— eventually was made a count of Flanders. We shall hear more about Adela and her daughters in the chapters on Denmark and Sweden.

Robert, like many other nobles of his time, made a pilgrimage to the Holy Land. He arrived by ship in 1087, and his expedition may be considered a precursor to the First Crusade. Upon his return, he made an alliance with Alexius Comnenus, the Byzantine emperor.

Robert aided Alexius in his efforts to build up the power of Byzantium by sending him troops. He also made an alliance with those foes of Byzantium in Sicily and Italy—the descendants of Tancred of Hauteville—by marrying his widowed daughter Adela to Roger Borsa, Duke of Apulia, the son of Robert Guiscard. She moved to Italy, where she became known as Alaine. It is interesting to note that both of Adela's husbands were of Scandinavian extraction, the first being a Dane and the second being a descendant of the Vikings who settled Normandy.

Robert le Frison's daughter Gertrude was also twice married. Her first husband was Henry III, count of Louvain, and her second husband was Thierry II, count of Alsace. "Thierry" is the French contraction of the good old Gothic name Theodoric, which means *ruler of the people*. German histories call him Dietrich, which connotes the same thing.

Robert remained on good terms with Philip I of France until 1092, when Philip (who had fallen in love with someone else's wife) repudiated Bertha, Robert's stepdaughter.

Robert le Frison, known as a battler and an adventurer who had explored many lands, died peacefully at home in 1093. He had outlived his brother-in-law and enemy William the Conqueror by six years.

### Robert II - Count of Flanders from 1093 to 1111

*"Nothing can stop me now! I will climb over the wall and help take Jerusalem from the infidels."*

Robert le Frison's son succeeded him as Robert II of Flanders. Robert II, like his father, was an adventurer who marched off to the Holy Land. He so distinguished himself in the First Crusade that he came to be known as "Robert of Jerusalem."

On November 25, 1095, Pope Urban made an impassioned plea to recover the Holy Land from the Muslims. No king was among those who responded to his challenge. (Possibly this was because Philip I of France, William II Rufus of England, and Henry IV of Germany were all officially excommunicated from the Church when the First Crusade was preached.)

Many lesser nobles, however, took the cross and set out with their armies to conquer Antioch first and then Jerusalem. One of these was Hugh of Vermandois, a brother to King Philip of France. Another very important figure in the First Crusade was Godfrey of Bouillon (a small territory in what is now Belgium). Godfrey was perhaps the crusade's most noble commander: brave in battle, humble in victory, skilled in administration, and unshaken in his commitment to what he perceived to be his holy mission.

Count Bohemund of Taranto (Robert Guiscard's son) and his

nephew Tancred represented the Normans from Sicily. Still another brave leader in the First Crusade was Raymond of Saint-Gilles, count of Toulouse. He had already fought the Muslims in Spain. Now, as an old man, he was determined to fight them once again in Jerusalem.

Robert II of Flanders and his troops joined the other crusading princes some time after the capture of Antioch. His mind must have been full of the stories his father had told him about the marvels of Byzantium, the treachery of the Saracens, and the treasures of the East.

On June 7, 1099, the Christian army camped outside Jerusalem. At first they made little progress in their goal of taking the city. The Muslim governor had plenty of supplies and was confident that he could withstand a long siege.

A month later, on July 8, the crusader army began to march around the city with the priests and monks leading the way. When they reached the Mount of Olives, all the men stopped and listened to a stirring sermon from Peter the Hermit, urging them to take the city. Meanwhile, the cocky Muslims stood on the city walls, scoffing at the 12,000 Christian foot soldiers.

The crusaders pushed their siege towers and ladders up against the walls of Jerusalem. On July 15, Godfrey's men took a section of the walls. The other crusaders followed. Among those who scaled the walls that day was Robert II of Flanders.

The Muslim governor of Jerusalem surrendered to Raymond of Toulouse in the Tower of David and was escorted out of the city. The 70,000 Muslims who remained in Jerusalem were slaughtered without pity, and the Jews were herded into a synagogue and burned alive. Godfrey of Bouillon, who was elected to govern the city, assumed the modest title of "Defender of the Holy Sepulchre."

Robert II of Flanders, along with most of the other nobles, gathered up his troops and returned home, where he was duly honored for his heroic deeds.

"Robert of Jerusalem" was a loyal vassal of the Capetian monarchy. The historian Suger reported that Robert sent 4,000 knights to serve King Louis VI in 1109. It was while fighting against Thibaut, count of Blois (an ally of Henry I of England) that Robert II was killed in 1111 at the bridge of Meaux, where the Seine and the Marne meet not far from Paris.

Robert II was survived by his widow, Clemence of Burgundy—a sister to Pope Calixtus II—as well as by their son, Baldwin VII of Flanders. Later, Clemence was remarried to Godfrey of Louvain.

Gautier of Terouanne, a contemporary of Robert II, wrote the following eulogy: "Such was his invincible power and valor that both Arabs and Turks called him the son of St. George."

We will now list briefly the next four rulers of Flanders, in order to bring the story up to 1168.

## Baldwin VII, count of Flanders from 1111 to 1119.

Robert II was succeeded in 1111 by his son Baldwin VII. Like his father, Baldwin VII was killed while fighting for Louis VI in his battles. (Louis VI's chief foe at this time was William the Conqueror's son, Henry I of England.) Wounded in 1113 at Bures-en-Brai, Baldwin VII never regained his health. When he died in 1119 without issue, the direct male line of Baldwin I came to an end. Flanders, nevertheless continued to prosper under rulers who came through the daughters of Baldwin VI.

The line of Baldwin I had not died out. Through the daughters and granddaughters of the counts of Flanders, the blood of the Baldwins continued to flow through the veins of the nobility of much of Europe. All the descendants of William the Conqueror are, of course, also descended from the counts of Flanders through William's wife Matilda.

## Charles the Good, count of Flanders from 1119 to 1127.

Charles was the only son of St. Knut of Denmark. Through his mother Adela, Charles was also a grandson of Baldwin VI and therefore he could claim the countship.

Charles, whose father Knut was the victim of an assassination, was himself assassinated in 1127. Charles was married to Margaret, the daughter of Renaud II, Count of Clermont, but he died without issue.

## William Clito, count of Flanders from 1127 to 1128.

Upon the death of Charles the Good, Flanders fell into turmoil. For a brief period (1127-28) it was ruled by William Clito, a grandson of William the Conqueror who could claim Flanders through his grandmother Matilda.

## Thierry of Alsace, count of Flanders from 1128 to 1168.

In 1128, William Clito died and was replaced by Thierry of Alsace, a son of Baldwin VI's daughter Gertrude. Thierry ruled Flanders for forty years, from 1128 to 1168.

Although Charles the Good had no direct descendants, the genes of his parents—St. Knut of Denmark and Adela of Flanders—were passed on through Charles' sisters: Cecilia and Ingegerd.

Both St. Knut's daughters married into the Swedish nobility. Cecilia married the great Västergötland jarl, Erik Göthe. Thus she became an ancestor of the Erik line of Swedish kings. Ingegerd married another Swede—Folke the Fat, who was jarl, or chief minister, to King Inge the Elder Stenkilsson. Ingegerd's descendants included many Swedish kings who were related to the Folkung family.

Through Ingegerd and Cecilia, the later kings of Sweden were able to trace their ancestry directly back to Karl the Great, for the princesses came from Baldwin I who had married a daughter of the Carolingian Charles the Bald. Because of the fact that Baldwin II had married a daughter of Alfred the Great, they could also trace their lineage to the Anglo-Saxon royal house. Because Baldwin V had married a Capetian, they were descended from Hugh Capet as well. And from their Billung ancestors, they had inherited plenty of Saxon blood. In this way, many royal lines converged in medieval Denmark and Sweden by way of the counts of Flanders.

## Chart 8 - The Family of Baldwin 1, Count of Flanders

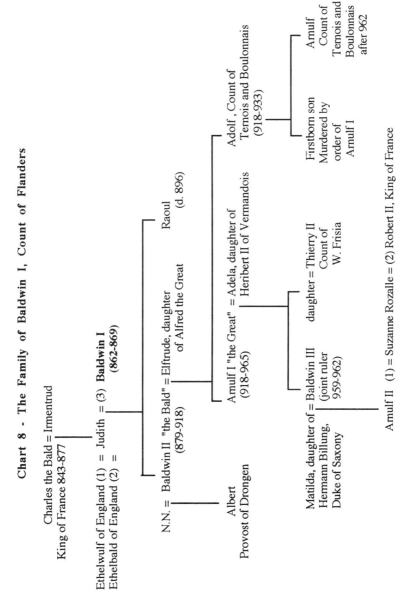

**Chart 9 - The Family of Baldwin IV, Count of Flanders**

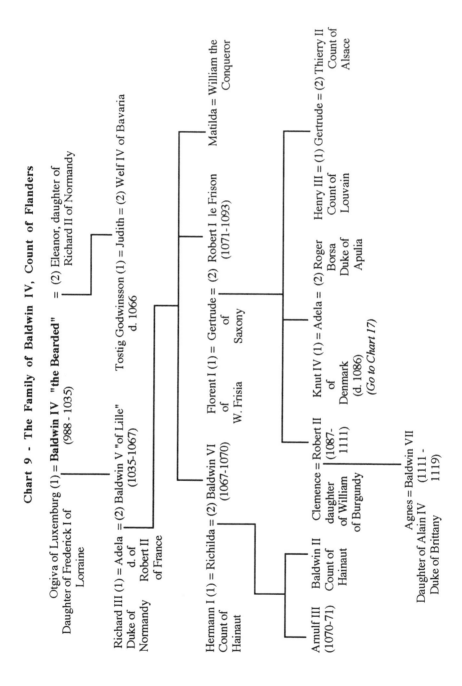

## Chapter 5

### The Kings of Denmark to 1035

Denmark's original inhabitants were closely related to other Germanic and Scandinavian peoples. Some of the early tribes said to have originated in Denmark were the Cimbrians, the Teutons, and the Vandals. The Cimbrians and Teutons marched south, ravaging the Roman Empire until they were defeated by a general named Marius in 102 B. C. The Vandals, every bit as hostile as the later Vikings, migrated south, gave their name to Andalusia (formerly Vandalusia) in Spain, founded a kingdom in Africa in the fifth century, and conquered Rome in 477 A.D.

Later we hear of still other tribes from Denmark—the Angles and Jutes—who along with their famous neighbors, the Saxons, invaded Britain in the fifth and sixth centuries. The languages of all these ancient tribes sprang from a common parent tongue, and the runic inscriptions from as late as 700 A. D. indicate that the Danish language at that time was exactly the same as that of Norway and Sweden. Gradually dialectical differences among the tribes became more pronounced, but members of the various Scandinavian tribes could still understand the speech of their neighbors without great difficulty.

#### A. Early legendary kings of Denmark

The kings of Denmark, like the Saxon, Norwegian, and Swedish rulers, all claimed descent from Odin. Odin's real name, according to the old stories, was Sigge Fridulfsson, but he called himself Odin so that people would worship him.

Odin is said to have come from Åsgård, the legendary home of the gods. (Interestingly, the twelfth-century Danish historian Saxo identifies Åsgård with Byzantium.) Traveling north from Åsgård in the first century A. D., Odin allegedly founded the Kingdom of the Svear in Uppsala sometime before the Christian era.

King Odin, we are told, had five sons. They reigned over various parts of Scandinavia, and at least two of them ruled in Denmark. (One must remember that Denmark at that time included Skåne. Although this region has belonged to Sweden in modern times, it was Danish from legendary through medieval times.) We shall not endeavor to mention all the legendary kings of Denmark, but rather highlight some of the more famous and interesting heroes of the sagas.

The Danish kings, like those of Norway and Sweden, did not always follow a direct line of succession from father to son. But they were required to be of noble blood, and they were elected by a gathering of nobles known as the *Thing*.

### Skjold—ruled Denmark at an uncertain date.

According to the *Ynglinga Saga*, Odin had a son named *Skjold* (meaning "shield"). Skjold led his followers to the Danish island of Sjaelland and became the father of the earliest Danish royal dynasty. Later Skåne, the Jutland peninsula, and the island of Fyn also submitted to Skjold. Thus the roughly-shaped borders of medieval Denmark were defined early on.

The Danish historian Saxo places Skjold's reign much later, making him the grandson of a ruler named Dan. And even *Beowulf* mentions Skjold, telling us that he mysteriously arrived in Denmark as a helpless but treasure-laden child. There he won many victories and established Denmark's royal line. What all these stories have in common is that a ruler named Skjold came to Sjaelland, added Fyn and Skåne to his domains, and became the progenitor of a Danish monarchy.

### Dan—ruled Denmark at an uncertain date.

Whether Dan was Skjold's descendant or ancestor depends on whether one reads Saxo or Snorri. Whatever Dan's family ties, he is alleged to be among the earliest of Denmark's legendary kings. We are told that he conquered many neighboring kingdoms and united them under his rule. It is from him that the country supposedly takes its name: *Dan-mark,* meaning the march or border of the Danes. Saxo Grammaticus states that from Dan "the pedigrees of our kings flowed in glorious series, like channels from some parent spring."

Dan's wife Grytha, according to the legends, bore him two sons: Humble and Lothar. Although Humble was elected king after his father, the cruel Lothar overcame Humble in war and took away his crown. According to Saxo, Lothar was "soon chastised for his wickedness, for he met his end in an insurrection of his country." Whether or not this legend is founded in fact, it certainly illustrates the all too familiar pattern of brother fighting brother for the crown.

### Frode—ruled Denmark at an uncertain date.

Another legendary descendant of Odin in Denmark was Frode, who is said to have made vassals of 225 other kings, thus extending his dominions from Russia to the Rhine. Frode, too, was beset with relatives who wished to take away his kingdom. One of these was Ubbe, who had married Frode's sister Ulfhild. While Frode was fighting wars in Russia and Ruthenia, Ubbe usurped the throne. Frode was forced to return to Denmark to reclaim his crown. He captured his brother-in-law Ubbe, took Ulfhild away from him, and wedded her to another man.

### Stoerkodder, Hrothar, and Hrolf Krake

Still another mythical king was Stoerkodder, a monarch with Herculean strength who was able to overcome any foe with the greatest of ease. However, like Samson, his strength left him when he committed a villainous act of treachery by murdering his brave and noble friend Hrothar. Other legendary kings include the stalwart and virtuous Hrolf Krake whose followers all loved him so much that they chose to die with him when he was treacherously slain.

### Ragnar Lodbrok—ruled at an uncertain date

It is difficult to date the reign of Ragnar, a semi-legendary folk hero who is the subject of many sagas and who is said to have ruled not only over Denmark, but also over Sweden and Northumbria. According to some sources, he ruled from about 770 to about 785. Some of the old sagas state that Ragnar's sons were the very men who attacked Lindisfarne in England in 793, destroying monks and manuscripts without remorse. If this is true, the 770-785 dates for Ragnar's reign would be about right.

According to other sagas, Ragnar was active in much later Viking raids and was still actively plundering the coast of England during the time of Ethelred I in the late ninth century.

*Lodbrok,* which means "hairy breeches," was called *Lothrocus* by the writer William of Jumieges, who Latinized the Scandinavian cognomen and mentioned his terrible deeds.

Some old Viking sagas place Ragnar's death in the 860s, during the reign of Ethelred I of England. Even if Ragnar lived an exceedingly long life, it is difficult to imagine that he could have ruled both during the Lindisfarne raid and the time of Ethelred I. Therefore we must conclude that the Ragnar Lodbrok of the sagas was at least partly fictional.

Leaving to one side the unsolved puzzle of Ragnar Lodbrok's chronology, we shall mention some old tales that are told about him.

Ragnar was married to the beautiful Tora, who bore him two sons: Erik and Agnar. Unfortunately, Tora fell ill and died. The heart-broken Ragnar vowed never to remarry, but instead to drown his sorrow in Viking excursions.

Eventually, Ragnar forgot his vow and married Kraka, a lowly Norwegian goatherd as beautiful as the deceased Tora. Some sources tell us that their five sons were Ivar the Boneless, Björn Ironside, Hvitserk, Ragnvald, and Sigurd *Orm-i-Oga* (which translates to the less-than-charming Sigurd Serpent-in-the Eye.) Still other legends list Ragnar's sons as Ivar the Boneless, Ubbi and Halfdan. These brothers all grew up to be strong warriors and became famous for their Viking raids and conquests.

Ragnar, making the rounds of his vast kingdom, visited his cousin Eystein-Beli who reigned as a Danish vassal in Uppsala, Sweden. There, the people began to whisper that Eystein's daughter Ingeborg, being high born, would make a much better queen for Ragnar than Kraka. Of course, as the story goes, Ingeborg was Ragnar's close relative (a first cousin once removed), but we note that no one seemed to worry about the engagement being invalid by reason of consanguinity.

Ragnar allowed himself to become engaged to Ingeborg, but then broke the engagement and returned to his peasant love, Kraka (who was also known as Aslög). Seeing that his lovely daughter Ingeborg was spurned, Eystein fell into a rage. Fighting broke out between Ragnar and his cousin Eystein, and in the battles that ensued, Ragnar's older sons—Erik and Agnar—perished. When the news was borne to Kraka, she vowed to avenge her stepsons as though they had been her own. She sent her own sons to ravage Sweden, where they overthrew and killed king Eystein.

While the sagas may not give the real causes of these Danish/Swedish battles, the fact that there were such conflicts in the seventh and eighth centuries is well attested. And certainly these wars involved brother fighting against brother and cousin against cousin.

We are told that Ragnar and his sons continued to ravage and conquer many other lands. They especially caused great devastation in England. The desperate King Ethelred raised a large army against the Vikings, and eventually Ragnar was taken prisoner and cast into a pit of serpents. (Some records tell us that was Aelle, king of Northumbria, who cast him into the snakepit.) There it is related that Ragnar died, singing:

*Now the gods call me,*
*And I mourn not to die.*
*Let us hasten hence.*
*The Valkyries whom Odin*
*Sends from his shield-polished hall*
*Beckon us home.*
*Joyfully I shall drink*
*The ale with the Aesirs on their thrones.*

When Ragnar died, his kingdom was divided among his four surviving sons: Ivar, Björn, Hvitserk, and Sigurd Orm-i-Oga. (Ragnvald had already perished nobly in battle.)

Ivar the Boneless got Ragnar's lands in Northumbria. According to some sources, Ivar headed the storming of York in 866; this was part of a raiding expedition in revenge for his father's death. We are further told that Ivar participated in the martyrdom of St. Edmund in 869 in England, and that he also took part at the siege of Dumbarton (in Scotland) in 870. At length his terrible deeds came to an end, and we read that in 873 Ivar, "king of the Norsemen of all Ireland and Britain" died. His sons and grandsons were among the Viking kings who at one time ruled Ireland. In 914 his grandson Ragnvald captured Waterford, and two years later another grandson, named Sygtrygg, reconquered Dublin for the Norsemen.

Ivar's brother Björn Järnsida (Ironside) received the lands of the Svear and the Götar in Sweden and "became the ancestor of many Swedish kings" according to the old chronicles. We shall hear more about him in the chapter on the early kings of Sweden.

Hvitserk got Jutland and the southern coast of the Baltic. Sigurd Orm-i-Oga (the youngest of Ragnar Lodbrok's sons) received Denmark, Skåne and the southern part of Norway. According to Snorri, Harald the Fairhaired was descended from this Sigurd's daughter Aslög.

We are told that Gorm the Old of Denmark was also descended from Sigurd Orm-i-Oga. Snorri tells us that, in fact, Gorm's father Hardeknut was a son of Sigurd and a grandson of Ragnar. If this is true, a very long line of Danish kings is descended from Ragnar Lodbrok, and the English monarchy is also descended from this great enemy of England!

## B. Early Historical Kings of Denmark

Leaving the descendants of Odin to the realm of folklore, we come to some historical Danish kings in the early ninth century. Thanks to their dealings with the Franks, who kept valuable records, we know at least a little about these early monarchs. Not surprisingly, we are told very little about their families, since the emphasis of the contemporary writers was on political developments as well as the spread of Christianity.

Besides the Frankish historians, the student of Danish history owes a great debt to two other medieval chroniclers: Adam of Bremen and Saxo Grammaticus. Adam, who headed up the cathedral school in Bremen, authored his invaluable *History of the Archbishops of Hamburg-Bremen* in the 1070s. In it, he tells not only about the archbishops, but also about the Danish kings, and what he says is not always complimentary! Saxo came later, composing his *Gesta Danorum* (Deeds of the Danes) about the year 1200. Although Saxo, like his Norse counterpart Snorri, includes much mythological material in his work, his comments about Denmark's historical kings are a valuable source of information.

Some of the historical kings from Denmark's early period are as follows:

### Sigfred—ruled Denmark in the late eighth century.

One of Denmark's earliest historically verifiable kings is Sigfred. He appears in the records of the times as an ally of the Saxons against whom Karl the Great (Charlemagne) waged such incessant warfare. And we even learn something about his wife: she was a sister of the Saxon chieftain Witikind. Due to this kinship, Witikind (who was growing weary of Karl's attacks), fled for refuge to Sigfred in 777.

Karl the Great intended to send Paul the Deacon to Denmark to negotiate a peace settlement with Sigfred. But Paul declined the offer, for he had no wish to endanger his life in a confrontation with a heathen Northman. As an excuse, he explained that since King Sigfred knew no Latin, communication might be a problem. Paul the Deacon was therefore excused from his mission, which might have yielded valuable spiritual fruit if he had pursued it.

### Godfred—ruled Denmark from about 800 to 810.

Sigfred died about 800 and was succeeded by Godfred, a ruler who was bold enough to withstand the great emperor Karl himself. The Danish and Frankish armies stood face to face in 804 at the Elbe, on the border between Denmark and Saxony. But negotiations saved the day, and a battle never materialized at that time.

In 808 Godfred, still bolder, invaded the lands of the Slavic Wends. He attacked the Abrodites of Mecklenburg, a Slavic tribe allied with the Franks. He captured their chieftain Drosuk and destroyed their city of Reric. Reric had been a busy commercial city; by destroying it Godfred knew he would increase business in his own marts.

Godfred forced the merchants of Rerik to move to Hedeby. This medieval Danish city, at the southeastern base of the Jutland Peninsula, had a rich trade in furs, textiles, iron and weapons, and even slaves.

After destroying Reric, Godfred ordered ramparts to be built on the border between Denmark and Saxony. The *Danevirke,* as the ramparts were called, served as a barrier to protect Hedeby from the Franks.

Everyone expected Karl the Great to retaliate against Godfred, for the ravaged Wends and their captured chieftain Drosuk had been allies of the Franks. But Karl was busy with greater matters—wars against the Moors, negotiations with Byzantium, and an alliance with Baghdad. He charged his son Charles of Neustria with the task of punishing the Danes, but Charles never carried it out.

Sensing that the old emperor would never actually take revenge, Godfred grew still bolder. Speaking like a madman, he vowed to make Frisia and Saxony into Danish provinces and to attack Karl in his very own palace at Aix-la-Chapelle.

Karl planned an unusual strategy against the Danes. He decided to take into battle the elephant Abu al-Abbas, which he had received as a gift from Harun al-Rashid, the caliph of Baghdad. Karl hoped that the very sight of the beast would frighten his foes, but much to his sorrow, the elephant died before the campaign could be carried out.

Karl the Great also ordered the building of a navy that would withstand Godfred's 200 Viking ships. He then gathered his army, camped by the river Weser, and waited for the Danish attack. But Karl's precautions proved unnecessary. In 810, before Godfred could carry out his threats, he was murdered by one of his own servants. His sons went into exile and his nephew Hemming succeeded him to the throne.

### Hemming—ruled from 810 to 811.

Godfred's nephew Hemming agreed to peace terms with Karl the Great. According to the agreement, Denmark's southern border was to be the Eider River which runs across the base of the Jutland Peninsula. The treaty was then signed and sealed, and witnessed by twelve nobles from the two kingdoms. The document is important for being the first written agreement between a Scandinavian nation and a non-Scandinavian nation in recorded history.

### Godfred's sons—ruled in the early ninth century

Godfred's sons returned from exile in Sweden to reclaim the throne. Their names—except for Horik—are lost to history.

The sons and nephews of an earlier king named Harald proved to be worthy rivals of Godfred's sons. A series of battles followed, and several pretenders to the throne were killed, including Godfred's nephew Sigfred and Harald's nephew Anulo. Adam of Bremen tells us that eleven thousand men lost their lives in the conflict. For a while Anulo's brother Reginfred was set upon the throne. But at last Godfred's sons gained the upper hand, taking over the kingdom about 814.

Karl the Great died that year, and the following year his son and successor, Louis the Pious, made an expedition into Jutland. Godfred's sons fled to the island of Fyn, where they felt protected by their strong fleet.

Louis the Pious had no wish to engage the Danes in a sea battle. He retreated and the Danes were left in peace.

### Harald Klak—died about 845.

Like that of Norway and Sweden, Denmark's early history is marked by internal wars between various ruling houses. At times, more than one man claimed the kingship. In the early 820s, both Horik the son of Godfred and Harald Klak (a nephew of the former king Harald and a brother of the deceased Anulo and Reginfred) were calling themselves kings.

Horik Godfredsson had no wish to share the throne of Denmark, so he forced Harald Klak to flee for his life. Harald found refuge with Louis the Pious in France. There, about 826, Harald heard the Christian message and was converted. He was baptized with much pomp in the royal palace at Ingelheim, near Mainz, with Louis the Pious serving as his godfather. At the same time his wife, his son, and 400 of his men were baptized.

After his baptism Harald prepared to return to Denmark to regain the throne. In response to Harald's plea for missionaries, Louis the Pious sent a missionary named Ansgar with Harald. It was a dangerous and heroic mission. The Danes were not anxious to leave off their pagan practices.

Ansgar is known as a thoroughly humble, pious man. At one time he is reported to have prayed, "I ask Thee, Lord, for only one miracle: that I would be a good man."

Ansgar founded a school to train young men in the Christian faith—probably at Hedeby—but the Danes were not yet ready for such a venture. After two years, the school folded and Harald Klak, hated by his people because he had become a Christian, once again lost his throne. Horik Godfredsson, a king completely opposed to Christianity, took his place.

The exiled Harald Klak, now a friend of the Franks, was given a fief in Frisia by Louis the Pious with the understanding that—as a loyal vassal of the empire—he would defend the Frisian coast against attacks from the North. Here Harald lived out the rest of his life, and there is evidence that he led attacks against the very Franks who had evangelized and befriended him.

When he died about 845, various relatives of his were given high positions in that part of the empire.

### Horik I Godfredsson— ruled from about 827 until about 854.

Having driven his rival Harald Klak out of Denmark about 827, Horik consolidated his royal power in Denmark.

In 829 Ansgar—whose mission to Denmark had seemingly proved futile— sailed to Sweden, but his ship and all his belongings were seized by Viking pirates. Refusing to be discouraged, Ansgar established a mission at Hamburg. It was conveniently located on what was then the border between Denmark and Germany, and there was easy access by sea to Sweden. His mission soon grew into an archbishopric, and he, of course, was the archbishop.

The devout Ansgar was destined to endure some terrible setbacks. His sponsor, Louis the Pious, was in open conflict with his three sons:

Lothar, Charles the Bald, and Louis the German. With the Empire thus weakened, the Danes streamed south to wreak havoc along the Rhine.

In 834, the Danes stormed the Frisian trading center of Dorestad, looting and plundering to their hearts' content while the defenseless inhabitants watched in horror. From Dorestad, they followed the Rhine southward and raided other towns.

In 838, Horik sent ambassadors to Louis the Pious making it known that he was in no way responsible for the atrocities on the Rhine. In fact, Horik explained, he had captured and killed the pirates who had perpetrated the raid. He asked for Frisia as a reward for this action, but Louis the Pious denied the request.

Lothar, the rebellious son of Louis the Pious, may have actually cooperated in the Danish raids in the late 830s, along with Louis' vassal and godson Harald Klak.

In 840 Louis the Pious died and his kingdom was fractured by the inevitable fratricidal wars that accompanied the Frankish inheritance system. The idea of primogeniture was unknown to the Franks, and so a monarch's heirs routinely fought each other for their father's lands and titles.

Eventually Lothar obtained the title of emperor and a 200-mile strip of land between the kingdoms of his brothers  Charles the Bald and Louis the German. (In time this middle kingdom disappeared although the modern name "Lorraine" survives as a contraction of "Lotharingia.")

Lothar decided to reward his ally Harald Klak. The Annals of St. Bertin for the year 841 state that Lothar gave the island of Walcheren (now in the Netherlands) in fief to his ally Harald Klak, who had aided Lothar in doing "so much damage to Frisia and other coastal countries of the Christian world in order to harm his father." The Annals then express the view that the giving of this island to Harald was "a deed which certainly deserves every abhorrence."

After the death of Louis the Pious, the confusion in the Empire gave the Danes a golden opportunity to invade the lands of Charles the Bald, who ruled what is roughly modern France. Led by the bold pirate Ragnar (who may or may not have been the legendary Ragnar Lodbrok) the Danes sailed up the Loire in 120 ships and defeated half of Charles the Bald's army on one side of the river. While the other half of the army watched in horror from the opposite bank, Ragnar strung up 111 of his victims as a sacrifice to Odin. He went on to thoroughly loot Paris on Easter Sunday, 845. Charles the Bald had to bribe him to depart with 7,000 pounds of silver.

That same year, under King Horik, the Danes conquered and sacked Hamburg. They completely destroyed Ansgar's church, his school, and his library, burning it all to the ground. Ansgar looked thoughtfully at the ashes and said, "The Lord gave and the Lord has taken away. Blessed be the name of the Lord."

Louis the German (the son of Louis the Pious who inherited Germany) was forced to send ambassadors to Horik to negotiate for peace. Then he had to find a new mission site for Ansgar. Since Hamburg had been destroyed, Louis the German made Bremen into an archbishopric and sent Ansgar there in 849. The persistent missionary, now given the title of archbishop of Hamburg/Bremen, determined not to give up on converting the Danes.

At last, Ansgar's forbearance paid off. In 850 Horik himself gave Ansgar permission to build a church in Hedeby.

The whole country was far from converted, however. When Ansgar died in 865, Denmark reverted to paganism. It was not until the time of Canute the Great, nearly two centuries later, that Christianity was made the official religion of Denmark.

Horik's long and violent reign in Denmark came to an end about 854. His sons and nephews had fought against him and against each other so long that at his death only one of them was left alive to take the throne: Horik II Horiksson, more commonly called Horik the Younger.

**Horik the Younger—ruled from about 854 to an uncertain date.**

Horik the Younger's subjects, who were on the whole opposed to the new religion, immediately urged him to destroy the Hedeby church. For a brief time, the church remained closed. Ansgar, however, persuaded the new king to reopen the sanctuary. The Hedeby church was then furnished with a bell tower and bell, and a second church was built in Ribe.

We are not told how long Horik the Younger ruled; what we know about the Danish monarchy at this period gradually peters out and comes to an abrupt stop in 888 with the death of Ansgar's biographer Rimbert.

Horik the Younger may have ruled over the whole country until Gorm the Old took over, or he may have shared the rule with Gorm.

**Rulers of Denmark in the late ninth century**

Still another possibility is that Denmark may have been fractured into many smaller kingdoms between the time of Horik II and Gorm.

Records from this period of time, although scanty, do mention a number of Danish kinglets. Most of them were probably pirates who were plundering the remains of Karl the Great's Holy Roman Empire and calling themselves kings in order to carve out their own petty realms.

It appears that before Gorm united Denmark, there were many "kings" ruling in various parts of the country. The Danish kings Sigfred and Halfdan appear in Frankish records from 873. We read that they sent gifts to the Frankish emperor Louis the German and made peace with him. And we hear of Danish kings named Sigfred and Godfred who perished in the bloody battle against the East Frankish Carolingian king Arnulf at the Dyle in 891.

Then there were the Danes who invaded England in the late ninth century. Halfdan, Guthrum, Oscetel and Andwend—all of them adventurers—called themselves "kings." Guthrum, the most famous, was defeated by Alfred the Great in a decisive battle at Edington in 878, and was then forced to make a peace treaty with him.

Southern Denmark came under Swedish domination about the year 900. Adam of Bremen tells us of "Olof, who came from Sweden and took possession of the Danish kingdom by force of arms." Snorri corroborates this account. The "Olof who came from Sweden" may have been a petty chieftain, or he may have come from the royal house of Uppsala. We have no way of knowing his ancestry.

This particular Olof of Sweden ruled southern Denmark for a period of time, followed by his sons Gnupa and Gurd, and his grandson Sigtrygg (the son of Gnupa). Two rune stones commemorating Sigtrygg have been found in Schleswig; they confirm the testimony of Adam of Bremen in regards to this Swedish family that ruled Hedeby for a brief generation.

In 934 Gnupa attacked the coast of Frisia. Henry the Fowler of Germany, unhappy with the pagan raid upon his land, immediately retaliated by invading Hedeby, defeating Gnupa, and forcing him to accept baptism.

In this way, the Swedish rule of Hedeby gave way to German rule under Henry the Fowler. This important medieval trading center remained in non-Danish hands until 983 when Gorm's son Harald Bluetooth regained it.

Adam of Bremen, a conscientious historian, states that from 850 to 950 no fewer than 50 kings ruled in Denmark, adding, "Whether of all these kings or tyrants in Denmark some ruled the country at the same time or one lived shortly after the other is uncertain."

Gorm the Old began a new dynasty of Danish rulers, one which can be verified and tracked down to the present time. It is not only Danish rulers who have inherited genes from Gorm; the rulers of many other nations, as well as commoners all over the world, can trace their family tree back to him.

### Gorm the Old (Knut I)—unified Denmark; died about 940.

*A man whose soul was ever hostile to religion.* Thus did the Danish historian Saxo sum up the life of Gorm the Old.

Gorm the Old, or *Gorm den Gamle,* appeared on the scene in the late ninth century and began unifying the country of Denmark.

Gorm's parentage is somewhat obscure, although we know that his father was named Hardeknut. As we have seen, Snorri tells us that this Hardeknut was the son of Sigurd Orm-i-Oga, who in turn was the youngest son of the legendary Ragnar Lodbrok.

According to other sources, Gorm's father Hardeknut came from Norway. While many Norwegian Vikings were seeking their fortune in the west, Hardeknut (according to this version) turned east and conquered the Danish island of Sjaelland. With little difficulty, he ousted the rightful heir to the throne, a young man named Siegric, and assumed the rule of the island.

When Hardeknut died, his son Gorm was accepted as king by the local inhabitants. Gorm is sometimes given the double name Hardeknut Gorm, and because of the *Knut* in his name, he may be listed as Knut I in the lists of Danish kings. The root *orm* seen in the name Gorm (and in our English word "worm") means serpent, and it is found in Orm-i-Oga and other royal names of the day.

Gorm was not content to rule only one small island, but began to extend his kingdom by conquest and barter. By the end of his reign he had unified Jutland, Schleswig, many islands, part of Holstein, and some provinces of Norway and Sweden under his rule. Thus Denmark under Gorm was larger than the Denmark we know today.

Gorm was every inch a Viking, and his subjects were given to the worst kind of piracy. The Danes plundered in Smolensk and Kiev in Russia. In 882 they journeyed to Aix-la-Chapelle where Karl the Great was buried, and stole the gold and silver decorations from his tomb. Over and over again, they harried France, and each time the ineffectual Carolingian king Charles the Fat was forced to pay them great quantities of silver in return for their agreeing to leave.

In 891, at the battle of Louvain, however, the tide turned against the Viking blackmailers. They were thoroughly defeated under the German forces of Arnulf, one of the last Carolingian emperors. It is said that the River Dyle was red with the blood of hundreds of thousands of slain Vikings, but that only one soldier was missing from Arnulf's troops.

Gorm may have already been on the throne of Denmark by the time of the Louvain battle. We are tempted to wonder how he received the news; perhaps he was grateful that he had personally escaped the carnage.

Gorm's wife was Tyra—of that there is no doubt. But her parentage is even more mysterious than Gorm's. According to an ancient tradition, she was the daughter of an Anglo-Saxon monarch, perhaps King Edward the Elder, who ruled Wessex from 904 to 924.

Snorri, on the other hand, informs us that Tyra was a sister of King Klakk-Harald of Jutland. (This Danish king is certainly not to be confused with the Harald Klak who was befriended by Louis the Pious a whole century before Gorm's time.)

There seems to be more evidence to support the tradition that Gorm's wife was English.

In the first place, Tyra was a Christian. It is far more likely that a Christian princess would have come from England, where the royal family were Christians, than from Jutland, which was still thoroughly pagan despite the early missionary efforts of Ansgar.

In the second place, several of Edward the Elder's daughters were married to royalty from the Continent. One daughter was married to Otto I of Germany, and another to Charles the Simple, the great-great-grandson of Karl the Great, so it certainly is plausible that Edward may have given a daughter named Tyra to Gorm, in an effort to secure peace between England and Denmark. *The Anglo-Saxon Chronicle* mentions that the Danes in England submitted to Edward, and it is possible that there may have been a marriage alliance between Gorm and the English royal family.

In the third place, the late twelfth-century historian—Saxo—tells us that Tyra was the daughter of an English king. (He calls her "the daughter of Ethelred," but then one is tempted to wonder whether Saxo used *Ethelred* as a title or generic term for all English kings. Ethelred I lived too early to have been the father of Tyra, and Ethelred II came much too late.)

We feel that Saxo, a Dane, was more likely to have his Danish history straight than was Snorri, an Icelandic Norwegian. Saxo states that Tyra "surpassed other women in seriousness and shrewdness, and laid the condition on her suitor [Gorm] that she would not marry him till she had received Denmark as a dowry. The compact was made between them, and she was betrothed to Gorm."

Whatever her ancestry, Gorm's Christian wife seems to have been a kindly woman, and very popular with her subjects. But she was unable to convert her husband to Christianity, and he remained a staunch pagan until his dying day.

Saxo goes so far as to state that Gorm was "a man whose soul was ever hostile to religion." And Adam of Bremen, in a play upon words, states that "over the Danes there ruled at that time Hardeknut Gorm, a savage worm, I say, and not moderately hostile to the Christian people. He set about completely to destroy Christianity in Denmark, driving the priests of God from its bounds and also torturing very many of them to death."

Adam further states that Henry the Fowler invaded Denmark and "so thoroughly terrified King Gorm that the latter... sued for peace."

Henry the Fowler, a German and a Christian, no doubt felt that he had every right to go to war against a heathen prince like Gorm. At the same time, he appears to have made an honest effort to convert the Danes through more peaceful efforts. For an entire century—since the days of Louis the Pious and Ansgar—missionary work among the Danes had been neglected. But Henry the Fowler sent Archbishop Unni of Hamburg/ Bremen to Denmark, and then to Sweden, on a mission. Unni died in 936 and his body was laid to rest at Birka in Sweden.

Gorm and Tyra had at least two sons. One was Knut and the other Harald *Blatand* or Bluetooth. Saxo, writing more like a plunder-loving Viking than a pious churchman says of Gorm's sons:

*When these princes had attained man's estate, they put forth a fleet and quelled the reckless insolence of the Slavs. Neither did they leave England free from an attack of the same kind. Ethelred [of England] was delighted with their spirit, and rejoiced at the violence his nephews offered him .... for he saw far more merit in their bravery than in piety.*

We may note in passing that Saxo seems once again to have used the term Ethelred generically. He may have been referring to Athelstan. If Tyra was a daughter of Edward the Elder, Knut and Harald would have truly been Athelstan's nephews.

About 936, Prince Knut died. The people of Denmark began to blame his younger brother Harald Bluetooth.

When Gorm, who was now old and blind, learned that his beloved eldest son had perished, he was overcome with grief.

There is no proof, at this date, that the cruel and crafty Harald killed his brother Knut. But if he did, one can see Cain killing Abel all over again, a story which was far too often repeated in medieval royal families.

This fratricidal streak can certainly be seen in the descendants of Gorm the Old and Harald Bluetooth. Erik Emune murdered his brother Harald Keisias in 1135. A century later, King Abel was suspected in the murder of his brother Erik Ploughpenny in 1250.

Tyra predeceased her royal husband, and he erected a memorial stone to her. Its runic letters read, "King Gorm raised this memorial to his wife Thyra, *Danmarkar bot.*" The runic words *Danmarkar bot* have been variously translated as Denmark's joy, saviour, restorer, benefactor, glory, or ornament. It is certainly a beautiful tribute to Queen Tyra. Very few medieval kings, whether Christian or pagan, were so devoted to their wives.

Gorm was survived not only by Harald, but also by a daughter— Gunnhild—who married Erik Bloodaxe of Norway. Gorm's descendants were destined to rule Denmark, conquer England, and marry into the royal families of many other nations.

After Gorm and Tyra died, their son Harald Bluetooth erected at Jelling the largest Viking monument known. It includes two rune stones, two huge mounds, the royal grave, and a church. The inscription on the larger rune stone was intended not only to honor Harald's parents, but also to make sure his own fame endured. It reads:

*King Harald commanded this monument to be made in memory of Gorm, his father, and in memory of Thorvi [Tyra] his mother—that Harald who won the whole of Denmark for himself, and Norway, and made the Danes Christian.*

### Harald I Blåtand (Harald Bluetooth)—from about 940 to 985.

*Harald ...won the whole of Denmark for himself, and Norway, and made the Danes Christian.* Harald Bluetooth's testimony to himself as a missionary is perhaps a bit exaggerated, since he did not even succeed in making his own son Sven a Christian, as we shall see.

Although there is some mystery surrounding the ancestry of both Gorm and Tyra, there is no question as to the historicity of their descendants. From the time of Gorm, the record of the Danish kings is well documented.

Harald made himself king of all Denmark about 940. He was not afraid to fight against those ancient enemies of the Danes: the Carolingians. He made an expedition to Normandy, where he gladly joined the Normans (after all, they were his fellow-Vikings) in opposing King Louis d'Outremer. In 945, on the banks of the River Dives, he met the French king in battle, overcame his armies, and took him prisoner. Whether Harald demanded a ransom for his enemy's release is unclear, but eventually Harald released King Louis and returned to Denmark.

Where and when Harald was given his surname Bluetooth is anybody's guess. Some historians have speculated that his name really means *Large Tooth,* and that he had protruding teeth. Or perhaps he had a discolored tooth (blue in the sense of "black and blue") as a result of some injury.

About halfway through his reign, King Harald turned to Christianity. A German bishop named Poppo baptized the king about 960. Adam of Bremen states that Harald "was baptized together with his wife Gunnhild, and his little son, whom our king raised up from the sacred font and named Sven Otto" in honor of the German emperor. If this account is to be trusted, we may note that Sven's baptism as an infant had little effect upon him as an adult, for he remained a strong pagan all his life.

An early thirteenth-century golden altar-piece at the Trandrup Church in Denmark commemorates Harald's baptism. Interestingly, Harald is shown naked from the waist up, being immersed in a large barrel of holy water.

Harald Bluetooth thus has the distinction of being the first ruling monarch of a Scandinavian country to formally turn from paganism to Christianity. (We don't count Harald Klak, since he was an exiled king or pretender when he converted.)

By 965, there were three bishoprics in Denmark: Schleswig, Ribe and Aarhus; the German ruler Otto the Great declared these sees "in the Danish marshes" to be exempt from taxes.

Harald, like nearly all the medieval monarchs, was beset with family problems. His deceased brother Knut had left a son called Guld or Gold-Harald. This nephew now demanded half the kingdom.

Snorri tells us that Harald Bluetooth flew into a rage, proclaiming, "No one asked King Gorm, my father, nor Hardeknut, my grandfather, to be half-king of Denmark! Under no condition will I yield up any of my claims."

At that time the Norwegian Jarl Håkan was at Harald Bluetooth's court. (He had found refuge there after fleeing from Harald's other nephews—the sons of Harald's sister Gunnhild.) Harald Bluetooth felt ready to murder his nephew Gold-Harald, but Jarl Håkan—burning with desire for revenge against Norway's rulers who had ousted him—advised the king to offer him Norway instead.

So the treacherous Harald Bluetooth told Gold-Harald, "I can't give you part of Denmark, but I'll help you conquer Norway. You can be king there instead."

Feigning friendship, Harald Bluetooth and Jarl Håkan tricked King Harald Graycloak of Norway into visiting Denmark. (Harald Graycloak also happened to be a nephew of Harald Bluetooth—a son to Gorm's daughter Gunnhild.)

The betrayal was carried out as planned. Harald Graycloak came to Denmark with three ships; his cousin Gold-Harald, hoping for a kingdom, met him with nine. The battle took place about 970 off the coast of Jutland, and Harald Graycloak was killed, as we have previously seen in our section on Norway.

But now Harald Bluetooth broke his promise to his brother's son. Instead of putting Gold-Harald on the Norwegian throne, the Danish king and his ally Jarl Håkan took him prisoner and had him hanged. Thus Harald Bluetooth was instrumental in the deaths of two of his nephews and namesakes: his sister Gunnhild's son Harald Graycloak, and his brother Knut's son Gold-Harald.

Harald Bluetooth then divided Norway with the Norwegian traitor Jarl Håkan. (Of course, Håkan was supposed to hold his part of Norway as a mere vassal of Harald Bluetooth.) But Harald Bluetooth suffered for his selfishness, for the jarl soon quarreled with his overlord and refused to submit to Denmark any longer.

Nevertheless, Jarl Håkan supported Harald Bluetooth in his quarrel with the German emperor, Otto II. Otto I "the Great" had died in 973, and Harald Bluetooth decided that this was his perfect opportunity to conquer some German lands beyond the Elbe and add them to Denmark.

Otto II retaliated by sending a large force against the Danes. Jarl Håkan came from Norway with his army, and the united Danes and Norwegians defeated the Germans at the Danevirke in Schleswig. Håkan then returned to Norway, leaving the Danes easy prey for the Germans. The Danes were defeated in a second battle, and Harald Bluetooth was forced to sue for peace.

Several Scandinavian monarchs in Harald Bluetooth's time had found their queens among the Slavs. (Erik the Victorious, Harald's Swedish contemporary, had married a daughter of Prince Mieszko of

Poland. And the Swedish king Olof Skötkonung had found both his queen and his common-law *frilla* among the Slavs in Wendland.)

Harald Bluetooth, likewise, was married to a Slavic princess—Tove Mistivojsdotter. Since he was married to Gunnhild at the time of his conversion, Tove was no doubt his second wife, and he probably married her after accepting Christianity. For those interested in the genealogy of the Scandinavian royalty, we have included Chart 12 which shows Tove's family line.

A rune stone, which can still be found in eastern Jutland, bears this inscription: "Tove, daughter of Mistivoj, wife of Harald the Good Gormsson, had this memorial made for her mother."

At least one of Harald's children preceded him in death. This prince was named Hiring; his father sent him to England on a Viking expedition and there he perished at the hands of Northumbrians.

We hear of at least three children of Harald who survived him. One—a daughter of Queen Tove—was named Tyra. She married Styrbjörn Starke, the exiled nephew of Sweden's king Erik Segersäll (Erik the Victorious). Styrbjörn had found refuge at Harald's court and perhaps had entered into a marriage alliance with Harald at that time. Harald Bluetooth is said to have supported Styrbjörn in his efforts to wrest Sweden away from Erik the Victorious, but the expedition failed.

Tyra and Styrbjörn became the parents of Thorgils Sparkalägger ("Kicking Legs") who in turn is said to have been the grandfather of the famous Sven Estridsson and thus an ancestor of a great many Danish monarchs, down to the present time.

Gunnhild—another daughter of Harald Bluetooth—was married to a nobleman named Pallig who settled among the Danes in England. Both Pallig and his royal wife were murdered in the 1002 St. Brice's Day massacre.

Harald Bluetooth's only surviving son was Sven *Tveskägg,* or Forkbeard. Snorri states that Sven was born to Harald in his old age, illegitimate, and little loved by his father the king. Some genealogists list Sven's mother's name as Söm-Asa, and state that she was Harald's concubine or *frilla;* Adam of Bremen suggests that Sven was the son of Gunnhild. Perhaps we will never know his true parentage, but the thoroughly unhappy and dysfunctional relationship between Sven and his father would seem to support Snorri's words rather than Adam's.

In Harald's old age, he was able to regain Hedeby, that important Danish trading center which the Danes had earlier lost first to the Swedes and then to the Germans. The German emperor, Otto II, was busy fighting wars in Italy, and Harald took advantage of this situation. He sent his army marching southward, under the leadership of his son Sven. As a result the Danes in 983 recaptured Hedeby, destroyed Otto's fortress in Schleswig, and drove the Germans south. No wonder Harald could boastfully state, in the runic stone he erected for his parents, that he was *that Harald who won the whole of Denmark for himself.*

Toward the end of Harald Bluetooth's life, his son Sven (like Gold-Harald before him) demanded a share of the kingdom. Once again Harald refused to divide his realm. As a result, young Sven found some powerful allies, gathered a navy (the Danes always preferred sea battles to engagements on land) and attacked his father about 985 at the Ise fjord in northern Sjaelland. It is said that Sven, who was thoroughly pagan, dealt the final blow to his own father.

Severely wounded, Harald fled to Jomsborg, a fortress he had erected in Wendish country (now on the north coast of Germany). There he died a few days later. According to his final wishes, he was buried in Denmark's first cathedral, the Church of the Holy Trinity at Roskilde.

Harald's long reign of almost fifty years was now ended. He is remembered for unifying Denmark, expanding its power over Schleswig and Norway, and being its first Christian monarch. His reign was marked not only by wars and conquests, but also by public projects such as the minting of coins based on Byzantine models and the building of bridges, fortresses, ramparts, and perhaps even churches. These were probably built through forced labor, which certainly did little to endear the monarch to his subjects.

### Sven I Tveskägg (Sven Forkbeard)—ruled from 985 to 1014.

*"I have conquered Olof Trygvesson of Norway. And now I am king of England as well!"* Sven may well have boasted in this way in 1014, little realizing how short his reign in England was destined to be.

Because he wore a long beard coming down to two points, Sven, (spelled Swein, Svein, Svend or Sweyn in some history books), is known as *Tveskägg* or Forkbeard. The name Sven means "youth" and is related to our English term "swain."

As we have seen, Sven spent his youth quarreling and warring with his father Harald Bluetooth, until at last the aged king was dead.

The Vikings of Jomsborg, in revenge for their king's death, took Sven prisoner. He had to bribe them with a large sum of silver in order to regain his freedom.

As Snorri tells it, Sven's marriage was also arranged by force—by the Jomsburg Vikings in an effort to make peace with the Slavs. Snorri states, "The king knew that they would torture him to death, and therefore he agreed to the peace."

As part of the peace arrangements, Sven was to marry the Polish princess Gunnhild, who had been the former queen of King Erik Segersäll of Sweden. It is hard to know just when this marriage took place. Snorri implies that Gunnhild married Sven almost immediately after he became king of Denmark. We may therefore safely assume that Erik Segersäll had repudiated Gunnhild and left her free to remarry considerably before his death in 995.

The Polish king, according to his part of the treaty, was supposed to marry Sven's sister Tyra (who had previously been married to Styrbjörn). The wedding was put off for a while, but eventually Tyra was forced to accept Boleslav's proposal.

According to the old stories, Tyra was miserable in this second marriage—first of all because her husband was a heathen, and secondly because he was old. She refused to eat and drink, and finally deserted Boleslav and fled to Norway. There—it is not clear just how much later—she found her third husband: Olof Tryggvesson.

Sven's forced marriage to Gunnhild seems to have lasted somewhat longer. Snorri writes, "King Sven returned to Denmark with Gunnhild, his spouse. Their sons were Harald and Canute."

Snorri tells us that Gunnhild was Boleslav's daughter. According to most genealogists, however, the princess was not Boleslav's daughter, but rather his sister, a child of the Polish prince Mieszko. What we can be sure of is that she was a Slavic princess, married to Sven as part of a peace agreement. Besides her sons Harald and Knut or Canute, Gunnhild bore Sven at least two daughters. One daughter, named Gyda, married Sven's ally Jarl Erik, the exiled son of Jarl Håkan of Norway. Another daughter was named Estrid. According to some of the old stories, she was briefly married to Robert I of Normandy (the father of William the Conqueror) and then repudiated by him. There seems to be little evidence for this tale. We do know that she married a jarl named Ulf. Three sons were born to this marriage: Sven (named for his grandfather, of course), Björn, and Osbern. These all inherited some Polish genes from their mother; and their Polish ancestry can be seen on Chart 11.

Despite the fact that it produced at least four children, the marriage of Sven Forkbeard to Gunnhild was not destined to last. Some sources say that King Sven repudiated Gunnhild; Snorri, on the other hand, reports that "Queen Gunnhild took sick and died; and a short time afterwards King Sven married Sigrid the Haughty."

Sven Forkbeard was heathen to the core. Saxo, who more than two centuries later was close to Bishop Absalon and may even have accompanied the cleric on his raids against the Wends, testifies that in the heathen Slavic temples there could be seen a wrought cup which Sven had brought as tribute to the gods. From this we may gather that Sven worshiped not only the Norse gods, but those of his Wendish neighbors as well.

Sven became a friend to Olof Tryggvesson of Norway. Together, Sven and Olof led raids against England. It hadn't bothered Sven to engage in battle against his own father, and he certainly didn't seem to feel the slightest compunction about warring against his grandmother Tyra's kinfolk. (As we have seen, Gorm's wife Tyra was very likely an English princess.) The Danes who had settled in northeastern England a century before, unhappy with their Saxon overlords, sided with the Vikings.

In 991, the Danes raided England. Instead of driving them off, Ethelred the Unready of England (acting on the advice of his cowardly archbishop Sigeric) bribed them to depart with 10,000 pounds of silver. It was a dangerous precedent, of course. Every time Ethelred made a payment to the Danes, they used their new resources to build up their invasion forces still further.

Ethelred's payments to Sven and Olof brought only temporary relief to England.  In 994, Sven Forkbeard and Olof steered ninety-four ships up the Thames and besieged London itself. When London successfully resisted the siege, the Vikings began raiding England's southern shores. Ethelred II was forced to come to terms with Sven's army; they were given winter quarters in Southampton and were paid 16,000 pounds of silver in cash.

Sigeric, the Archbishop of Canterbury, advised Ethelred to make a peace treaty with Olof Tryggvesson. (After all, Olof Tryggvesson had recently become a Christian.) The Anglo-Saxons confirmed the Norwegian king in his faith, bestowed royal gifts on him, and made him promise never to invade England again.

Olof Tryggvesson then returned home to Norway in peace—to rule his subjects and convert them by the sword. Sven Forkbeard returned to Denmark, with no intentions of giving up his Viking raids. He made expeditions against Frisia and Saxony, minted coins patterned after English models, and planned still further invasions of England.

Sven also made friends with the Swedish king, Olof Skötkonung. The Swedish Olof even suggested that Sven might care to marry his mother, Sigrid the Haughty. In Chapter 2, we have already made reference to Snorri's story about how Sigrid rejected her suitor Olof I Tryggvesson of Norway rather than renounce her pagan faith and be baptized as a Christian. We are told that Sigrid then promptly married Sven Forkbeard. If the chronicles are to be trusted, both Sven's first wife (Gunnhild) and his second wife (Sigrid) had been previously married to Erik the Victorious, king of Sweden. Probably both of them had also been repudiated by that much-married Swedish king.

Olof Tryggvesson, meanwhile, having been rejected by Sigrid, turned around and married Tyra, Sven's sister. Tyra persuaded the Norwegian Olof to make an expedition to Wendland to claim the lands she had been given as a dowry in connection to her brief marriage to Boleslav. Olof Tryggvesson built a large ship, christened it the *Long Serpent,* and sailed to Wendland, where he was able to come to agreeable terms with Tyra's ex-husband.

But there would be no peace between Olof Tryggvesson and Sven Forkbeard. The battle lines were clearly drawn. On one side was Sven Forkbeard of Denmark, together with his stepson Olof Skötkonung of Sweden, and his son-in-law Jarl Erik of Norway. On the other side was Olof Tryggvessen, fighting against his former friend and present brother-in-law, Sven Forkbeard.

As we have seen, the historic battle took place at Svölder, off the coast of the island of Rügen, in the year 1000. The three victors— King Sven of Denmark, Sven's stepson Olof Skötkonung of Sweden, and Sven's son-in-law Jarl Erik of Norway—divided the kingdom of the defeated Olof Tryggvesson.

Olof Skötkonung of Sweden probably ruled Bohüslan (which was formerly a part of Norway) as well as Ranrike on the east coast of the Oslo fjord. The rest of Norway now belonged to Sven Forkbeard, under the regency of Jarl Håkan's sons Erik and Sven, who remained loyal vassals of the Danish throne.

Not content with Norway and Denmark, Sven continued raiding England and bleeding her people for gold. In 1001, the Danes invaded England and extorted 24,000 pounds of silver from the Anglo-Saxons. During Ethelred's reign, he was forced to tax his people six times in order to buy off the blackmailing Vikings. The tax was called the "Danegeld" and it did nothing to increase Ethelred's popularity among his subjects.

On November 13, 1102—St. Brice's Day—Ethelred's hatred of the Vikings led him to order a massacre of English settlers of Danish descent.

The thirteenth-century John of Wallingford writes:

*This day was Saturday, on which the Danes are in the habit of bathing; and accordingly, at the set time they were destroyed most ruthlessly, from the least even to the greatest. They spared neither age nor sex, destroying together with them those women of their own nation who had consented to intermix with the Danes, and the children who had sprung from that foul adultery.*

Among the casualties were Sven Forkbeard's sister Gunnhild and her husband. (Pallig had been in the service of Ethelred but had sided with the Danes in their invasion in 1001.) As she lay dying, Gunnhild predicted that her death would bring England nothing but sorrow.

To no one's surprise, her prophecy was soon fulfilled. The news of the cruel atrocities drove Sven to revenge; he swore on his Viking "bragging cup" to punish Ethelred, he raised the largest fleet possible, and in 1003 he landed at Exeter in southwest England to wreak vengeance.

In 1004, according to *The Anglo-Saxon Chronicle*, Sven completely ravaged Norwich and Thetford in England. In 1007, Ethelred was obliged to pay the Danegeld for the fourth time, and Sven sailed home with 36,000 pounds of silver.

In 1011 the Vikings sailed to England again. This time Sven stayed home, placing his men under the leadership of a Jomsborg chieftain named Thorkel the Tall. With the Danes was Olof Haraldsson of Norway (known to posterity as Olof the Stout, or St. Olof). Other famous Danish figures in the 1011 raid included Thorkel's brother Hemming and a captain named Eilaf, a brother of the Jarl Ulf who married Sven's daughter Estrid.

The Vikings took Canterbury and captured Archbishop Alfheah, the very man who had earlier baptized Olof Tryggvesson. He had angered the Danes by condemning paganism and the slave trade, so they kept him prisoner on a ship at Greenwich for seven months. The beleaguered Anglo-Saxons raised 48,000 pounds of silver for the cleric's ransom, but their efforts were futile.

On April 19, 1012, the drunken Vikings killed the old man anyway, first pelting him with bones and oxheads, and then dealing him a final blow with an axe. Thorkel the Tall is said to have done all he could to stop the Danes from killing the archbishop, but his efforts were unsuccessful. Most of the Danish troops then sailed home, but Thorkel the Tall and Olof the Stout (perhaps feeling remorseful over Alfheah's death) remained in England and switched their allegiance to Ethelred.

In 1013 Sven Forkbeard set sail again, determined to conquer London itself. He had many accounts to settle with the English: They had killed his brother Hiring, they had killed his sister Gunnhild, and they had killed many of his men.

The learned Flemish monk who wrote the *Encomium Emmae Reginae* poetically described Sven's navy with metaphors borrowed from classical literature:

*When at last the soldiers were all gathered, they went on board the towered ships. . . On one side lions molded in gold were to be seen on the ships, on the other birds on the tops of the masts indicated by their movements the winds as they blew, or dragons of various kinds poured fire from their nostrils. . . .*

*The royal vessel excelled the others in beauty as much as the king preceded the soldiers in the honor of his proper dignity . . . The blue water, smitten by many oars, might be seen foaming far and wide, and the sunlight, cast back in the gleam of metal, spread a double radiance in the air.*

With Sven was his eighteen-year-old son. The youth's Danish name was Knut, but since he later became king of England we shall call him by the English form of his name—Canute. (As king of Denmark he was known as Knut II, the first Knut having been Gorm Hardeknut.)

Sven left his son Canute in charge of the Danish fleet at Gainsborough, and it was probably at this time that the young prince took as his mistress Alfgifu of Northumbria.

Little by little Sven took over more and more English territory, much of it without bloodshed, as the English yielded to him. The helpless and "unready" Ethelred paid the Danes 21,000 pounds of silver and then fled to Normandy with his sons and his wife Emma.

London was now open to Sven. With the help of his fellow-Dane, Thorkel the Tall (who had been in Ethelred's service but now switched sides again), Sven entered the city. Sven was promptly proclaimed King of England. Five weeks later, however, on February 3, 1014, he died very suddenly at Gainsborough. He was only about fifty-five years old.

Sven's death—at the very height of his conquests—was caused either by apoplexy or by a fall from his horse. Whether his demise was a mere accident or a skillfully disguised murder is anybody's guess. *The Anglo-Saxon Chronicle* refers to his death as a "happy event" for the people of England.

Sven was buried in England (some sources say at Gainsborough and others say at York), but later his remains were brought home to Denmark and buried in the church at Roskilde.

Despite his heathen ways and his unforgettable patricide, Sven Forkbeard was one of Denmark's greatest kings. He was responsible for taking back Hedeby from the Germans during his father's time. Later, as king in his own right, he made Denmark into an empire by defeating Olof Tryggvesson, adding part of Norway to his dominions, and then conquering the great land of England. Now he was dead, but destined to be succeeded by a son who would be even more famous— and certainly more Christian—than himself.

Upon his death, Sven's realm was divided up. Denmark went to his son Harald; and England went to his son Canute. His Norwegian territories went to Olof the Stout Haraldsson (St. Olof)—a descendant of Harald the Fairhaired—who in 1015 returned to Norway and reclaimed the throne that rightfully belonged to his family.

### Harald II Svensson—King of Denmark from 1014 to 1018.

*Of course I'll help my younger brother Canute outfit his fleet and sail off to England. I want him out of Denmark while I'm on the throne!* We can well imagine that Harald may have said this to himself when Canute asked him for aid.

Harald, Sven's eldest son, succeeded his father as king of Denmark. Meanwhile, young Canute had been ousted from England by forces which were loyal to Ethelred. Canute set the sails of his father's fleet toward Denmark. Stopping at Sandwich in Kent, he released the hostages he had been given at the peace agreements; but not without first mutilating them by cutting off their hands, ears and noses.

When Canute got back to Denmark, his brother Harald decided to help him refurbish the Danish fleet. Harald hoped to help Canute regain the throne of England (and also hoped to keep Canute out of Denmark!).

In 1015 Canute sailed again for England with two hundred ships and many seasoned warriors, including the Danish chieftain Thorkel the Tall. The bard Ottar the Black wrote:

*You were but a boy, ship-batterer,*
*When you launched your boat,*
*No king younger than you*
*Yet cast off from his country.*
*Helmed one, you hacked*
*The hard-cased ships.*

Leaving Harald on the throne of Denmark, let us turn to see what his brother Canute was doing in England. Despite his youth, Canute showed the determination and decisiveness of a skilled leader. He also was extremely lucky. In early 1016, Ethelred the Unready died, and Canute found it easy to overcome the English king's son Edmund Ironside at the great battle of Ashingdon.

After the battle, a peace treaty was arranged, and Edmund and Canute agreed to divide England. Edmund was to have Wessex, and Canute was to rule Mercia and the Danelaw. However, before the end of 1016, young Edmund mysteriously died. Rumor had it that he was poisoned, but the reports were never verified. Canute, now the sole ruler of England, was duly crowned and set upon the throne.

Harald Svensson died in 1018. Canute was now king of both England and Denmark.

**Canute—ruled Denmark and England from 1018 to 1035.**
*The mighty ruler of England, South Scotland, Denmark, Norway, and the Wendish lands.* Thus was Canute praised by his contemporaries, and the praise was amply justified. He may not always have been kind and fair; in fact he was sometimes downright cruel, but he was certainly a skilled leader of men and nations.

Canute the Great was only a teenager in 1013 when he accompanied his father, Sven Forkbeard, on the expedition to England. By 1014, upon his father's death, he was leader of the army. Two years later, as we have seen, upon the untimely death of Edmund Ironside, young Canute found himself proclaimed king of England by the nobles.

An Icelandic saga describes Canute in the following way: "Cnut was of great size and strength and very handsome, except that his nose was thin, high, and slightly bent. He had a light complexion and fair, thick hair, and his eyes surpassed the eyes of most men in their beauty and keenness."

Canute was a masterful organizer. To provide a more efficient government, he divided England into four earldoms. For himself he kept Wessex, from whence had sprung the great Saxon dynasty of Egbert and Alfred the Great. East Anglia was given to the Danish chieftain Thorkel the Tall. Canute's brother-in-law, Jarl Erik of Norway, was placed in charge of Northumbria; and a double-dealing Anglo-Saxon nobleman named Edric Streona was given Mercia.

Edric advised Canute to kill off Ethelred's sons. Edwig, a son of Ethelred by his first marriage, was thus soon dispatched. Edric also counseled Canute to kill Ethelred's grandsons — Edmund and Edward — who had survived their father Edmond Ironside. Instead of killing them, Canute sent them into exile in Sweden. From there, they were sent to Solomon, king of Hungary. There they made many Continental connections. For example, Edward married Agatha, a niece of Germany's emperor Henry II.

Only a year after being crowned, Canute had the murderous Edric Streona killed as a traitor. Yet in spite of the blood he shed, Canute was basically a reasonable king who kept England under its Saxon laws and was kinder to the English people than many of their own Saxon dynasty had been.

In 1017 Canute married Ethelred's widow Emma. (Edward the Confessor and Alfred, her two sons by Ethelred, remained in Normandy.) The marriage was a superbly calculated move designed to insure continuity in the government and endear the new king to the Anglo-Saxons. It was not the first time a Viking had married the widow of an enemy; history is full of such examples. Emma was thirty-four, ten years older than Canute, but still capable of bearing children.

Canute was no saint when it came to his love life. Scandinavian custom permitted kings to have a *frilla* or paramour as well as a legitimate queen. Canute's *frilla* was Alfgifu, the daughter of a certain minor official of Northumbria named Alfhelm. Queen Emma probably was aware that she had to share Canute's affections with her rival. Alfgifu bore two sons to Canute: Sven and Harald Harefoot.

By his queen — Emma, widow of Ethelred — Canute also had two children: a son named Hardecanute, and a daughter Gunnhild (who married Henry III of Germany). These family relationships may be seen on Charts 13 and 14.

Canute, unlike his father Sven, claimed to be a Christian. He made laws forbidding worship of idols, sun moon, stones or trees. He even sent English clerics overseas to Denmark to help finalize the evangelization of his native land. In an effort to make Denmark's church independent from Hamburg/Bremen, Canute established bishoprics at Odense on the Island of Fyn, at Roskilde in Sjaelland, and at Lund in Skåne. These sees were all governed by English bishops whom Canute had invested and who took it upon themselves to spread Christianity throughout the nation. From Canute's time on, Denmark could be considered as an officially Christian nation.

In 1020, Canute chose a man named Godwin to be earl of Wessex and Kent. For fifteen years, Godwin was the most powerful man in the kingdom next to Canute himself. Godwin may have been of Danish extraction; his wife Gyda was most certainly Danish, a sister to Jarl Ulf, as can be seen on Chart 10. Godwin and his wife gave some of their children Danish names: Sven, Tostig, Harald, and Gunnhild. The best known of these children, ironically named in honor of Canute's son Harald, is Harald Godwinsson who was defeated by William the Conqueror in 1066.

Much could be said about Canute as a ruler of England. He actually became more English than Danish, and only three times during his reign did he return to his native land.

The first time was when his older brother Harald died, and he went to Denmark to claim the throne. Lest the English people should forget who their real king was, Canute sent a letter from Denmark back to England, reminding them of his role as the Christian king and protector of England.

The second time Canute returned to Denmark as king was in 1023, to make peace with Thorkel the Tall. Thorkel had at first been Canute's most trusted advisor; his name appears on several charters issued between 1017 and 1020. In fact, Thorkel the Tall had been left in charge of England during Canute's first absence.

For some unknown reason, Thorkel the Tall was exiled to Denmark in 1021. Evidently Canute thought highly enough of him to seek him out and effect a reconciliation in 1023. Thorkel was then made regent in Denmark, and was appointed guardian of Hardecanute, Canute's son by Emma.

Thorkel appears to have died a year or two after the reconciliation in Denmark. Ulf Thorgilsson, Jarl of Skåne—who was married to Canute's sister Estrid—was made Denmark's new viceroy about 1024. He also took Thorkel's place as the guardian of young Hardecanute.

The Danes were unhappy because Canute, their real king, was never at home. Perhaps because of this, Jarl Ulf (his name means "wolf") made plans to seize the royal power. Treacherously obtaining a royal seal, he forged a document that would place Canute's young son Hardecanute on the Danish throne.

Jarl Ulf even joined the anti-Danish alliance led by King Anund Jakob of Sweden and King Olof the Stout of Norway. (Apparently Anund and Olof were worried about the balance of power, fearing that the Danish/English kingdom had grown far too strong.) Ulf's brother Eilaf, who had been given an English earldom by Canute, joined the conspiracy.

This serious situation led to King Canute's third royal visit to Denmark, in 1026. He sailed eastward and surprised Anund Jakob and Olof the Stout with a large fleet near the coast of Denmark. The Swedes and Norwegians, seeing Canute's impressive ships, retreated to the mouth of the Helga, or Holy River, on the east coast of Skåne, and there a furious battle took place. It appears that the double-dealing Jarl Ulf may have aided both sides in the fray. Neither side gained much in the battle; and after the fighting, a peace treaty was made.

Now Canute had to deal with Ulf. He sailed back to Denmark and crushed Ulf's rebellion. Many stories are told about the hostility between the brothers-in-law. According to one tale, Canute challenged Jarl Ulf to a game of chess one day, and had him murdered the following day in the Roskilde Cathedral. Once more a medieval king, fighting to preserve his power, had caused the death of a near relative. But he did not forget his widowed sister. Perhaps out of pity, or perhaps in an effort to atone for the murder of her husband, Canute bestowed large estates upon Estrid.

The Danish royal power reached its zenith in Canute. His ancestors, in a sense, had been little more than roving pirate chieftains. But he was a real king, recognized as a peer among the European monarchs of his time. Like many other medieval kings, he made a pilgrimage to Rome. Writing to his English subjects, he stated, "I do call you to witness that I have traveled to Rome to pray for the forgiveness of my sins and for the welfare of the peoples under my rule."

His pilgrimage coincided perfectly with the coronation of the Emperor Conrad II. On Easter Sunday, 1027, at St. Peter's Church in Rome, King Canute stood alongside Conrad of Germany, who was being crowned Holy Roman Emperor. Both Rudolph of Burgundy and Canute of England were there as official attendants and witnesses. It was perhaps Canute's moment of greatest glory.

It may have been at this time that Canute arranged the marriage of his daughter Gunnhild to Conrad's son Henry, who was destined to become emperor. The marriage didn't actually take place until 1036, after Canute's death, and Gunnhild—a sickly girl—died only two years after the wedding.

In 1028 Canute extended his vast empire still further by driving Olof the Stout out of Norway. Canute had astutely prepared the way by generously dispensing large gifts to the Norse nobility ahead of time. When he sailed up Norway's west coast, therefore, he received a royal welcome wherever he landed. And when he reached Nidaros, he was formally acknowledged as king of Norway.

Malcolm II and two other kings of Scotland also did homage to Canute. The Dane was now more than a king; he could well have been called an emperor.

Canute installed Jarl Håkan, son of the famous Jarl Erik, as his viceroy in Norway. When Håkan died shortly afterward, Canute put his mistress Alfgifu and their son Sven on the throne of Norway. Olof the Stout attempted to return to Norway, but fell at Stiklestad in 1030 and was later canonized. Alfgifu and Sven, never very popular in Norway, were eventually forced to flee to Denmark. There Sven, Canute's son, passed away in 1035.

Canute the Great died that same year, on November 11, 1035; he was only about forty years old. He was greatly mourned in Denmark and England, and was buried in Winchester Cathedral. He was praised as the "mighty ruler of England, South Scotland, Denmark, Norway, and the Wendish lands."

**CHART 10 - The Family of Gorm the Old, King of Denmark**

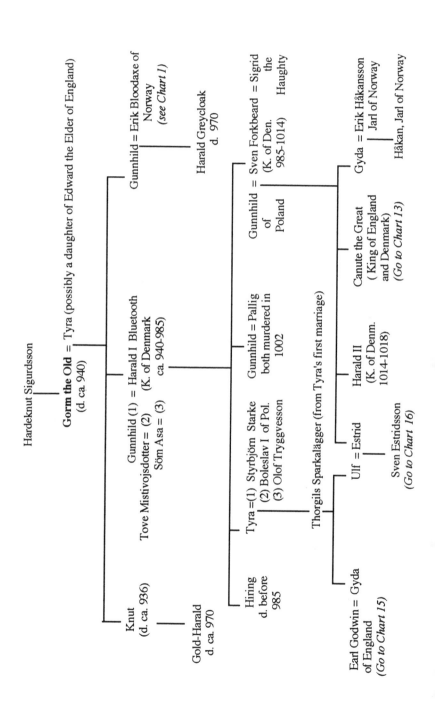

# CHART 11 - The Family of Mieszko I of Poland

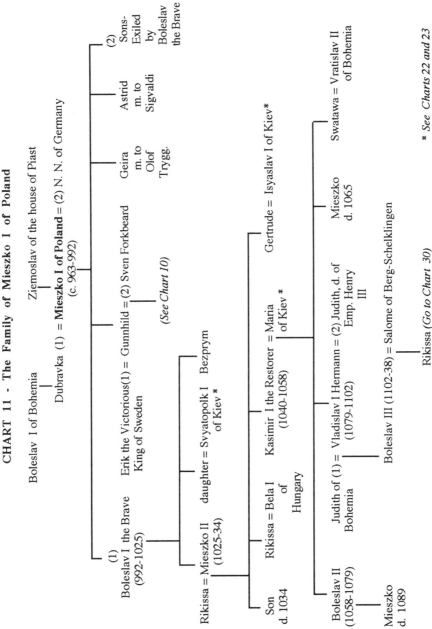

Boleslav I of Bohemia    Ziemoslav of the house of Piast

Dubravka (1) = **Mieszko I of Poland** = (2) N. N. of Germany
(c. 963-992)

(1)
Boleslav I the Brave
(992-1025)

Erik the Victorious(1) = Gunnhild = (2) Sven Forkbeard
King of Sweden

(See Chart 10)

Geira
m. to
Olof
Trygg.

Astrid
m. to
Sigvaldi

(2)
Sons-
Exiled
by
Boleslav
the Brave

Rikissa = Mieszko II
(1025-34)

daughter = Svyatopolk I    Bezprym
of Kiev *

Rikissa = Bela I
of
Hungary

Kasimir I the Restorer = Maria
(1040-1058)    of Kiev *

Gertrude = Isyaslav I of Kiev*

Mieszko
d. 1065

Swatawa = Vratislav II
of Bohemia

Son
d. 1034

Boleslav II
(1058-1079)

Judith of (1) = Vladislav I Hermann = (2) Judith, d. of
Bohemia    (1079-1102)    Emp. Henry
III

Boleslav III (1102-38) = Salome of Berg-Schelklingen

Rikissa (Go to Chart 30)

Mieszko
d. 1089

* See Charts 22 and 23

**CHART 12 - The Family of Mistivoj, King of the Wends of Mecklenburg**

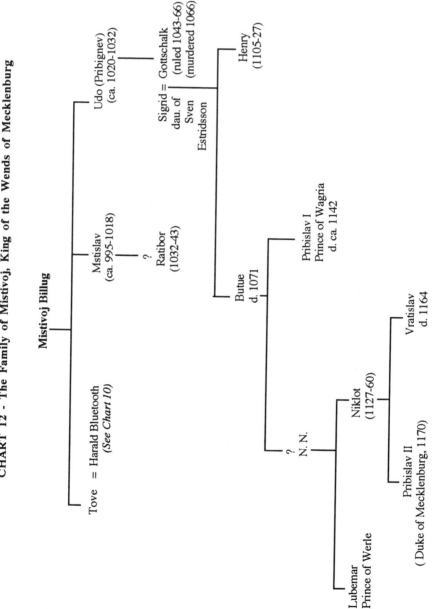

**CHART 13 - The Family of Canute the Great, King of England and Denmark**

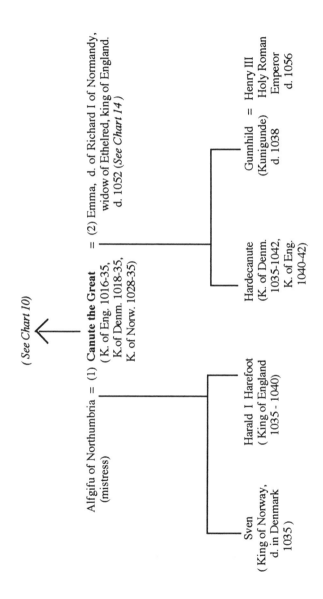

Alfgifu of Northumbria = (1) **Canute the Great** = (2) Emma, d. of Richard I of Normandy,
(mistress)                        (K. of Eng. 1016-35,             widow of Ethelred, king of England.
                                      K. of Denm. 1018-35,          d. 1052 (*See Chart 14*)
                                      K. of Norw. 1028-35)

(*See Chart 10*)

Sven
(King of Norway,
d. in Denmark
1035)

Harald I Harefoot
(King of England
1035 - 1040)

Hardecanute
(K. of Denm.
1035-1042,
K. of Eng.
1040-42)

Gunnhild = Henry III
(Kunigunde)   Holy Roman
d. 1038          Emperor
                     d. 1056

**CHART 14 - The Family of Emma of Normandy**

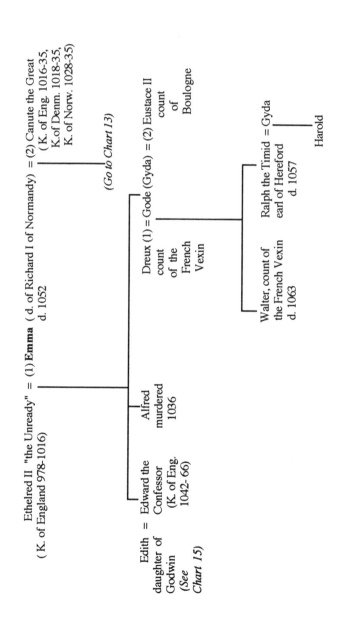

## CHART 15 - The Family of Godwin, Earl of Wessex

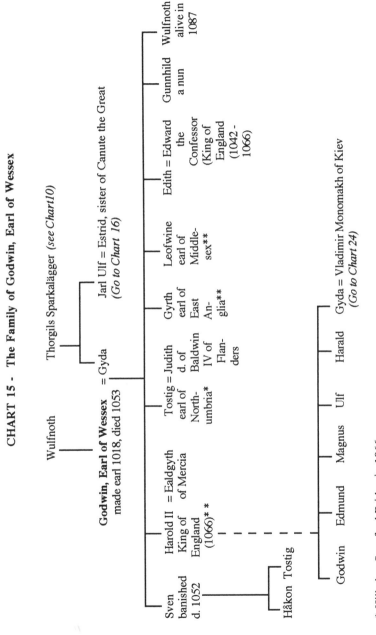

* Killed at Stamford Bridge in 1066
** Killed at Hastings in 1066

## Chapter 6

### The Kings of Denmark from 1035 to 1241

**Hardecanute (Knut III)—ruled Denmark from 1035 to 1042 and England from 1040 to 1042.**

*He did nothing worthy of a king as long as he ruled.* Thus does *The Anglo-Saxon Chronicle* summarize Hardecanute's life.

Hardecanute, as we have seen, was Canute's only legitimate son. On his father's side he was descended from Gorm the Old, and on his mother's side he was descended from the dukes of Normandy. Because of the *Canute* in his name, he is sometimes called Knut III in the list of Danish kings. (His father, Canute the Great, is Knut II.)

Hardecanute was made regent of Denmark in 1029, so he was in Denmark when his father passed away in England. At that time, the young prince was only seventeen.

The great North Sea empire which Canute the Great had built up was now destined to break up. Denmark continued to be ruled by Hardecanute. Norway went to Magnus, son of the slain St. Olof. And England, once more separate from Scandinavia, went to Canute's illegitimate son Harald Harefoot.

Hardecanute's mother Emma had lost both her husbands. To add to her trials, Alfred—a son from her first marriage—had been murdered. Now exiled from England, she had found asylum with Count Baldwin V in Flanders and commissioned a Flemish monk to write a history of Canute and his deeds: *Encomium Emmae Reginae*.

As long as they both lived, there was bitter rivalry between the half brothers Harald I Harefoot of England and Hardecanute of Denmark.

But Hardecanute had more amiable relations with Magnus of Norway. They made peace, pledged to be foster-brothers, and agreed that if either died without heirs, the other would succeed to his throne.

Hardecanute next sailed to Bruges, to visit his mother Emma and perhaps to make plans to get England back from his half brother Harald.

Hardecanute did not have to fight. In 1040 Harald conveniently died without heirs, and Hardecanute was summoned to England to be made king. A fleet of sixty-two ships accompanied him.

Hardecanute promptly alienated his subjects by levying grievous taxes. He also shocked them greatly when he ordered that the body of his paternal half brother Harald should be dug up and thrown into the river. Then he sought revenge for the death of his maternal half brother Alfred, since murder charges had been brought against Earl Godwin and the bishop of Worcester. The bishop was deposed, and Godwin had to gain his freedom with a bribe of a splendid warship manned with eighty warriors.

Having avenged Alfred's death, Hardecanute invited his remaining half brother Edward to England, made provision for him, and named him as his heir.

After only two years as King of England, Hardecanute died of overdrinking at a wedding feast at Lambeth. With his death the Danish dynasty in England came to an end after less than 30 years. All four of Canute the Great's children were now dead. Sven had died in Denmark in 1035, Gunnhild in Germany in 1038, Harald in England in 1040, and now Hardecanute was dead in 1042. And all four died without descendants. The genes of the great Canute were not destined to be passed on to posterity.

The English throne passed to Edward the Confessor, Hardecanute's half brother on his mother Emma's side. But Denmark was invaded by Magnus the Good of Norway, who claimed the throne by virtue of his treaty with Hardecanute.

**Magnus I—ruled Denmark and Norway from 1042 to 1047.**

*Hardecanute promised me that if he died without heirs, I should succeed to his throne. Now's my chance to make Denmark a part of my Norwegian kingdom!*

While Hardecanute was succeeded in England by Edward, he was succeeded in Denmark by Magnus I (Magnus Olofsson or Magnus the Good) King of Norway.

Snorri informs us that the Danish nobles readily welcomed Magnus. Not only was there no son of Canute the Great left alive to take the throne, but they hailed the available candidate as a son of a real saint, for "the sanctity of Holy King Olof and his miracles had become known in all the lands."

Not everyone, however, was interested in honoring the foster-brother treaty that Hardecanute and Magnus had sworn. Harald, son of Thorkel the Tall, attempted to seize the Danish throne, but he was killed by Magnus' brother-in-law Ordulf, son of Bernhard, the duke of Saxony.

Another contender for the throne was Sven Estridsson, a son of the murdered Jarl Ulf. Sven had a legitimate claim to the Danish throne through his mother, a sister of Canute the Great.

Rather than fighting against Sven Estridsson, Magnus decided to make peace with him, naming Sven as his regent in Denmark. Sven, in turn, swore allegiance to Magnus.

Snorri tells us that King Magnus, sitting on his high throne, called the nobles to him and proclaimed, "I have promised to give you a chieftain for the protection of the land and for governing it. I do not know of any man as well suited for that, in every way, as is Sven Ulfsson. He has the birth to be a chieftain. Now then I shall appoint him my jarl and give into his hands the Danish realm to rule while I am in Norway."

Soon after being appointed regent, Sven attended the Viborg *Thing,* where the Danes to all intents and purposes named him their king. Magnus, unhappy with this turn of events, moved swiftly against his vassal, and Sven Estridsson was forced to flee to his father-in-law, Anund Jacob, in Sweden.

Magnus may have felt that he needed to prove to the Danes that he was a worthy king, and that he could protect them against the raids of the neighboring Slavic Wends. In 1043 Magnus stormed and burned the Wendish city of Wollin. According to Snorri, he also destroyed Jomsburg, and "many people in Wendish lands offered their submission to King Magnus, but many more fled."

The sagas celebrate Magnus' battles in alliterative poetry, telling of his great victories over the Wends with his father's battle-axe, called "Hel." (We may note in passing that although Magnus' father Olof had been made a saint, his axe was ironically named for the ancient heathen goddess of death.)

*With both his hands the haft of*
*Hel he grasped ...*
*Unscathed in skirmish,*
*Skulls he cleft and obtained the victory.*

More about Magnus, his family relationships, and his effort to obtain England will be found in the chapters on Norway. Magnus died in Denmark in the autumn of 1047, as the result of a fall from a horse. He was not even thirty years old, and he left no heirs.

In Norway Magnus was succeeded by Harald Hårdråde, his father's half brother. In Denmark, the obvious successor was Sven Estridsson. Sven, who had fled to Skåne, now returned to the Danish mainland. Once more he was proclaimed King of Denmark at the Viborg *Thing* in Jutland, and this time there was no one to oppose him.

### Sven II Estridsson—ruled Denmark from 1047 to 1074.

*Sven made himself master of all the land ... he took possession of all the islands. The people all submitted to him.* Thus Snorri summarized Sven Estridsson's rise to power.

Sven is sometimes surnamed Ulfsson after his father Ulf Thorgilsson, the jarl of Skåne who in 1027 was cut down in his prime at the Roskilde church by Canute the Great's royal order. On his father's side, Sven claimed descent from Styrbjörn Starke, that rebellious nephew of the Swedish king, Erik the Victorious. Sven seems to have inherited plenty of Styrbjörn's independent and adventuresome spirit. Since Styrbjörn's wife was said to be Tyra, the daughter of Harald Bluetooth, Sven could trace his paternal as well as his maternal ancestry back to Gorm the Old of Denmark.

At other times Sven is called Sven Estridsson after his mother, Canute the Great's sister. On his mother's side, Sven was not only a descendant of Gorm the Old, but also grandson of Sven I Forkbeard, a nephew of Canute the Great and a cousin to Hardecanute. He therefore had a claim to the throne of Denmark through his mother.

Sven was born in England about 1020 and spent part of his childhood there, at the court of his uncle Canute the Great. At the time that his father Ulf was murdered, Sven was only about seven years old.

Neither England nor Denmark seemed like a safe haven for Sven after his father's murder, so the boy was taken to Sweden for asylum. There he lived for twelve years serving king Anund Jakob. When he reached marriageable age, he was given Anund Jakob's daughter Jutta (Gyda) as a bride.

As we have seen, Sven was first made a Danish viceroy by King Magnus the Good, but became king in his own right in 1047.

The following year Sven joined Edward the Confessor of England and the Emperor Henry III of Germany in an alliance against Baldwin V of Flanders. The reader may remember that Sven's first cousin Gunnhild (a daughter of Canute the Great) had been married to Henry III.

Upon seeing the great fleets that were assembled against him, Baldwin surrendered to the emperor without a fight.

About this same time, another English/Danish drama was being played out. Sven Estridsson's aunt Gyda (a sister to Jarl Ulf) had married the powerful Godwin of Wessex. One of their children (whose name also happened to be Sven) got into trouble in England for seducing an abbess. Sven Godwinsson was put to public shame, forced to go into exile, and ended up seeking refuge with his first cousin Sven Estridsson.

While the English/Danish/German forces were preparing to blockade Flanders, Sven Godwinsson sailed into Chichester with eight ships and tried to make his peace with Edward the Confessor. Edward refused to listen to Sven Godwinsson's pleas, so the exile sought the aid of his cousin Duke Björn, a brother to Sven Estridsson.

Björn and his brother Osbern came to their cousin's aid, but he soon quarreled with them. Sven Godwinsson murdered Björn, forced Osbern to flee, and was once more exiled from England. This time he fled to Baldwin of Flanders, who always seemed ready to receive pirates, political refugees, and even criminals.

For seventeen years—from 1047 to 1064—Sven Estridsson's reign was marked by constant warfare against Harald III Hårdråde of Norway. It is pointless to recount all the details of their many battles; suffice it to say that in most of them Sven was defeated.

In 1049, Harald Hårdråde burned Denmark's primary mart, Hedeby, to the ground. The poets mourned the occasion with alliterative verse:

*All Hedeby was blazing,*
*Fired by Harald's fury ...*
*King Sven now feels the dire damage*
*Of Harald's valiant vengeance.*
*At dawn on Hedeby's outskirts*
*The high flames of the houses whirled.*

Peace between Norway and Denmark finally came in 1064, after a battle at the Nissa River. Although the Danes lost the battle, Harald Hårdråde was willing to sign a treaty which restored to Norway and Denmark their ancient boundaries. The poets breathed a sigh of relief and one of them wrote:

*I have heard how happily*
*Harald and Sven gave hostages.*
*May the pact of peace*
*Remain unbroken.*

It was perhaps after this treaty that marriage alliances were made between Harald and Sven. Harald's son Olof (later known as Olof Kyrre) married Sven's daughter Ingegerd. And Sven's son Olof (later known as Olof Hunger) married Harald's daughter Ingegerd.

Two years later, Harald Hårdråde was killed at the battle of Stamford Bridge in England, and Sven was spared further threats from this "lightning bolt of the north."

In 1067 Sven, not content with Denmark, sent a message to William the Conqueror, asserting his right to the English throne by virtue of the fact that he was Canute's nephew, and insisting therefore that William pay homage to him as a vassal.

William made a polite reply to his "friend and cousin," sending along some rich presents. Sven, however, was not moved by William's diplomacy. In 1069, allying himself with some Anglo-Saxon and Anglo-Danish rebels against William the Conquerer, Sven sent a fleet of 240 Danish ships to England under the command of his brother Osbern. Sven's two older sons—Harald and Knut (Canute)—were also sent on the expedition, but Sven himself remained at home.

Sven's brother and sons, of course, were cousins to the sons and grandsons of Godwin of Wessex. (Godwin had married Gyda, a sister to Sven's father Jarl Ulf.) The Danish/Wessex connection could have meant big trouble for William, and he was unprepared for a sea battle.

Sven's forces were nevertheless repulsed in skirmishes at Dover, Sandwich and East Anglia. In early September, the Danish fleet entered the Humber; it had been just three years since Harald Hårdråde had met his final defeat there. Here Sven's persistent troops were finally victorious at York. The Danish fleet settled down for the winter on the Isle of Axholme near the south shore of the Humber, erected fortifications, and made friends with the Anglo-Danes who lived in the area.

In the spring of 1070, Sven himself came from Denmark to join his fleet. From the Humber the Danish forces sailed south, seized the Isle of Ely, and plundered the abbey and monastery at Peterborough in true Viking style.

William was forced to make an agreement with Sven that summer. Like his predecessors, William paid the Danes off and as a result Sven withdrew his troops from England. Both kings were probably relieved at the arrangement; it meant there would not be a full-scale war. Neither side was really ready for such a catastrophe; the Danes were not prepared for battles on land and the Normans did not have a sufficient navy to be sure of a victory at sea.

Sven worked to establish the independence of the Danish church. His uncle, Canute the Great, had hoped that the Danish church would be under the jurisdiction of Canterbury, but this was not meant to be, for England and Denmark went their separate ways after Canute's death. Instead, Denmark remained under the jurisdiction of the Archbishop of Hamburg/Bremen. Sven, an astute diplomat, cooperated with Archbishop Adalbert, although he hoped to make Denmark eventually independent under a separate archbishopric in Lund.

Adam of Bremen describes the meeting between Adalbert and Sven in Schleswig which took place about 1050:

*Finally, as is the custom among the barbarians, they feasted each other sumptiously on eight successive days to confirm the treaty of alliance. Dispositions were made there of many ecclesiastical questions; decisions were reached about peace for the Christians and about the conversion of the heathen. And so the prelate returned home full of joy and persuaded the emperor to summon the Danish king to Saxony that each might swear to the other a perpetual friendship.*

In addition to establishing and organizing hundreds of churches, Sven founded six bishoprics. Two of these were in Skåne, which is now Swedish but at that time was Danish. Sven also was known as a patron of learning.

Despite his interest in the church, Sven was in many ways a real Viking at heart, always ready to conquer his neighbors and wreak revenge upon his foes. It is said that one New Year's Eve, the king's servants, having had too much wine, were making fun of his lack of valor in battle. Sven grew so angry that he ordered the scoffers to be killed while they were at church on New Year's Day.

When the bishop reproached Sven for desecrating God's House

with murder, he responded with deeds of penitence and gave a large grant to the Church.

What shall we say about Sven Estridsson's family life? Adam of Bremen, who knew Sven personally, was appalled by the king's morals. Sven had at least four wives, and many mistresses as well.

There are several different accounts of his marriages, none of them clear. According to one Swedish source, Sven's first wife was Jutta (also called Gyda), the daughter of King Anund Jakob of Sweden, whom Sven had served for twelve years in his youth.

Jutta is said to have died around 1045, and Sven is said to have married Anund Jakob's widow Gunnhild shortly thereafter. (Gunnhild was the second wife of King Anund.) Sven was therefore taking his first wife's stepmother as his second queen.

Adam of Bremen supports the view that Sven's second wife was Anund's widow, but he indicates that Sven had an earlier queen also named Gunnhild. He tells us that Sven "married a blood relative from Sweden." Then he states:

> *This mightily displeased the lord archbishop, who sent legates to the rash king, rebuking him severely for his sin.... At length the Danish tyrant was prevailed upon by letters from the pope to give his cousin a bill of divorce. Still the king would not give ear to the admonitions of the priests. Soon after he had put aside his cousin he took to himself other wives and concubines, and again still others. And the Lord raised up against him many adversaries on all sides as He had against Solomon.*

Adam furthermore calls Sven's repudiated wife "the most saintly queen Gunnhild," and tells us that "after her separation from the king of the Danes on the ground of consanguinity, she lived on her estates across from Denmark, devoting her time to hospitality and almsgiving."

A later scholar added a footnote to Adam's work, stating that "there was another Gunnhild, the widow of Anund."

Still another addition to Adam's account tells us that Sven had a legitimate queen named Gyda, who was poisoned to death by her rival, a concubine named Tora. The note adds: "When King Sven sent Tora's son, named Magnus, to Rome to be consecrated there for the kingship, the unhappy youth died on the way. After him the wicked mother did not have another son." It may well be that the poisoned Gyda was Anund Jakob's daughter.

Another of Sven's wives, we are told, was named Elizabeth. Some sources state that Sven later married the widow of his former foe Harald Hårdråde, so it may be that it was Elizabeth of Kiev who married Sven.

Louda and McLagan's *Lines of Succession* show Sven Estridsson's first wife as Gunnhild, the daughter of a minor jarl named Sven. They show his second wife as being the widow of Anund Jakob. They entirely leave out Jutta or Gyda, Anund's daughter.

What all these accounts have in common is that Sven married more than once, that at least one of his wives was named Gunnhild, and that he married Anund Jakob's widow. It is completely possible that there were two Gunnhilds, two Gydas, and two Toras! We can also read between the lines and see that there was a great deal of jealousy among the monarch's wives and concubines.

Sven had fifteen sons, all or most of them out of wedlock. There is a great deal of debate as to the identity of the mothers of these sons. Louda and McLagan's *Lines of Succession* show Knut IV, Olof Hunger, and Erik Ejegod as legitimate sons of Queen Gunnhild (not the Gunnhild who was Anund Jakob's widow, but rather Sven's earlier wife—the pious cousin who was repudiated on the grounds of consanguinity).

When one compares the dates of Sven's sojourn at Anund Jakob's court with Knut's birth (about 1043), it appears that Knut may have been the son of Jutta Anundsdotter. If this is true, the line of King Anund Jakob of Sweden did not really die out. Through his daughter Jutta, many future kings may have descended from Anund Jakob.

We may not know the names of the mothers of all Sven's sons, but we can be sure of the fact that they quarreled over the succession. Five of them succeeded Sven to the Danish throne—Harald Hejn, Knut IV, Olof Hunger, Erik Ejegod, and Niels.

Sven's male descendants ruled Denmark for three hundred years after his death, until in 1375 Valdemar III died without sons. However, through the daughters of Valdemar III and through subsequent Danish kings, the descendants of Sven Estridsson have continued to inherit the throne of Denmark up to the present time.

It is also interesting to note that the present royal family of England is descended from a long line of Danish kings, including Sven Estridsson. This is because James I of England (an ancestor of Queen Elizabeth II) was married to Anne, a daughter of King Frederick II of Denmark.

And so the blood of Sven Estridsson continues to flow in the veins of many European monarchs and also in many common folk whose distant ancestors were royalty.

Many kings of Sweden also claim descent from Sven Estridsson. Sven's great-granddaughter Margaret, a daughter of Prince Knut Lavard, married into the Swedish nobility. From her line came Karl VII Sverkersson, who ruled Sweden from 1161 to 1167, and all his descendants.

Besides his many sons, Sven Estridsson also had four daughters, all of them illegitimate. Through them, his genes were passed on to still other royal families. As we have seen, Sven's daughter Ingegerd married Olof Kyrre, the son of the Norwegian Viking Harald Hårdråde.

Another daughter of Sven Estridsson was named Sigrid. As part of a political alliance, Sigrid was given to Prince Gottschalk of Mecklenburg, a Wendish city. Their son was Henry. Gottschalk has gone down in history as something of a saint and martyr; Adam of Bremen tells us that in 1066 he was "slain by the pagans [the Slavs] whom he was trying to convert to Christianity." Gottschalk's ancestry may be seen on Chart 12.

Still another daughter of Sven Estridsson was named Gunnhild.

Sven Estridsson fell ill and died in 1074. He was one of Denmark's most colorful monarchs. Although often defeated by his powerful foe Harald Hårdråde, he showed an invincible spirit of tenacity. He was tough and persistant, and he refused to be discouraged. In the end, he outlived his foes.

With his death, the Viking age in Denmark came to an end.

## Harald III Hejn—ruled from 1074 to 1080.

*Let us have peace! There is no need to fight the Norwegians.* This attitude of Harald Hejn (sometimes called Harald III) led to his nickname *Hejn* or "the Softstone." He was somewhat timid, disinclined to war, devoted to the church, and ready to give in easily to the demands of the peasants.

When Sven Edstridsson died, his two older sons began to quarrel, quite predictably, over the throne. Harald and Knut had fought unitedly in the 1069 expedition against England, but now they had become enemies.

The victor in the fraternal contest was Sven's oldest son Harald, who won the throne by the approval of the nobles. The disappointed Knut decided it was best to get away from Denmark, so he sailed away on a second expedition to England with two hundred ships. His purpose was to support a rebellion led by some English earls against William the Conqueror. But the rebellion was quelled before Knut arrived, and so his expedition came to nothing.

When it came to defending Denmark against the Norwegians, Harald was lacking in energy and decisiveness, and therefore his popularity was short-lived. His reign was brief, but he did accomplish two noteworthy things. He reformed criminal law, and he updated the coinage of the country.

Harald died on April 17, 1080. He left no heirs, so his second brother Knut, who had been his rival, succeeded him as king.

History was repeating itself. In 1018, Denmark's first Harald Svensson had died without direct heirs, leaving the throne to a brother named Knut (Canute the Great). Now in 1080, a second Harald Svensson had died without heirs, leaving the throne to a brother named Knut—who, like Canute the Great before him—was a forceful leader and an invader of England. There the resemblance ends, however, for Knut IV never realized his dream of sitting upon the English throne.

### Knut IV "den Helige" (St. Knut)—ruled from 1080 to 1086.

*Bring your tithes and your taxes! You are required to pay ten percent of all your harvested corn.* With such demands, King Knut alienated his subjects, but he is remembered more as a saint than as a tyrant.

Knut was the second of the five sons who succeeded Sven Estridsson. Since Danish kings with the name of Hardecanute (including Gorm) are included among those listed as Knut, Saint Knut is sometimes called Knut IV. Other historians list him as Knut II.

As we have seen, Knut spent his youth taking part in Viking raids and expeditions. When he became king, he showed something of his father's tenacity and strong will. He defended the legal system and worked to abolish slavery. He also supported the church, and brought to Odense the bones of St. Alban, a Briton who was martyred in the days of Diocletian.

In 1082 St. Knut married Adela, the daughter of Robert I le Frison, Count of Flanders. A medieval scribe, writing in Latin, called her Ethela, and stated: "A divine spirit inspired [St. Knut] to despise the lascivious embrace of concubines, and he chose for his wife Ethela from the [Holy] Roman Empire."

St. Knut's marriage in many ways marked a new day for the Danish royal family. Instead of marrying a Scandinavian or Slavic princess, he was marrying into the royal lineage of mainline Europe— the Holy Roman Empire, if you wish. For Adela was descended from the Great Karl—from Charlemagne himself.

St. Knut and Adela, during their brief four-year marriage, became the parents of two daughters—Ingegerd and Cecilia—and a son named Karl or Charles.

Knut was in many ways the opposite of his timid brother Harald. He was brave and even despotic; a strong rather than a weak ruler. He attempted to exact from his people a tithe for the church—ten percent of all harvested corn. Not surprisingly, the peasants became angry at being forced to contribute this instead of giving voluntarily.

Knut reminds us in some ways of King John of England, who also angered his subjects by excessive taxes. Knut, like John, wished to keep the royal forest exclusively for the crown and to make fishing on the Danish coast a royal monopoly.

Knut made his brother Erik jarl of Sjaelland, the island where the great dynasty of Gorm had sprung up. Another brother, Olof, was made duke of Schleswig. Eventually this duchy became almost independent from Denmark.

Knut also attempted to get back England from the Normans, hoping to succeed where his father had failed eighteen years before. With his end in view, in 1085 he established an alliance with Count Robert le Frison of Flanders (his father-in-law). Joining these two was Knut's brother-in-law Olof Kyrre (the Quiet) of Norway, who had married Knut's sister Ingegerd. Knut hoped that the three of them could be strong enough to overcome William the Conqueror. He hoped that the Danes, who had claimed the English throne for just twenty-six short years— from 1016 to 1042—could get it back.

The Danish/Norwegian/Flemish fleet that the three leaders mustered was immense—1,660 ships. Sixty of them were Norwegian; 600 were Flemish, and 1,000 were Danish.

The fleet gathered at Limsfjord in Jutland, but Knut was forced to postpone the expedition in order to halt a a rebellion in Schleswig.

While Knut was away trying to quell the trouble on his southern borders, the troops in the fjord grew restless. By the time he returned, the fleet had broken up; only the Norwegian ships were left in the harbor. Knut decided to send them home with thanks for their loyalty. It was the last time the Danes attempted to conquer England.

William the Conqueror, fearing that Knut might attempt another invasion of England the next year, hired a great host of merceneries to meet the Danes. But William's immense army never had to fight, for Knut never left his homeland.

Knut's own people were angry with their king on several accounts. He had severely punished the troops who had abandoned ship while he was in Schleswig. And he had levied yet another tax to benefit the Church. It was just too much for the peasants, and they rose up against him. The rebellion began among the peasants in northern Jutland. Knut and his brothers Benedict and Erik fled from the rebels, seeking refuge at St. Alban's church at Odense.

Odense, the largest city on the island of Fyn, was named for the pagan god Odin, but Canute the Great had sent English missionaries there, and they had founded a monastery. It was in the Odense cathedral that Knut had placed the relics of the English saint, Alban, but now his prayers to St. Alban seemed to go unheeded.

The pursuers surrounded the church, crying out, "Where is Knut, our god-forsaken king? Let him come forth and show himself!" The angry peasants, shouting out curses and insults, grew bolder and began to throw whatever was at hand through the church windows. There is considerable evidence that the mob's fury was incited at least in part by Knut's brother Olof, who because of his designs on the throne had turned many Danes against their king. Olof could not have led the mob, however, because he was at that moment in exile.

According to some sources, Knut was killed by a spear thrown in from outside through a window. According to other accounts, it was a stone that took his life.

So it was that on July 10, 1086, after receiving communion, Knut and his brother Benedict (whose name is sometimes shortened to Bengt) were slain before the altar; they never had a chance to defend themselves. Erik, however, escaped and eventually became king.

Ironically Knut, who in his life was hated by his people, became a hero to them after being martyred. Miracles were reported at his tomb, and he was later canonized as a saint. His feast day is January 19.

As we have seen, Knut's widow, Queen Adela, was left with three small children. We know that she returned for a while to her childhood home in Flanders, taking little Charles with her. Later, in a marriage arranged by her father, she was wed to another ruler of Scandinavian descent—the Norman Roger Borsa, who had succeeded his adventursome father Robert Guiscard as Duke of Apulia in 1085. A new life began for Adela in sunny, southeastern Italy. There she gave birth to William, destined to succeed his father as Duke of Apulia in 1111.

Little is known about the childhood of St. Knut's children. The boy may have been raised in Flanders, and the girls may have remained in Denmark to be raised by relatives, rather than moving to

Italy with their mother. In the Middle Ages, royal children were considered property of the state. Royal daughters, particularly, were viewed as government assets, to be given in marriage as part of political alliances. A case in point is Eleanor of Aquitaine. When she divorced Louis VII of France and married Henry II of England, she was not allowed to take her two daughters by Louis with her. They remained in France, as property of the state.

Interestingly, the compilation known as *Vitae Sanctorum Danorum,* ("Lives of Danish Saints"), which includes papal epistles, prayers to Danish saints, and other tributes to St. Knut, does not mention his daughters. The encomiums do mention his son, who eventually became Charles the Good, Duke of Flanders (and was later tragically murdered, much like his father).

It is from Saxo as well as Swedish sources that we learn of St. Knut's daughters and their husbands. Ingegerd married into the Folke family of Sweden, and Cecilia also married into the Swedish nobility, becoming the wife of the Jarl Erik Göthe. We shall trace their royal descendants in subsequent chapters, for many Swedish kings are descended from these daughters of St. Knut and Adela.

### Olof I Hunger—ruled from 1086 to 1095.

*"This famine is sent from God as a punishment upon Denmark! You have murdered the holy King Knut, and now you will suffer."* With these words, the clergy of Olof Hunger's time berated their congregations and sought to bring them to repentance.

When Knut died, his brother Olof was chosen as the next king. This was because the nobles deemed him, out of all Knut's many brothers, to be the one least likely to try to avenge his death. It will be remembered that Knut had designated Olof to be duke of Schleswig. However, Olof was not to be found in Denmark; he was in Flanders with Knut's father-in-law, Robert le Frison, where he had been exiled by Knut for treason.

Taking her young son Charles with her, Knut's widow returned to Flanders, and persuaded her father to release her brother-in-law. Olof was brought back to Denmark and assumed the throne.

There was a severe famine in Olof's day. Because of this, he was known as Olof Hunger. The priests declared to the faithful that the famine was sent directly from God as a punishment for the death of the holy Knut.

Olof did little to relieve the distress of his hungry subjects. While they went without basic necessities, he lived in luxury at his court. When he died in 1095, there were few to mourn him.

Olof's queen was Ingegerd, a daughter of Harald III Hårdråde of Norway. There was a double family connection between the royal houses of Norway and Denmark at this time. The Danish king Olof Hunger was married to Harald Hårdråde's daughter Ingegerd. And the Norwegian king Olof Kyrre was married to Sven Estridsson's daughter Ingegerd. How confusing! Two King Olofs, two Queen Ingegerds, and all of them in-laws!

Upon Olof's death, his brother Erik, who had stood by St. Knut to the bitter end at St. Albans, was called home from Sweden to be crowned.

### Erik I Ejegod—ruled from 1095 to 1103.

*"Farewell, my people. I have taken the cross and shall go forth to the Holy Land!"* Erik, the third son of Sven Estridsson to come to the throne, lived from about 1056 to 1103. His surname, *Ejegod,* means "Evergood" or "Good for the Eyes". Because of this, he is often called "Erik the Good" in English.

He probably earned his nickname because of his handsome looks; he was blue-eyed, blond, and tall, with the long fair hair which was considered a badge of nobility among the Vikings. He was also said to be stronger than any four other men, and skilled in riding, swimming, and other athletic accomplishments. Furthermore, we are told that he was an excellent harp player and poet, and such a good linguist that he could converse with any foreigner in his native tongue.

Although Erik was said to be a pious man, he became embroiled in the church-state controversies which were so prevalent in medieval times. As a result, he was excommunicated.

Erik was not willing to accept this verdict, and promptly traveled to Rome to appeal his case before Urban II, the famous pope who preached the First Crusade. Erik's efforts were successful, and he was reinstated in the church. In 1101, Pope Paschal II even consented to canonize Erik's brother Knut.

King Erik, of course, solemnly supported the canonization. A Benedectine monastery was established in Odense and monks were brought over from England to maintain the shrine. At the same time, Erik succeeded in getting Lund established as an archbishopric, thus freeing the Danish church from the its long domination by Hamburg/ Bremen.

Denmark's first archbishop was Asser, and he just happened to be a nephew of Erik's wife Bothilda. This cleric set about to organize the Danish church and to ensure its support through exacting tithes from the citizens.

Erik, now the brother of a martyred saint, generously supported the Church. However, he angered the clerics a second time by hot-headedly murdering a servant who had displeased him. According to the historian Saxo, Erik was not really to blame; it was all the fault of some stirring music which had driven him mad.

To atone for his sins, Erik insisted on going on a crusade to the Holy Land. Perhaps his earlier contact with Urban II in Rome had inspired him with the crusading spirit. Unfortunately, he died in Cyprus in 1103 before he ever reached Palestine. His wife Bothilda Trugotsdotter, who accompanied him, passed away not long afterward, in Jerusalem.

Erik left at least three sons. One was Knut Lavard, and he was thoroughly legitimate. Another was Harald Keisias. We are told that Harald was "the bastard son of Erik the Good, and a wild and dissolute man."

Erik the Good also left another illegitimate son (later known as Erik Emune) and an illegitimate daughter named Ragnhild. None of Erik the Good's sons succeeded him immediately to the throne of Denmark. It was not until two years later that a successor was chosen with the election in 1105 of Erik's brother Niels.

### Niels Svensson—ruled from 1105 to 1134.

*My son, my son! Magnus is dead, and I must flee for my life.* Niels Svensson's long life and reign was destined to end on this tragic note.

Niels' name is the shortened, Danish form of Nicholas. The Swedish form of his name is Nils.

Niels is pictured by Saxo as a weak and ineffectual king, but he managed to keep the throne for thirty long years. The Slavic Wends, under their King Henry, invaded Schleswig and would have conquered it had not Niels placed his nephew Knut Lavard in charge of that part of the kingdom. Like Olof Hunger before him, Knut Lavard was made duke of Schleswig and ably defended his duchy from the Wends. He also helped to defend Holstein.

Niels' nephew Knut, the son of Erik Ejegod and his queen Bothilda, could have been called Eriksson, after his father. But he is more commonly known as Knut Lavard. The surname *Lavard,* in its original form, is identical to the Anglo-Saxon *Hlaford.* In its simplest roots, it merely means *loaf-ward,* or the guardian of bread ... the husband or master of the house. Later, the word evolved into the feudal title *Lord*. So we can think of Knut Lavard as "Lord Knut."

Knut had received his military training at the court of Lothar, Duke of Saxony. In 1125, when Lothar was named Emperor, he made Knut king of the Wends, in gratitude for Knut's help in defending Holstein. (The Wendish king, Henry, had died, and so the emperor bestowed his title upon Knut.) Thus Knut obtained titles and respect from both the German emperor and the Danish king, Niels.

King Niels was married twice. His first wife was Margaret Fridkulla, a daughter of King Inge I of Sweden. His second wife was Ulfhild, King Inge II's widow.

By his first wife, the Swedish princess Margaret, Niels had a son named Magnus, a handsome and gifted youth. Magnus, being the grandson of King Inge the Elder of Sweden, succeeded to the Swedish throne and ruled that country (at least in name) for a brief period. But Magnus was obviously more interested in the throne of Denmark than in that of Sweden. And he felt that his right to that throne was being threatened! The Emperor had already heaped honors upon his cousin Knut Lavard. Next Knut might be given the whole kingdom of Denmark! Magnus decided he would have to do something about the situation.

The treacherous Magnus invited Knut to spend Christmas at the royal castle at Roskilde. As Knut was returning to his own lands after the celebration, he was ambushed and murdered by Magnus' men. The murder took place in Haraldsted wood near Ringsted, on January 7, 1131. How often in that century had cousin murdered cousin in a jealous rage!

Knut Lavard left a widow named Ingeborg. Her father was Mstislav, Grand Prince of Kiev; and her mother was Kristina, a daughter of King Inge the Elder of Sweden.

Just one week after Knut Lavard died, his widow Ingeborg gave birth to a son, destined to rule Denmark one day as Valdemar the Great. Knut Lavard also had three older daughters: Kristina, Margaret, and Katrina. Kristina was briefly married to Magnus the Blind of Norway; Margaret married Stig Hvide, a nobleman from Skåne and became the grandmother of Sweden's king Sverker II.

If murder was endemic in medieval royal families, so was revenge. As soon as Knut's half brother Erik Emune heard of the murder, he appealed to the *Thing,* begging the nobles for men and money so that he could avenge Knut Lavard's death.

Many Danes willingly joined the army Erik was raising. Among them was Archbishop Asser, Erik's relative. When the bishops and priests saw that Asser was supporting Erik, they joined his side.

Magnus marched forth against Erik's coalition; the rivals met at Fodevig in Skåne on July 4, 1134. Magnus and a great host of his men were slain. Five of Denmark's seven bishops perished in the fray, along with sixty priests who had sided with the rebels. Archbishop Asser, however, survived. Since he was almost eighty, he had not gone into the battle even though he supported Erik.

While his son Magnus lay dying, old King Niels retreated to his ship and escaped to Schleswig where he rode boldly into his deceased nephew's palace. There he was murdered by Knut Lavard's loyal subjects. He was nearly seventy years old.

Niels' only son, Magnus, had fallen in battle, and so there appeared to be no immediate heir to sit upon Denmark's throne. However, the handsome and ill-fated Magnus did not die without issue. He was married to Rikissa, a daughter of Boleslav III of Poland, and their son Knut would later become a contender for the Danish throne. (More about the widowed Rikissa and her several marriages will be found in the chapters on Sweden.)

Ironically, Niels, who was the fifth and last of Sven Estridsson's sons to assume the throne, had the longest reign. He died a full sixty years after his father. During his time trade flourished, Denmark began to accept the ways of southern Europe, and Christianity made great progress. Stone churches began to replace the old wooden ones, and monasteries sprang up in many places.

**Erik II Emune—ruled from 1134 to 1137.**

*"My cousin Magnus and my uncle Niels are out of the way. Next I must get rid of my brother Harald."* In Erik Emune, who must have said something like the above to himself, we see a prime example of the fratricidal tendencies of medieval monarchs.

After the murder of King Niels, the Danish throne went to the nephew who had risen up against him. This was Erik Emune, whose surname can mean "the Boaster". He was a son of Erik Ejegod, but there was little about him to remind one of his repentant father who had died while on a pilgrimage to the Holy Land.

Erik was brave in battle and won many victories over the Wends, but his reign was marked by unspeakable cruelties, many of them directed toward his relatives.

In 1135, fearing that his remaining half brother would steal his power, Erik put Harald Keisias to death in the Riksforest. Then he seized Harald's ten sons—his own nephews. He took them over to

Skåne, and there had them murdered. Only one survived—Olof, who became a rival of Erik Lamb and is listed in some history books as Olof II of Denmark.

The line of Harald Keisias, however, did not die out. One of Harald's sons—Björn Haraldsson—was killed along with his brothers in the massacre. But he left a ten-year-old daughter named Kristina, who later married St. Erik of Sweden, and thus became a queen in her own right.

Erik Emune had a history of not being able to get along with his relatives. At one point, when fleeing from his father's brother Niels, he had found refuge with Harald Gille, who had designs upon the throne of Norway. At that time, Snorri informs us, "they had sworn brotherhood to one another."

After Erik Emune became king, he invited his ally Harald Gille to Denmark. Harald, who was fleeing from his rival King Magnus Sigurdsson, was happy to find refuge in Erik the Boaster's court. There Harald Gille—ever the charmer—lured Erik into giving him eight warships, as well as revenue and men from the Danish province of Halland (now part of Sweden).

Erik Emune and his deceased brother Knut Lavard had married sisters. (Their wives were both daughters of Mstislav I of Kiev.) Erik's wife was named Malmfrith. She had previously been married to Sigurd Jerusalem-farer of Norway, and then had been repudiated by him. Thus, when Erik was aiding Harald Gille of Norway, he was conspiring against his wife's stepson Magnus.

With the naval and military aid from Erik, Harald Gille won a great victory over King Magnus Sigurdsson of Norway. Harald Gille then mutilated and blinded Magnus so cruelly that the defeated king has gone down in history as Magnus the Blind. Harald Gille, for his part, was soon out of the picture—murdered in 1136.

Now it was Magnus the Blind who sought refuge at Erik Emune's court, persuading Erik to give him aid against the ruling sons of Harald Gille. King Erik and Magnus the Blind sailed together to Norway with hundreds of ships. There Erik's men made brief forays into Oslo, burning down many buildings, including St. Halvard's Church. But the Danes were not able to establish their troops on land. The Danish fleet retreated before the forces of Harald Gille's son Inge, and Erik returned to Denmark "ill-pleased with Magnus" who had tricked him into the ill-fated expedition.

The Danes were not happy with their cruel tyrant. They had not forgotten his atrocities against his own brother and nephews, and they were daily more enraged by the burdens he placed upon his subjects. The peasants of Sjaelland rose up in open revolt, under the leadership of Eskil, Bishop of Roskilde. (Eskil was related to the royal family; he was a nephew of Denmark's first archbishop, Asser, who was also related to the Danish monarchs.)

In 1137 Erik was murdered at a meeting of the *Thing* in Jutland; a nobleman nicknamed Black Plow dealt him the death blow.

A contemporary used the words "arrogant" and "full of wickedness" to describe him and wrote: "Erik acted in all matters as if he were emperor, swept all hindrances aside, endured no equal."

As far as we know, Erik Emune and his wife Malmfrith of Kiev had no children together, but Erik (who himself had been born out of wedlock) left an illegitimate son named Sven. Since the boy was doubtless too young to rule, Erik Emune's nephew and namesake, Erik Lamb, succeeded to the throne.

### Erik III Lamb—ruled from 1137 to 1146.

*"I am giving up the throne and going into a monastery to serve God."*

Erik Lamb's claim to the throne came through his mother Ragnhild, an illegitimate daughter of Erik I Ejegod. Erik Lamb's father was Håkan Sunnevasson, a nobleman from Jutland.

While Erik Lamb ruled most of Denmark, the people of Skåne chose his first cousin Olof (a son of Harald Keisias who had managed to survive the recent massacre) as their monarch. Olof II, as he is known, died in 1143 and Skåne then turned its allegiance to Erik Lamb.

Erik Lamb's surname gives us a clue to his personality. He was a weak monarch, better suited for the cloister than the throne. He cooperated closely with Bishop Eskil, who had now become Archbishop of Lund, and seemed more interested in building up the church than in protecting his people. His subjects, who were hoping for relief from the harrying of the Wendish pirates, found themselves in even greater trouble than they had been under his uncle, the despotic Erik Emune.

Yet Erik Lamb was not entirely as meek as his name implies. When the Danes in England called upon him for help, he decided to launch an expedition against England in good old Viking style. He even took horses with him—something his predecessors had never done before.

Erik Lamb's troops and horses reached England without problems, but the Danish army was soon defeated. He retreated in shame, and like his Spanish contemporary Ramiro the Monk, he abdicated in order to take holy orders. He joined St. Knut's monastery in Odense in 1146 and there he died about 1147.

Erik Lamb (before becoming a monk) was married to Luitgard, a daughter of Count Rudolph of Stade. This marriage shows how vastly improved were the relationships between Germany and Denmark by the twelfth century. Gone were the days when Henry the Fowler and other Germans made raids upon Denmark in order to "convert" the heathen and take their territory. Now German and Danish royalty were intermarrying, and it was Danes against Danes—all relatives— who were fighting for the throne.

## Sven III Grathe, Knut V Magnusson, and Valdemar I—ruled from 1146 to 1157.

With the abdication of Erik Lamb, Denmark entered a period of civil war. Three claimants to the throne—all of them great-grandsons of Sven Estridsson—were vying for the crown.

The first of these was Sven III Eriksson (also called Sven Grathe), an illegitimate son of Erik Emune. The second was Knut Magnusson, grandson of the murdered King Niels. Eventually Sven and Knut were named co-regents. Sven was married to Adelaide, a daughter of Conrad of Meisse; and Knut was married to a daughter of Sverker I, King of Sweden.

Shortly after the two second cousins agreed to share the kingdom, a third rival appeared on the scene in the person of Valdemar, son of the murdered Knut Lavard.

His name, a variant of the Russian Vladimir, came to him through his mother. We remember that she was Ingeborg, the daughter of Mstislav I of Kiev, and thus a descendant of Vladimir the Great, Russia's first Christian king.

Now the plot thickened. Knut and Valdemar decided to join forces against Sven. Since Knut's father had murdered Valdemar's father, this may seem a bit unusual, but no doubt both were hoping to benefit by the strange alliance. Besides, they were related by marriage, since Valdemar's wife Sofia was a half sister to Knut V. (Both Sofia and Knut V had Rikissa of Poland for their mother.)

In the struggle for the throne, each side sought help from the Emperor Frederick Barbarossa. The emperor (as Denmark's feudal overlord) responded by dividing the country into three parts, one for each of the three contenders. This arrangement was supposed to preserve the peace, but nobody was happy about it.

In 1157, a few days after Denmark was officially partitioned, the three kings attended a banquet at the royal palace in Roskilde. That evening some armed men forced their way into the banquet hall, extinguished all the lights, murdered Knut, and wounded Valdemar.

No one doubted that the master mind behind the "Bloody Banquet of Roskilde" was Sven Eriksson. After all, the other two kings were attacked, and he was not. The peace agreement evaporated into thin air. With Knut Magnusson now out of the way, Valdemar and Sven resumed their rivalry for the throne.

Valdemar, although wounded, fled with his men to Jutland. The power-hungry Sven followed him with an armed fleet. The two armies clashed in a battle near Viborg, and Valdemar emerged victorious. His second cousin Sven lay dead on the battlefield, killed by a peasant's axe. Valdemar now could claim the throne without being contested.

### Valdemar I the Great—ruled from 1157 to 1182.

*"We grew up together, Absalon. I shall make you the new arch-bishop of Denmark."* In this way, Valdemar I invested his foster brother as archbishop of Lund.

Valdemar, the posthumous son of Knut Lavard, was raised in Sjaelland in the home of a nobleman named Asser Rig, a member of the aristocratic family of Skjalm Hvide (Skjalm the White).

The Hvide family had helped to raise Valdemar's father Knut, so it was logical that they should raise the tiny orphaned prince. Asser Rig was married to Inga, a daughter of the Swedish Jarl Folke the Fat. Inga's mother was Ingegerd, a daughter of Denmark's St. Knut. So Valdemar's foster mother was his own kinswoman, a first cousin once removed. The young prince Valdemar grew up with Asser Rig's sons, Esbern and Absalon, and he became close to his foster brothers. (They were, of course, also his distant cousins.) Of Absalon we shall hear more. As for Esbern (surnamed *Snare* or "the Quick"), we shall briefly mention that he became an ancestor of Benedikta Ebbesdotter, who married King Sverker II of Sweden.

Valdemar was married twice. His first wife was Kristina, the daughter of Magnus IV, king of Norway. They were married in 1132, they were divorced in 1133, and she died in 1139. Since they were both literally very young children when all this occurred, the marriage hardly counts at all.

Valdemar's second wife, whom he married in 1154, was the

Russian princess Sofia. This was a real marriage, and it was blessed with a number of children.

Sofia was the daughter of Volodar (sometimes called Vladimir) Glebovitz, Prince of Minsk. Sofia's mother was Rikissa, a daughter of King Boleslav III of Poland. Rikissa of Poland had been married successively to Magnus Nielsson of Denmark, Volodar of Minsk, and Sverker I of Sweden, so Sofia was related to many royal dynasties of the times. In fact, she was a half sister to the murdered Knut V, who had so briefly shared the Danish kingdom with Valdemar.

Valdemar and Sofia had two sons: Knut VI and Valdemar II. They also had at least three daughters: Ingeborg (who married Philip II Augustus of France), Helena (who married William, Duke of Brunswick), and Rikissa (who married the Swedish king Erik X Knutsson).

Having dealt with Valdemar's upbringing and marriages, let us look at his reign. We have already seen how, after twenty-five years of civil war, Valdemar I emerged as the victor, claiming the Danish throne in 1157. He was about twenty-six years old at the time. The German emperor Frederick Barbarossa, Denmark's archbishop Eskil, and the powerful Hvide family were all on Valdemar's side.

One of Valdemar's first actions after ascending the throne was to invest his foster brother Absalon as the new bishop of Roskilde. Together they set about to restore the unity and prosperity of Denmark.

About one third of Denmark had been ravaged by the Wends, those Baltic Slavs who had migrated north. Valdemar I conducted no less than seventeen campaigns against these pagan tribes. In 1169 he ended Wendish power in Denmark by capturing their stronghold, the island of Rügen. The great temple of the Wends was razed to the ground and the many-headed Slavic idols were chopped up and burned.

Saxo vividly describes some of the idols that Valdemar and his foster-brother, Bishop Absalon, destroyed. One monstrous oaken statue had seven human faces. The swallows had built their nests in its features. The statue was so large that "Absalon, standing a-tip-toe, could scarce reach its chin with the little axe he was wont to carry." Nevertheless, this statue of a war god was chopped up and burned along with many others. The Wends were forced to accept Christianity.

Valdemar greatly increased the Danish defenses and army. Baked bricks had been recently introduced into Denmark, and Valdemar used them to build strong castles, fortresses, and churches. He fortified the Danevirke, that ancient rampart wall in southern Schleswig. With the aid of Bishop Absalon, the king turned the fishing hamlet of *Havn* into a fortified city called *København*, which means *Merchant's Haven*. It is known to us today as Copenhagan.

Early in his reign, Valdemar acknowledged the German emperor Frederick I Barbarossa as his overlord. But troubles were brewing between church and state all over Europe, and Denmark was not spared in the conflict.

Denmark's archbishop Eskil, like his English contemporary Thomas a Becket, was unwilling to bow to his king. To add to the confusion, two popes had been elected in 1159. One was the reformer Alexander III and the other was the anti-pope Victor, backed by none other than the Emperor Frederick Barbarossa himself.

Archbishop Eskil, naturally and wholeheartedly, sided with Alexander III. Valdemar, wishing to remain loyal to his overlord Frederick, backed Victor. Absalon and most of the other Danish bishops supported Victor, Frederick and Valdemar.

It wasn't long before the ecclesiastical disagreement turned into open war. Eskil, archbishop of Lund, took up arms against Valdemar and Absalon. Valdemar retaliated by conquering the archbishop's fortress and forcing him into exile in France.

Valdemar, Absalon, and most of Denmark's bishops then attended a Church council where Victor was officially recognized as pope. Once again, Valdemar swore fealty to Frederick Barbarrosa, doing homage according to the custom of the times when he "put both his hands in the Emperor's and hailed him as his lord."

In the papal struggle which ensued, Alexander III soon won out over the anti-pope Victor. Now Valdemar and his bishops were obliged to change their allegiance. Valdemar meekly recalled the exiled archbishop Eskil in 1168.

Valdemar and Absalon began to work in harmony with Eskil. The archbishop, on his part, agreed to canonize Knut Lavard, Valdemar's murdered father. The canonization took place in 1170, in the newly built brick church of Ringsted. Many important bishops and archbishops from as far away as Uppsala and Oslo attended the service, which was led by Eskil. The bones of Knut Lavard were ceremoniously carried up to the altar and placed in an ornate shrine, and Knut was declared to be a saint.

Denmark now could be said to have not one, but two saints named Knut. However, Knut Lavard is usually called "Knut the Pious" to distinguish him from Knut IV Svensson, the earlier St. Knut. Interestingly enough, both St. Knut and Knut Lavard were probably canonized more for political expediency than for real piety during their lives. A successor who could say, "My brother was a saint," or "My father was a saint," had an unquestionable tactical advantage over any rivals to the throne.

Valdemar did not stop with the canonization of his father. During the same great ecclesiastical gathering, he strengthened his royal authority still more by having Eskil anoint and crown his seven-year-old son Knut. Like most Teutonic monarchies, the Danes were now turning away from the power of the *Thing* ... away from an elective monarchy ... and toward a strong hereditary kingship sustained by the church. Valdemar, of course, was very happy to have things going in this direction.

In 1171 the Wends once more raided the shores of Denmark. Valdemar was forced to seek the aid of the Saxon duke Henry the Lion in his battles against the Wends. Valdemar and Henry made a treaty, and to seal the agreement the duke's daughter Gertrude was betrothed to the eight-year-old Danish prince Knut. Valdemar's treaty with Henry the Lion (and his support for Pope Alexander III) predictably caused a break in his good relations with Frederick Barbarossa.

Valdemar's restored relations with Archbishop Eskil were not destined to last, either. Eskil's kinsmen joined in a conspiracy against the king, and consequently Eskil once more went into exile in France. Here he stayed from 1177 until he died.

With Eskil gone, the way was clear for Valdemar to install his foster brother Absalon as the new archbishop of Lund. The king, now nearing the end of his reign, was still strengthening the monarchy, putting down rebellions, and extending Denmark's international influence. And he was still fortifying the country, everywhere erecting buildings made of brick rather than stone or wood. It is no wonder that he is called Valdemar the Great, and that his reign is said to have introduced the "Great Period of the Valdemars."

Valdemar I died very suddenly in 1182 at Vordingborg Castle. He was only fifty-one. He was "lamented by all Denmark" according to the chronicles of the times. Bishop Absalon, who headed the funeral procession, wept openly along with all the peasants who followed the bier. "Denmark's shield and the pagan's scourge has departed," he mourned. "I fear that, without Valdemar, the Wends will conquer us again." Valdemar's body was then laid to rest in the large brick church at Ringsted, which he had built.

Valdemar's eldest son, Knut VI, succeeded him as king. The second son, Valdemar II, was made Duke of Schleswig, a title that his grandfather Knut Lavard had held before him.

### Knut VI—ruled from 1182 to 1202.

*"What shall I reply to the emperor? I had better let Archbishop Absalon decide what to say."*

Knut was about nineteen years old when he ascended to the the throne, but he showed little of the leadership qualities that an earlier Knut—Knut II, better known as Canute the Great—had displayed at that age.

A pious man and meek man, Knut VI let Archbishop Absalon make most of his decisions for him.

The Holy Roman Emperor, Frederick Barbarossa, sent word reminding Knut VI, that as a newly appointed king, he should come south and do homage to his overlord.

Knut himself did not respond to the demand; but Absalon was ready with a quick reply. He told the emperor in no uncertain terms that if he wanted Knut's oath of fealty, he had better give him some of northern Germany in return. He also explained that in Denmark, Knut was king, and therefore on an equal footing with Frederick himself. This reply put a stop to any hopes Frederick may have had of making Denmark into a German vassal state.

With the help of his brother Valdemar and his foster uncle Absalon, Knut VI managed to conquer Pomerania and Holstein, so that the gloomy predictions made at his father's funeral never came to pass.

By 1184 Knut earned the title of "King of the Danes and Wends." After annexing Pomerania, he seized Mecklenburg and other important German territories. He was able to do this for two reasons: In the first place, Germany had been weakened by civil strife. In the second place, Knut VI had the help of his valiant younger brother, Valdemar Duke of Schleswig.

In 1192 Count Adolf of Holstein, who had lost much of his land to Denmark, retaliated by invading Schleswig. Valdemar Duke of

Schleswig led a brilliant counter-offensive and not only held off the count, but conquered Hamburg and Lübeck as well. He began to be known as *Valdemar Sejr,* or "Valdemar the Victorious."

Like all medieval monarchs, Knut was beset with family problems. His distant cousin Valdemar (who was Bishop of Schleswig and a grandson of the Magnus Nielsson who had murdered Knut Lavard) had joined forces with the count of Holstein and had actually proclaimed himself king of Denmark.

With the aid of his brother Valdemar the Victorious, King Knut captured Bishop Valdemar and threw him into the dungeon of Soborg Castle along with his ally, Count Adolf of Holstein.

In Knut's time, the Danes also tried to conquer and Christianize Livonia and Estonia, but they were less successful in those lands, which remained predominantly pagan.

Absalon by this time was growing old. He retired to Soroe Abbey, reminisced about his past military successes, and gave to his secretary Saxo the task of recording Denmark's history. Absalon had served as the real power behind the Danish throne all during Knut's reign. It is somehow ironic that the king seemed more interested in the church than in his kingdom; while the bishop spent more time in battles and affairs of state than in religious exercises.

Knut was beset with quarrels with his brother-in-law, Philip Augustus of France. Knut had given his sister Ingeborg to Philip in 1193, but the French king repudiated her almost immediately after the wedding.

When Danish ambassadors tried to effect a reconciliation, Philip expelled them from his country. He even had Queen Ingeborg clapped into prison! All this put a severe strain upon Danish/French relations during Knut's time, and later his brother Valdemar inherited the problem along with the throne.

According to the agreement made in his boyhood, Knut was married to Gertrude, a daughter of Henry the Lion, duke of Saxony. The marriage was childless. Since Knut VI left no descendants when he died in 1202, he was succeeded by his brother Valdemar II.

## Valdemar II the Victorious—ruled from 1202 to 1241.

*"I am planning a crusade against Estonia! Each village must send me its quota of ships, and each warrior must bring provisions to last five weeks, as well as a sword and a shield, a crossbow and five dozen arrows."* This was the call that Valdemar II sent out before launching his Estonian expedition.

We have already mentioned Valdemar's early life and victories. In

1188, at the age of 18, Valdemar II was made Duke of Schleswig; he helped conquer Holstein and Hamburg before the year 1200. In 1202 he succeeded his brother Knut VI as king of Denmark.

Valdemar, like his ancestor Sven Estridsson, had a number of illegitimate children by various women. One of these mistresses was Helena Guttormsdotter. Their son Knut was made Duke of Estonia. Knut's son Svantepolk (a grandson of Valdemar II) married into the Folkung family of Sweden. His descendants are shown on Chart 28.

Valdemar also is said to have had an affair with the widow of Esbern Snare, Bishop Absalon's brother.

By the time he was in his mid-thirties, Valdemar was ready to settle down to marriage. He chose as his queen a daughter of Ottokar I of Bohemia. Her Bohemian name was Dragomir, but her Danish name was officially Margaret. She was only about fourteen when they were married in 1205, and the marriage lasted until her death in 1212 or 1213.

The Danes loved Queen Margaret. Playing upon her Slavic name, they nicknamed her *Dagmar,* "maiden of the day". We know little about her life, but many stories are told about her death. It is said that as she lay dying, her priest urged her to confess her sins. She was so pure and holy, however, that the only sin she could think of was the excess of having braided ribbons into her long golden hair before attending mass.

Valdemar II and Margaret had only one son, and they named him Valdemar for his father.

About a year after Margaret's death, Valdemar the Victorious took for a second wife Berengaria, a daughter of King Sancho I of Portugal. The people of Denmark, who had adored the gentle Dagmar, came to loathe the tall, dark-haired Berengaria. Deliberately mispronouncing her name, they called her *Bengjoerd*—a vile woman. She bore three sons: Erik, Abel and Christopher to Valdemar. She also gave him a daughter named Sofia, who married John I, Margrave of Brandenburg.

So much for Valdemar's wives. Now we will mention something about his campaigns.

Valdemar, trying to make good his surname "the Victorious," sought to seize power in Norway and Sweden, but was unsuccessful in these efforts. Perhaps in hopes of adding Sweden to his own domains, he tried to meddle in the conflict between the royal families of St. Erik and the Sverkers. In 1208 at Lena, and again in 1210 at

Gestilren, Valdemar sided with Sverker II in battles against Erik X. Both times, Valdemar and Sverker were defeated by Erik, and many Danish soldiers lost their lives. A folk ballad speaks of the mourning in Denmark that followed the defeat in Sweden.

*The ladies stood in Highloft,*
*Their lords' return to see,*
*But every steed with gore was red,*
*And empty each saddle tree.*

To make peace, Valdemar gave his sister Rikissa as a bride to the victor—Erik X of Sweden.

Shortly after this, Valdemar had the satisfaction of seeing his other sister, Ingeborg, vindicated. It took the intervention of Pope Innocent III for the French king, Philip, to take Ingeborg back and thus avert the possibility of war between Denmark and France. After many disputes she was restored to her place as queen of France in 1213. But she lived separately from her husband.

This was a period when several different monarchs were vying for the title of Holy Roman Emperor. Early in the struggle Valdemar supported Otto IV and the Welf faction, but later switched his allegiance to Frederick II, the great king of Sicily who united Italy.

As a reward for his allegiance, Frederick II in 1214 gave Valdemar title to all the territories north of the Elbe. Denmark was once again a powerful empire, although not as extensive as it had been in the days of Canute the Great.

Having been defeated in Sweden, Valdemar was determined to be victorious elsewhere. In 1219, with the approval of the pope, he set forth on a crusade against the pagans of Estonia. He was far more successful in his campaign than his brother Knut had been, According to legend, at one point the Danes lost their banner to the enemy and became disheartened by the advances of the heathen Estonians. But their despair turned to hope when suddenly a red flag bearing a white cross dropped from the sky. Rallying to this miraculous standard, they defeated the enemy and have kept the red and white banner to this day.

Before long, Valdemar had conquered the entire country. He established bishoprics at Reval (Tallinn) and Dorpat, built the Tallinn-Reval Castle, and named his illegitimate son Knut as Duke of Estonia.

Just when things seemed to be going really well for Valdemar, a terrible blow befell him. In the spring of 1223 Valdemar II and his oldest legitimate son, also named Valdemar, were hunting on the little island of Lyoe, south of Fyn. While they were there, they received a visit from Henry, Count of Schwerin.

That evening the king gave a banquet for his guest. Unfortunately, both Valdemar and his son got rather drunk. Later that night, while the two Valdemars lay sleeping, Count Henry kidnapped them, pulling sacks of wool and straw over their heads, and carrying them off without awakening their servants. Gagged and bound, they were taken to a prison in the castle of Danneberg in Hanover. There they were kept for more than three years.

Valdemar's nephew, Albert count of Orlamunde, set out with an army to rescue his uncle, but he was defeated and thrown into the dungeon with his uncle and cousin.

The royal prisoners were finally released on very severe conditions. Valdemar was required to pay a ransom of 40,000 marks, and he was forced to leave his three younger sons in the prison as hostages until the money was paid.

His sister Ingeborg must have felt great sympathy for Valdemar. After all, she knew what it was like to be kept in prison! She wasted no time in sending a large contribution toward the funds needed for Valdemar's ransom.

But the ransom money was not the only condition for Valdemar's release. He was also forced to give up his German holdings north of the Elbe, including Holstein and Pomerania. Valdemar was left, however, with Denmark, Estonia and Rügen.

Returning to his diminished kingdom, Valdemar tried to make order out of the chaos that had occurred during his absense. He made a couple of unsuccessful raids into the German provinces he had lost, and in one of them he lost an eye. Valdemar had to come to terms with the fact that he was no longer "the Victorious." The Danes would have to stay north of the Danevirke.

Valdemar II had made sure that his oldest legitimate son was crowned as his co-regent, and he expected the prince to succeed him as Valdemar III. But this was not to be. Dagmar's son died in 1231 at the age of twenty-three, in much the same way that William Rufus had died in England. He was wounded by a stray arrow while hunting, and died shortly afterward. His young wife (a daughter of Alfonso II of

Portugal) and his tiny son had died just three months before this tragedy.

The broken-hearted Valdemar II decided to devote the rest of his life to codifying Denmark's unwritten laws. He ordered a census similar to the Domesday Book prepared by William the Conqueror, and revised and codified the rules and regulations that had governed the Danish *Things* since time immemorial. His Jutlandic Law was enacted at Vordinborg in 1241; it remained valid in Jutland and Fyn until 1683, and in Schleswig until 1900.

On Maunday Thursday, 1241, only a few days after the enactment of his code of laws, Valdemar passed away at the age of seventy-one. He was mourned by all his people. Despite the troubles of his later life (which almost made a saint and martyr out of him) his subjects remembered him chiefly for his great conquests.

With his death, the "Great Period of the Valdemars" came to an end. As had happened so often in medieval royal families, his sons by Berengaria began to fight one another. Erik, Abel, and Christopher all took the throne at one time or another between 1241 and 1259.

### Erik IV Ploughpenny—ruled from 1241 to 1250.

The first son, Erik, was called "Ploughpenny" because he imposed a tax on plows. His wife was named Jutta but apparently they had no children.

Erik IV gained the throne upon his father's death, but was assassinated in 1250, most likely by his brother Abel. Prince Abel, who was married to Matilda of Holstein, had the support of his brother-in-law, the count of Holstein; and he was also supported by the clergy, the Swedes, and the city of Lübeck.

### Abel—ruled from 1250 to 1252.

Abel took over the kingdom, suspected of murder by all the people but declared innocent by the archbishop.

Abel lost his life only two years later while on an expedition against Frisia. He thus became the only Danish king since Harald Bluetooth to perish in battle.

He was survived by several children (among them Erik, Valdemar, and a young son also named Abel). Also surviving him was his widow, Matilda of Holstein, who later became the wife of Sweden's famous Birger Jarl.

**Christopher I—ruled from 1252 to 1259.**

Christopher, the third son of Berengaria and Valdemar II, took the throne in 1252, only to endure a sudden death in 1259 after taking communion, supposedly having been given a poisoned wafer by a power-hungry prelate.

**Erik V Glipping—ruled from 1259 to 1286.**

Christopher was succeeded by his ten-year-old son, Erik Glipping or "Erik the Blinker." While Erik was still a child, his widowed mother (Margaret, a daughter of Sambor duke of Kaussuben) ruled as his regent. From Erik Glipping came many famous Danish kings, as well as a daughter, Marta (sometimes called Margaret) who married the Swedish king Birger.

Erik Glipping is remembered chiefly because, like King John in England, he was forced to sign a "Magna Carta," a document which made the king subject to the law. It was also in Erik Glipping's time that Denmark lost Skåne to Sweden.

The reigning sons and grandsons of Valdemar the Victorious—and through them the subsequent kings of Denmark—could trace their roots back to many prominent families. To begin with, they were descended from Gorm the Old who had united Denmark some three centuries earlier. If we hold to the ancient tradition that Gorm's wife was an English princess (and there seems to be good evidence for this), we can also assume that Valdemar's sons were all descended from Alfred the Great and the house of Wessex.

Plenty of Russian and Slavic blood also coursed through the veins of Valdemar's sons. Through Knut Lavard's wife Ingeborg, they were descended from Vladimir I the Great and Yaroslav the Wise of Kiev. (We'll say more about these Russian rulers in the next chapter.) Valdemar's sons were also descended from Vladimir II Monomakh, whose mother came from a long line of Byzantine rulers. Thus Greek heredity and culture also came into their lineage.

Through their grandmother Sofia, Valdemar II's sons could claim descent from many Polish kings as well. And there were so many connections with Swedish and Norwegian royalty that it would be hard to enumerate them all.

Through their mother Berengaria, the ruling sons of Valdemar II could trace their ancestry back to many ancient lines of Spain. Berengaria's father, Sancho I of Portugal, was a great-grandson of

Alfonso VI of Castile and León. Alfonso VI could claim as ancestors the early kings of León. Since the rulers of León had intermarried with the houses of Navarre and Aragon, there was even Basque and Navarrese blood in Valdemar's sons, and they could trace their family tree back to that shadowy ninth-century ruler, Aznar Galindo of Aragon.

Berengaria of Portugal not only descended from Alfonso VI of Castile and León, but also from Henry of Burgundy who had married Alfonso's daughter Teresa. Henry of Burgundy was descended from Robert II the Pious, the Capetian King of France. So it could be said that Valdemar's sons were Capetians.

Hugh Capet's mother happened to be a daughter of Henry the Fowler of Germany. Therefore, the sons of Valdemar and Berengaria were descended on their mother's side from that famous Saxon ruler who fought against their father's people in the time of Gorm.

And Hugh Capet's wife, Adela of Poitiers, was directly descended from Karl the Great through his son Louis the Pious. By virtue of this connection, all the Capetians could claim Carolingian descent. So the sons of Valdemar the Victorious, like virtually all the medieval rulers of their time, were also Carolingians. The Danes had come a long way since the time when Karl the Great planned to frighten them into submission with the elephant he had received from the caliph of Baghdad!

Having dealt with Norway, Flanders, and Denmark, we are now ready to turn our attention to Sweden. But before we look at the medieval rulers of that country, we will focus on the Swedes who migrated to Russia and established the house of Rurik.

CHART 16 - The Family of Sven Estridsson, King of Denmark

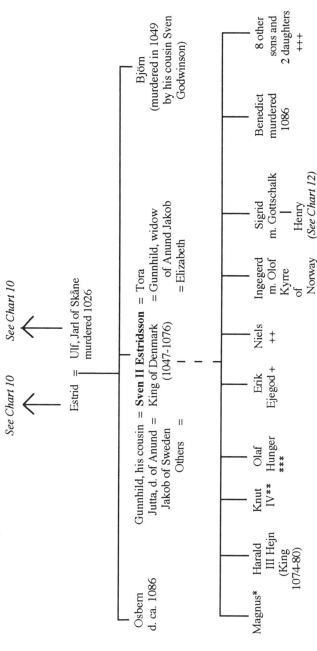

See Chart 10    See Chart 10

Estrid = Ulf, Jarl of Skåne murdered 1026

Osbern d. ca. 1086

Björn (murdered in 1049 by his cousin Sven Godwinson)

Sven II Estridsson = Tora
King of Denmark (1047-1076)
= Gunnhild, widow of Anund Jakob
= Elizabeth
Gunnhild, his cousin = 
Jutta, d. of Anund = Jakob of Sweden
Others =

Magnus*    Harald III Hejn (King 1074-80)    Knut IV**    Olaf Hunger***    Erik Ejegod +    Niels ++    Ingegerd m. Olof Kyrre of Norway    Sigrid m. Gottschalk | Henry (See Chart 12)    Benedict murdered 1086    8 other sons and 2 daughters +++

* Died young, en route to Rome.
** King from 1080-86; Go to Chart 17.
*** King from 1086-95; Married to Ingegerd, daughter of Harald Hårdråde of Norway (See Chart 3).
+ King from 1095-1103; Go to Chart 18.
++ King from 1105-1134; Go to Chart 19.
+++ Includes one son Sven who died in 1097, another son Sven who died in 1104, and daughters Gunnhild and Gyda.

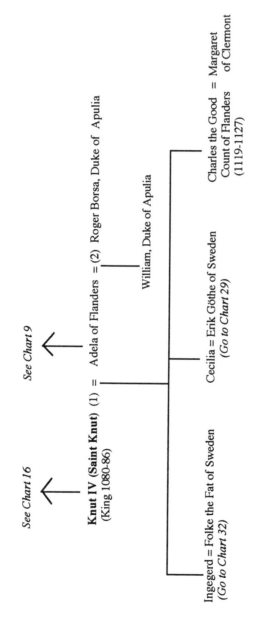

CHART 17 - The Family of Knut IV, King of Denmark

# CHART 18 - The Family of Erik I Ejegod, King of Denmark

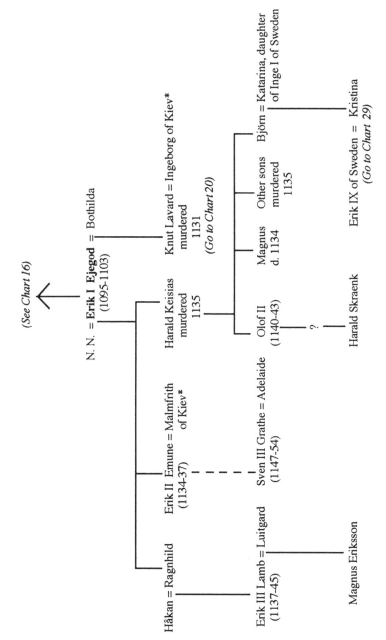

(See Chart 16)

N. N. = **Erik I Ejegod** = Bothilda
(1095-1103)

Håkan = Ragnhild

Erik II Emune = Malmfrith
(1134-37)       of Kiev*

Sven III Grathe = Adelaide
(1147-54)

Erik III Lamb = Luitgard
(1137-45)

Magnus Eriksson

Harald Keisias
murdered
1135

Knut Lavard = Ingeborg of Kiev*
murdered
1131
(Go to Chart 20)

Olof II
(1140-43)

?

Harald Skraenk

Magnus
d. 1134

Other sons
murdered
1135

Björn = Katarina, daughter
of Inge I of Sweden

Erik IX of Sweden = Kristina
(Go to Chart 29)

* See Charts 5 and 24.

**CHART 19 - The Family of Niels Svensson, King of Denmark**

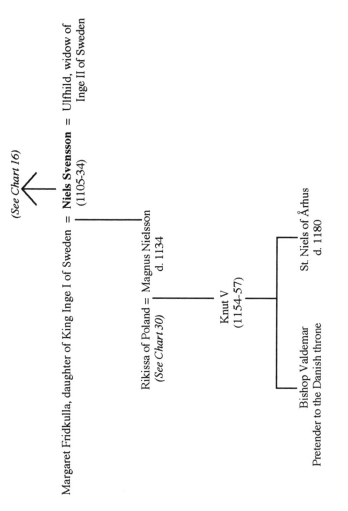

*(See Chart 16)*

Margaret Fridkulla, daughter of King Inge I of Sweden = **Niels Svensson** = Ulfhild, widow of
(1105-34)                              Inge II of Sweden

Rikissa of Poland = Magnus Nielsson
*(See Chart 30)*       d. 1134

Knut V
(1154-57)

Bishop Valdemar          St. Niels of Århus
Pretender to the Danish throne          d. 1180

**CHART 20 - The Family of Knut Lavard, Duke of Schleswig and King of the Wends**

*(See Chart 18)*

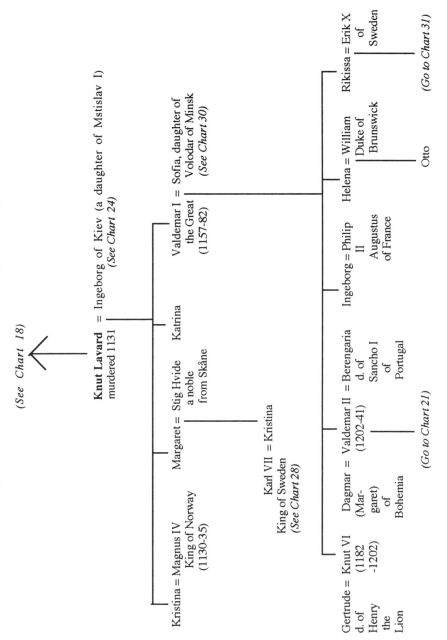

**CHART 21 - The Family of Valdemar II the Victorious, King of Denmark**

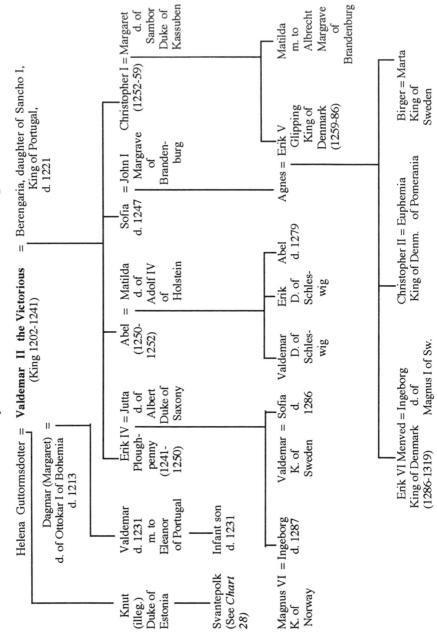

## Chapter 7

### The Princes of Kiev from 862 to 1132

Not far from the Gulf of Finland and the present city of St. Petersburg, lies Lake Ladoga. There is a water highway from this inland lake, south along the Volkhov River past Novgorod. One can continue past Smolensk on down the Dnieper and over the the Black Sea to the great city once known as Constantinople. Or one can follow the Volga to Persia by way of the Caspian Sea.

Throughout the world, great cities have often grown up along navigable rivers, and Russia is no exception. People of many tribes and nations found the waterways made up of the Volkhov, Dnieper, Desna, Pripet, Dvina and Lovat. At the north of this system the city of Novgorod grew up; at the south end was Kiev. Midway between was Smolensk.

The Scandinavians were among the earliest of peoples to discover this water highway. Not far from Smolensk lies the vast burial field of Gnezdovo with 3000 grave mounds, many resembling Scandinavian grave mounds. At Bereganji on the mouth of the Dniester a Norse Runic stone was found.

What native peoples did Scandinavian traders and settlers find along the great water highway?

To the west, of course, lived the Latvians and the Estonians. There were also many Finns, who spoke a Ural-Altaic language related to Mongolian. And there were the Lithuanians, speaking a tongue believed to be closer than any other to the original Indo-European.

Between Estonia and the great eastern steppes, all up and down the rivers, were many fractured, feuding Slavic tribes. By language and ancestry they were related to the Poles, to the Moravians (ancestors of the modern Czechs), to the Wends who settled in Northern Germany along the Elbe, and to the powerful Bulgarians to the southwest.

To the east of the Slavs were the Khazars, a confederation of Turkish and Iranian tribes. By the year 700 they had occupied the area north of the Caucasus mountains all the way to the Volga River and were ruling the valleys of the Dnieper and the Don. The Alani (an Iranian tribe), some groups of Magyars, the Greeks who had settled in the Crimea, the Volga Bulgars and many Slavic tribes submitted to the Khazar khan.

In the middle of the eighth century the Khazar rulers embraced the Jewish faith, but remained tolerant of other religions. The Khazars were traditionally trading partners and allies of Byzantium, whose emperors Justinian II and Constantine V married Khazar wives. But we shall see that as Kiev waxed in power, the Khazar kingdom waned.

Another powerful kingdom to the southeast of the Slavs was that of the cruel Pechenegs. The Greeks called them Patzinakoi, hence their alternate name, Patzinaks. These were nomadic people of Turkish origin who occupied the steppes north of the Caspian Sea, all the way down to the Volga River. Traditionally they were enemies of the Khazars, Byzantium and the Hungarians. Like the Norsemen who invaded France, the Pechenegs were known as raiders and marauders, making repeated incursions upon Thrace and Bulgaria.

It was to the borders of this land of Slavs, Khazars and Pechenegs that the Viking Rurik, eager to carve out a domain for himself, came in the middle of the ninth century. And because his descendants married into the royal houses of Scandinavia, we have included him in our narrative.

### Rurik—ruled from 862 to 879.

*"Come and be our ruler, Rurik!"*

Rurik, the traditional founder of the Kievian dynasty, may well have come from Birka, a city and trading post on an island in Lake Mälaren in eastern Sweden. Birka and the neighboring town of Helgö have been excavated, and coins of many nations have been found there, indicating its importance as a commercial center. The Viking traders (often called Varangians) went all the way to Constantinople and brought back valuables to sell in their native Sweden.

The Varangians from Birka sailed east and landed on the Baltic shore. Leading their forces against the coastal inhabitants, they secured the surrender of Seeburg, Grobin and Apuole in Kurland, now Latvia. There are many grave fields with Swedish and Gotlander weapons and artifacts to be found in Grobin.

Not content to remain on the coastlands, the Vikings rowed their long ships up the Gulf of Finland until they reached the inland sea known as Lake Lagoda. There they found the land that is now Russia. According to the Hypatian codes, "They took with them all the Russes and came first to the Slovenes (Slavs) and they built the city of Ladoga."

The site was occupied before the Swedes arrived, probably by a Finnish community. Old burial grounds that have been examined appear to be of Swedish and Finnish origin. The early name given to Russia by the Swedes was *Gardarik* (Land of Homesteads).

It is from the Swedish rowing men, famous for their long ships, that modern Russia derives its name. *Rus* is related to *Ruotsi*, the Finnish name for Sweden, to the Estonian *Rootsi*, and to the Old Norse *rothr* (a rowing-way or water-way). The rowers were called *Rothmen* and their rowing law at Lake Mälaren was called *Roslagen*.

We learn of Rurik and his brothers from an old document called the *Russian Primary Chronicle*. It tells us the following:

*These particular Varangians were known as Russes ... for they were thus named. The Chuds, the Slavs, the Krivichians, and the Ves then said to the people of Rus, "Our land is great and rich, but there is no order in it. Come to rule and reign over us." They thus selected three brothers, with their kinsfolk, who took with them all the Russes and migrated. The oldest, Rurik, located himself in Novgorod; the second, Sineus, at Beloozero; and the third, Truvor, in Izborsk. On account of these Varangians, the district of Novgorod became known as Rus.*

Although some historians have consigned the tale to legend, we see no particular reason to doubt its basic truth, which is that men of Viking descent made their way to Novgorod and Kiev, ruled over the local inhabitants, and gave their name to modern Russia. Certainly there exists much archeological evidence of Scandinavian influence in what is now Russia.

The *Chronicle* further relates that after two years Sineas and Truvor both died, and Rurik assumed the whole leadership.

Rurik thus established the city of Novgorod ("New City") south of Lake Ladoga, on Lake Ilmen. Here he ruled over the people who had invited him: the Ves (a Finnish tribe), the Chud (probably Lithuanians or Finns), and the local Slavs. Although he proclaimed himself king, he does not seem to have been unkind to the people he found there. His purpose, like the hunters and trappers who settled west of the Mississippi centuries later, seems to have been trade and money-making rather than conquest and pillage.

With Rurik were two men—Askold and Dir—who served as his aides. They asked Rurik for permission to go to Constantinople with their families. As they sailed down the Dnieper, *The Russian Chronicle* tells us, they came to a small city on a hill. "Whose town is this?" they asked.

The local people—southern Slavs called Polyane (meaning "people of the plain")—were quick to reply, "This city was built by Kiy and his two brothers, but since their deaths we have had to pay tribute to the Khazars."

Askold and Dir decided they would make better rulers than the Khazars. They remained in the city of Kiev, sent for more of their Scandinavian relatives to help colonize it, and established their dominion over the Polyane at the same time Rurik was ruling in Novgorod.

They did not, however, forget their original purpose to sail to Byzantium. In the early 860s they rowed south, raided the coastal towns of the Black Sea and appeared at the very gates of Constantinople. The terrified Byzantines engaged in fervent prayer; and a storm came up which helped repel the invaders. The Scandinavians were forced to retreat and did not return until 907 under Oleg.

### Helgi (Oleg the Knowing)—ruled from 879 to 912.

*"Welcome to my ship, Askold and Dir! Come aboard and let us celebrate."* Thus did the treacherous Oleg trick his fellow-Vikings in order to obtain their Russian lands.

Rurik died in 879. Since his infant son Ingvar was too young to rule Novgorod, a kinsman was named as regent. The new ruler's Scandinavian name was Helgi, but the Slavs called him Oleg. He has gone down in history as "Oleg the Knowing" but a better name might be Oleg the Treacherous.

Around 882 Oleg followed the water road south to Kiev. He invited his countrymen Askold and Dir to come aboard his ship, where he murdered them. He then set himself up as prince in Kiev, and proclaimed that it should be the mother of Russian cities.

By 900 the two Swedish colonies were united as the state of Kievan Rus. The Varangians, Slavs, Finns and others in Oleg's troops all became known as Russes. Oleg began to build stockaded towns and impose tribute on the Slavs, the Krivichians who lived in Smolensk, and the Merians who lived along the Volga.

### Ingvar (Igor)—ruled from 912 to 945.
*"My first invasion of Byzantium was a failure. But I shall try again!"*

Although Oleg's rule was a long and powerful one, eventually Ingvar Ruriksson came to power. By this time the Scandinavian colonists were adopting Slavic speech and ways, and Ingvar is usually known by his Slavic name, Igor. He married a wife of Scandinavian descent, whose family had established itself at Pskov. Her given name was the Teutonic Helga, but she (like her husband) is better known by her Slavic name, Olga.

Like Askold in 865 and Oleg in 907, Igor decided to invade Byzantium. His first attempt, in 941, was a disaster. The pagan Swedish-Russians ravaged the coasts of Thrace and Bythinia. Like their Norwegian counterparts who destroyed the monasteries of Ireland, these descendants of Vikings murdered many Christian priests. Some were crucified, others were buried alive, and still others had nails driven through their heads.

Once again the Byzantine navy routed the pagans, and very few Varangians escaped back to Russia.

But Igor was not easily discouraged. In 944 he was back, appearing on the Danube with a large battle force of his loyal Russians as well as blood-thirsty Pechenegs, who had allied themselves with the Russians. The deputy Eastern Emperor Romanus I (who ruled for Constantine VII) thought it wise not to fight such a force. Instead, he made peace with the Russians, renewing a commercial treaty with them.

The treaties between Byzantium and the Russians (two under Oleg, one under Igor, and a fourth under Svyatoslav I) have been preserved. Licensed Russian merchants were allowed into Constantinople. Some lists of merchants have also been preserved and it is interesting that most of them had Scandinavian names. The Emperor was to give them free food, lodging, use of his steam baths, and even rigging for their return trips.

The treaty also included provisions favorable to the Byzantines. The merchants were to come into the city unarmed, and only by a certain gate. No more than fifty at one time would be allowed to enter.

Disputes were to be settled by a mixed court under Roman law and Scandinavian custom.

Igor died in 945 died at the hands of the Drevlyane, a Slavic tribe who lived along the Prepet river. He had come to them once before to collect tribute, and the Drevlyane decided not to let him get away with it again. On his second expedition to secure tribute, Igor was ambushed and killed.

As Igor's son Svyatoslav was a minor, the boy's mother Olga became regent. An energetic and determined ruler, she punished the Drevlyane severely for the murder of her husband. We are told that she falsely promised them peace if they would send her a tribute of pigeons. Upon receiving the birds, the vengeful widow fastened torches to them and sent them back to burn the Drevlyane cities.

Many Scandinavian immigrants to Russia had left off worshiping Thor, Odin and Frey, and instead were praying to the Slavic gods Perun, Sverog and Veles. But Olga was not satisfied with idol worship. She kept up her husband's policy of travelling around the country to collect tribute, and her travels brought her into contact with Christians. At one point she seemed ready to accept the Roman Catholic faith from St. Adalbert of Prague. However, it was later, on a visit to Constantinople, that she was baptized in 957. The eastern emperor, Constantine VII, was willing to act as her godfather. Later, when he proposed marriage to her, she reminded him that it was against Church law for a man to marry his goddaughter.

Olga, the first of the house of Rurik to accept Christianity, was unable to convert her son to her new faith.

### Svyatoslav I—ruled from 957 to 972.

*"I can't become a Christian, Mother,"* Svyatoslav told Olga. *"My soldiers might make fun of me; I don't want to lose the respect I need as king."*

Svyatoslav's thoroughly Slavic name shows how Rurik's family were gradually being absorbed into the culture of the Slavic majority.

This pagan ruler, we are told, subsisted on the flesh of horses and wild beasts, and made it his custom to sleep out under the stars.

He took as his wife one of the ladies who waited upon the queen mother Olga. Her Scandinavian name was Malmfrith, but she is usually called by her Russian name, Malusja. She bore several sons to her royal husband, the most famous being Vladimir the Great.

Svyatoslav is known as a great warrior. In 965 he destroyed the powerful Khazar empire along the lower Volga, a feat equally desired by Byzantium and Novgorod. In its place, he set up a Scandinavian/

Russian type of government.

In 968 Svyatoslav invaded Bulgaria, conquering the inhabitants and taking the capital Preslav for himself. But his conquest of Bulgaria was not destined to last long. In April 971 the brilliant Byzantine general and emperor John Tzimsces stormed the Bulgarian capital and set up as ruler a deposed tzar. This made the Bulgars happy and they began to desert from Svyatoslav. Tzimsces then marched against the Danube town of Silistria where Svyatoslav had shut himself up. At the same time the Byzantine navy sailed up the Danube and further strengthened the siege. By the end of July after two months of siege and the loss of many men, Svyatoslav surrendered to Tzimsces. He promised to withdraw from Bulgaria and never to appear in the Balkans again. He also promised to help Byzantium against any foe. Tzimsces then provided supplies to Svyatoslav's starving soldiers and renewed the old trading agreements with the Russians.

After a personal interview with the victor, Svyatoslav returned home with his greatly weakened army. On his way, he found the rapids of the Dnieper blocked by the Pechenegs. Svyatoslav, who had lived by the sword, was destined to die by the sword. When he resisted the Pechenegs, they killed him and made a drinking cup for themselves out of his skull.

### Yaropolk and Oleg Svyatoslavsson—ruled from 973 to 980.

Svyatoslav, according to ancient Teutonic custom, had divided his kingdom among his three young sons: Yaropolk, Oleg Svyatoslavsson and Vladimir. Predictably, they were not content with the divided inheritance, and began to quarrel among themselves. Yaropolk, the eldest, was easily led by unscrupulous advisors. He was stirred up to fight his brother Oleg who was killed as a result. Later, Yaropolk himself was betrayed by Blud, another advisor, who brutally murdered him. The kingdom was left to Vladimir.

### Vladimir I the Great—ruled from 980 to 1015.

*"I am ready to abandon my idols and worship only one God. But which religion shall I follow? The Jewish? The Muslim? The Christian?"*

Thus spoke Vladimir, son of the barbaric Svyatoslav, but grandson of the pious Christian, Olga. Let us trace the story of his life.

Like his father, Vladimir was given a thoroughly Slavic name, even though both his parents were of Nordic ancestry. The name, which can be translated as "world-ruler," later came back to the Scandinavian royalty as Valdemar. The English equivalent is Walter.

Before he died, Svyatoslav named Vladimir as prince of

Novgorod. Upon his father's death, Vladimir's brother Yaropolk attempted to seize the city. Vladimir was forced to flee to his kinsmen in Sweden, where he obtained arms and men from a powerful uncle.

As we have seen, the weak Oleg and the scheming Yaropolk were soon out of the way, and Vladimir returned to Russia. In 980, with support from the Varangians of Novgorod, he established himself as Prince of Kiev. He began his reign by conquering another Viking prince, Ravolod (Ragnvald), who "had come from across the sea" and who ruled in Polotsk. Vladimir then took Ragnvald's daughter as one of his wives.

Vladimir was every inch a heathen. At the beginning of his rule, he lined the front of his palace with statues of Slavonic gods: Svarog the father of the gods, Dazhd-Bog the sun god, Veles the cattle god, and Perun the thunder god. The wooden statues were lavishly adorned with gold and silver.

To thank the gods for his military victories, Vladimir offered human sacrifices. Two of the victims (named Theodore and Ivan) were Christians, and they cried out just before their death, "Yours is not a god, but just a piece of wood!"

Perhaps the martyrs' words sunk deeply into Vladimir's conscience. At any rate, he became disillusioned with Slavic paganism and began seeking a new religion.

The eleventh-century monk Jacob (not too far removed from Vladimir's time) tells the story of how Vladimir chose Christianity. There were people of many religions living in and around Kiev, and Vladimir investigated them all. Islam had no appeal, due to its prohibition against the wine which the Russians so enjoyed. "Islam is a religion without joy," he decided.

There were also Jews in Kiev and among the neighboring Khazars. "Why are you scattered over the earth?" Vladimir is said to have asked them. When they replied, "For our sins," the Jewish faith likewise lost its appeal for Vladimir.

Vladimir chose to accept Christianity. But should he align himself with the eastern or western branch? The king of Poland, Mieszko I, had had converted to Rome in 966, and so Vladimir was familiar with the Roman Catholic ritual. But Vladimir found the pomp and ceremony of the church in Byzantium to be even more attractive. Besides, Constantinople was nearer than Rome, and there was the example of his Christian grandmother, Olga. Vladimir is reported to have said, "My grandmother, being the wisest of mortals, must have made the best choice."

There were other ties to Byzantium. When the Emperor Basil II appealed for help in crushing his opponents in 988, Vladimir sent him six thousand choice Varangian troops who remained in the imperial service. The prince of Kiev was then promised as his bride Anna, the purple-born sister of the emperor.

The people of Byzantium were in shock. No princess born in the purple chamber of the Eastern Roman Empire had ever before been married to a barbaric foreigner. Basil's people felt that he had made too hasty a promise and should retract it. While the controversy over Anna was raging, it appears that nobody bothered to ask her how *she* felt about the warlike and polygamous prospective bridegroom.

But Vladimir was not about to cancel the marriage plans. In an attempt to gain his bride by force, he marched against the Greek colony at Kherson on the Crimea. After a long siege, he conquered it.

Vladimir then sent word to Basil II and Constantine VIII that he would offer peace in return for the promised hand of their sister Anna. Basil must have realized that he would be better off with Vladimir as a brother-in-law than as a foe. He agreed to give Anna to Vladimir if the later would become a Christian. Vladimir was already anxious to do this, and so he was baptized before the wedding in 989.

Vladimir returned to Kiev not only with his bride but also with the priests who had baptized him. Like Saul of Tarsus, the former persecutor became ardently zealous for his new faith. He ordered his idols to be whipped and then cast into the river. Then he ordered all the people of Kiev to go into the river as well. There they were baptized en masse while the priests stood on the shore and read the liturgy.

Vladimir at first forced Christianity upon his empire by the sword. Like the Saxons and other tribes before them, the Slavs adapted Christianity to their existing beliefs. Perun, god of thunder, became associated with Elijah and his chariot of fire. Veles became St. Blaise, still the patron saint of cattle. Far later there remained many blends with the old religion.

The conversion of Kiev to Christianity was a great boost to the Eastern Church. Thus the largest and most important of the Slavic states became subject to the spiritual guidance of the Patriarch of Constantinople.

Vladimir himself became a transformed person. Instead of treating conquered peoples with cruelty, he devoted himself to administering justice for all. He established schools, and he supported the reading of Scripture in the Slavic tongue.

Vladimir commissioned Byzantine architects to build several beautiful churches. One was erected on the site previously sacred to Perun, and another at the place where he had sacrificed Theodore and Ivan. He became known as "Vladimir the Joyous" because of his Christian faith.

The importance of Vladimir's conversion cannot be under-estimated. Russian Christianity spread all the way to Siberia, to Alaska, and eventually even to California.

Vladimir was a powerful ruler. His domain reached from the Baltic to the Ukraine, and extended westward as far as Poland and eastward to the Don and the Upper Volga.

Before his conversion, Vladimir had at least five royal wives (some historians tell us that he had eight). These were princesses from neighboring kingdoms, married for the sake of political advantage. He is also said to have kept 800 concubines in various parts of his realm. But when he married Anna, he abolished polygamy and re-mained faithful to her until she died in 1011.

When Anna died, Vladimir took a new bride who bore him a daughter. The little girl's Slavic name was Dabrogneva, but she is more commonly known by her Christian name, Maria. She later became the queen of Kasimir I of Poland, and their descendants intermarried with the Swedish royalty.

Vladimir had twelve sons by various mothers, most of them born before his conversion. When he died in 1015, his kingdom was divided among the twelve sons and a nephew. The peace and joy of his reign gave way to terror until 1019, when Yaroslav became the undisputed ruler of Kiev.

## Svyatopolk I—ruled from 1015 to 1019.

*"I must get rid of those Christian brothers of mine! I refuse to share my throne with them."*

According to some sources, Svyatopolk was an adopted son or stepson of Vladimir I. But his royal father treated him no differently from the others, giving him a portion of the realm when he divided the kingdom. Svyatopolk inherited Turof, but he was not content with this. A very unscrupulous man, he hoped to expand his dominions by taking away territory from his brothers. In particular, he was cruelly jealous of Boris and Gleb, sons of Princess Anna. In 1015 he made plans to murder them.

Boris was warned of the plot, but because of his Christian convictions, he refused to raise his hand against his brother. Instead of fleeing or defending himself, Boris spent the night in prayer. While he was still at his devotions, the followers of Svyatopolk fell upon him with spears and began dragging his body back to Kiev. When they discovered that he was still alive, they finished the job with swords.

Gleb, the second son of Princess Anna, was slain by treachery. Svyatopolk, pretending friendliness, invited him to Kiev, but had him murdered along the way. As he was being butchered, Gleb cried out, "I am being slain; I know not why, but thou, oh Lord, knowest."

Having dispatched Boris and Gleb, Svyatopolk set his hopes upon taking the high throne of Kiev away from his brother Yaroslav, who had inherited that city. To do this, Svyatopolk decided that he needed foreign aid, so he made an alliance with Boleslav II of Poland. The pact was sealed by his marriage to Boleslav's daughter.

On July 21, 1018, Boleslav defeated Yaroslav in battle, and sent him into exile. The Polish king then placed his son-in-law Svyatopolk on the throne. But the Polish victory in Kiev was brief. The exiled Yaroslav gathered the fighting men of Novgorod and together they set sail for Kiev. With them were also some Varangians "from across the sea"—possibly relatives from Sweden.

Yaroslav was successful, and his troops drove Svyatopolk out of Kiev. Many of Boleslav's troops perished in in the fray, and Boleslav was forced to retreat.

Svyatopolk next turned for help to the Pechenegs, but they betrayed and killed him on the very spot where Boris had been murdered. Yaroslav the Wise became the uncontested ruler of Kiev in 1019.

### Yaroslav the Wise—ruled from 1019 to 1054.

*"Now that I've vanquished my foes, I'll build a library and order Greek manuscripts to be translated into Slavic."*

Some historians date Yaroslav's rule as 1015 to 1054; others date the beginning of his reign at 1019, after his usurping brother Svyatopolk was out of the way.

Besides trying to gain back his throne, Yaroslav had to deal with the marauding tribes which surrounded him. After many battles, Yaroslav finally conquered the barbaric Pechenegs in 1036. He also fought the Poles and recovered territory which they had taken from Kiev.

His rule, however, is remembered more for peace and scholarly achievements than for war. Yaroslav gathered a large library, ordered Greek religious texts translated into Slavic, and codified the legal system of Russia much as Leo the Philosopher had done in Byzantium, as Karl the Great's scholars had done in France, and as Alfred the Great had done in England.

Yaroslav is also remembered for carrying out religious duties. Early in his reign, he buried the bodies of his martyred half brothers Boris and Gleb at Vyshgorod. Miracles were reported at their tomb, and they were canonized by the church as models of brotherly love and "turning the other cheek." The murdering brother Svyatopolk, on the other hand, has gone down in history as "the accursed."

Following his father's example, Yaroslav continued to make of Kiev a city of beauty with Constantinople as a model. He built the Church of St. Sophia and the Monastery of St. George. He commissioned artists to fill the city with beautiful paintings and scholars to record the city's history.

Yaroslav was married to Ingegerd, a daughter of Olof Skötkonung, Sweden's first Christian king. By this means, Yaroslav entered into a marriage alliance with his Scandinavian kinfolk. We read that he was thus able "to secure Varangian auxiliaries from across the sea" in his battles.

When Ingegerd came to Yaroslav, she was accompanied by Ragnvald, jarl of Västergötland, who was given lands in Russia as a reward for chaperoning the princess. This further strengthened the close ties between the Swedish nobility and Russia's ruling class. Ingegerd lived until about 1058 and bore many children to Yaroslav.

Like countless kings before him, Yaroslav made foreign alliances by marrying off his sisters and daughters to neighboring monarchs. As we have mentioned, he gave his baby sister Maria in marriage to Kasimir I of Poland. And as we have seen in previous chapters, his daughter Elizabeth was given to the adventurous Harald Hårdråde of Norway, a guest in his court.

Advantageous marriages were also arranged for his other children. His daughter Anna was married to Henry I of France. By this marriage Yaroslav is a direct ancestor of many present-day royal persons, including Queen Elizabeth II of England.

The youngest daughter, with the Byzantine name of Anastasia, was married to King Andrew I of Hungary.

Yaroslav's favorite son, Vsevolod, was married to Irina, a daughter of Constantine IX Monomach of Constantinople.

Before his death, Yaroslav set up a complicated system for succession. The kingdom was apportioned among his five living sons and Rostislav, an orphaned grandson. They were to accept Izyaslav as Grand Prince of Kiev.

**Izyaslav I and Svyatoslav II—ruled from 1054 to 1078.**

Like the Franks, the house of Rurik had the custom of dividing the kingdom among the sons of a deceased sovereign. Much has been written about the problems this caused for the Carolingians. There, with the passage of time, the vast empire of Karl the Great was fractured into ever smaller splinters as more and more heirs were born to fight over their increasingly smaller dominions.

In the same way, the Teutonic method of succession caused the Scandinavian-Russian royalty no end of problems. Byzantium, on the other hand, remained a united empire because the throne passed either from father to son (or daughter), or to sons who ruled as co-emperors without splitting up the empire.

In Yaroslav's system of succession, sons were given different cities, where they reigned as princes, under the leadership of the Grand Prince of Kiev. Each time a brother died, the younger brothers were all to move up one rung on the hierarchical ladder. Thus a prince of Minsk or Novgorod might eventually move up to become Prince of Kiev, if he could get rid of his brothers. Naturally, such a system leads inevitably to fratricide. The wise Yaroslav had hoped to keep his descendants united by his rule of succession, but instead Kiev entered a period of civil war which eventually led to its decline.

When Izyaslav became Prince of Kiev, its citizens were unhappy because he was unable to protect them from the Polovtsy, a powerful Turkish tribe which had moved into the area formerly occupied by the Pechenegs. His subjects expelled him from Kiev in 1073.

Izyaslav was succeeded by Svyatoslav II, the second brother. When Svyatoslav II died in 1078, he was succeeded by Vsevolod, Yaroslav's third son, and his favorite.

**Vsevolod—ruled from 1078 to 1093.**

Vsevolod had been named Prince of Pereaslavl (close to Kiev). He was also given the province of Suzdal, close to modern Moscow. He later became Prince of Chernigov as well.

On Svyatoslav's death, Vsevolod (as the next brother in line) succeeded him as Prince of Kiev. But Izyaslav returned from exile with Polish assistance and Vsevolod was forced to retire. Not until Izyaslav died, was Vsvevold back again as Grand Prince of Kiev.

We learn something of Vsevolod's scholarly bent from his son, Vladimir II, who wrote in his his *Testament*, "Without ever having left his palace, my father could speak five languages: it is this that makes us admired by foreigners."

**Svyatopolk II and others—ruled from 1093 to 1113.**

The years after Vsevolod's reign were marked by terrible family strife. We will skip over most of the bloodshed and violence as power-hungry brothers, cousins, and nephews quarreled with each other. Some of these rulers are shown on Charts 23 and 24; others have been omitted since our concern is primarily to show the interconnecting marriages between Kiev and Scandinavia, rather than to dwell on all the fighting between the various cousins.

Perhaps the worst junior prince was the cruel David, son of Svyatoslav II, who hired four ruffians to tear out the eyes of his cousin and rival Vasilko. He then carried Vasilko off in a cart to his own territory, where he could finish him off at his leisure. Vasilko's relatives, predictably, called for revenge; and eventually David lost his title and died in disgrace.

During these bloody years the Grand Prince of Kiev was Svyatopolk II, son of Izyaslav. He did little to stop the feuding. Svyatopolk II died without sons and finally a worthy descendant of Yaroslav the Wise, Vladimir Monomakh, came to the throne.

**Vladimir II Monomakh—ruled from 1113 to 1125.**

*"The people want you as their king!"* Vladimir was told when his cousin Svyatopolk II died. *"I don't want to break my grandfather Yaroslav's rule of succession,"* the humble Vladimir replied. *"Let the throne go to my cousins."* Despite his protests, the throne became his, and he proved to be a wise and benevolent ruler.

Vladimir II Monomakh was born about 1053, the only son of Vsevolod and his Byzantine wife Irina. (As previously mentioned, she was the daughter of Constantine IX Monomach.) No doubt Vladimir's surname came from his maternal grandfather.

Vladimir showed ability to rule early in life. He helped his father defeat his usurping cousins Oleg (son of Svyatoslav II) and Boris (son of Vyacheslav) at Chernigov. When his father Vsevolod became Grand Prince of Kiev, Vladimir was named Prince of Chernigov. He ruled there from 1078 to 1094, showing wisdom and diplomacy in his dealings with his feuding cousins. Twice his advice helped avert further bloodshed when the Russian princes held meetings to try to solve their problems.

Vladimir Monomakh also distinguished himself as a brave soldier. In 1101 and 1103 he carried out two successive expeditions to the Polovtsy country where the Russians triumphed. After the victory,

Monomakh quoted the familiar benediction from Psalm 118, "This is the day which the Lord has made; let us rejoice and be glad in it."

When Svyatopolk II, son of Izyaslav, died in 1113, the people demanded that Vladimir Monomakh be made Grand Prince of Kiev. It took all their powers of persuasion to finally get him to agree to put aside the rules of succession and take the throne.

For twelve years there was peace and victory in the kingdom under Vladimir Monomakh. He was a fair ruler, an able administrator, and an energetic builder, founding the city of Vladimir on the Klyazma River.

Vladimir Monomakh was married to Gyda, a daughter of that Harald Godwinsson who so briefly ruled England until overcome by William the Conqueror in the famous battle of Hastings. Snorri calls her "Gyda the Old." As we have previously noted, Queen Gyda was related on her mother's side to the royal house of Denmark. Thus many lines: Swedish, Danish, and Greek, came together in Mstislav and the other children of Vladimir and Gyda.

Like Alfred the Great of England, Vladimir left a written legacy for posterity. In the *Testament* which he wrote for his sons he recounted eighty-four "long journeys" in which he slept in the open, traveled through dangerous forests, was thrown by a bull, attacked by a wild stag, bitten by a bear, and kicked by an elk. He also recounted his military triumphs over 200 Polovtsy princes.

In a final charge to his descendants, Vladimir urged them to pray before bedtime, to rise early in the morning, to judge the poor fairly, and never to shed blood except in battle. He even opposed capital punishment. "Do not have either an innocent or a guilty man put to death," he preached, "for nothing is more sacred than the life and the soul of a Christian."

"Children," he exhorted his sons, "fear neither man nor beast. Play the man. Nothing can hurt you unless God wills it. God's care is better than man's."

## Mstislav I—ruled from 1125 to 1132.

*"I am a Varangian by ancestry; I have a Swedish wife; and my daughters shall marry Scandinavian princes. This will strengthen my alliance with Sweden, Norway and Denmark."*

When Monomakh died his son Mstislav succeeded him. He appears to have heeded his father's advice, for he maintained peace, ruled fairly, and kept the family united against the invading pagans.

Although by the twelfth century the house of Rurik was thoroughly Russian in culture, Mstislav was doubtless aware of his Viking roots. Like most rulers of Kiev, he had both a Slavic and a Scandinavian name. His Nordic name was Harald Valdemarsson, and it is by this name that Snorri refers to him.

Given all the connections between Kiev and Sweden, it is not surprising that Mstislav married a Swedish princess—Kristina, a daughter of King Inge the Elder. Good relations with Scandinavia were strengthened still further when Mstislav's two daughters married into the Scandinavian royal families. His daughter Ingeborg married Prince Knut Lavard of Denmark, and his daughter Malmfrith married Sigurd Jerusalem-farer. After this Norwegian ruler (in a sort of mid-life crisis) divorced her, Malmfrith was married to yet another Scandinavian king—Erik Emune of Denmark.

Mstislav I died in 1132, and the era of Kiev's greatest glory came to an end. New family feuds emerged. Brothers, cousins, uncles and nephews argued endlessly over the order of succession. The wise advice of Yaroslav and Vladimir Monomakh was forgotten, and Russia entered a new period of bloodshed and civil war. Eventually the kingdom disintegrated into ever smaller city-states, divided and ruled by an ever increasing number of Rurik's descendants. It is no wonder that by the thirteenth century they became easy prey for the invading Mongols.

Meanwhile, through the line of Maria—a daughter of Vladimir I—as well as through Mstislav's daughters Ingeborg and Malmfrith, the descendants of Rurik were also increasing in Scandinavia where his dynasty had originated some 300 years before.

This brings us to our final chapters, which deal with Sweden's medieval monarchs and their descendants.

CHART 22 - The House of Rurik

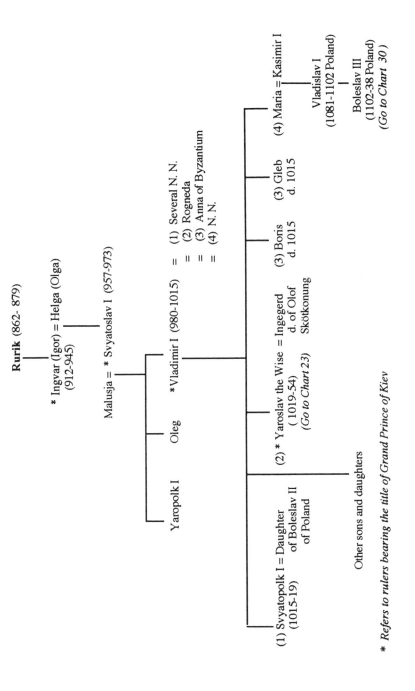

**Rurik** (862- 879)

* Ingvar (Igor) = Helga (Olga)
  (912-945)

Malusja = * Svyatoslav I (957-973)

Yaropolk I

Oleg

*Vladimir I (980-1015) = (1) Several N. N.
              = (2) Rogneda
              = (3) Anna of Byzantium
              = (4) N. N.

(1) Svyatopolk I = Daughter
    (1015-19)      of Boleslav II
                   of Poland

(2) * Yaroslav the Wise = Ingegerd
      ( 1019-54)          d. of Olof
      *(Go to Chart 23)*   Skötkonung

(3) Boris
    d. 1015

(3) Gleb
    d. 1015

(4) Maria = Kasimir I

Vladislav I
(1081-1102 Poland)

Boleslav III
(1102-38 Poland)
*(Go to Chart 30 )*

Other sons and daughters

\* *Refers to rulers bearing the title of Grand Prince of Kiev*

## CHART 23 - The Family of Yaroslav I the Wise

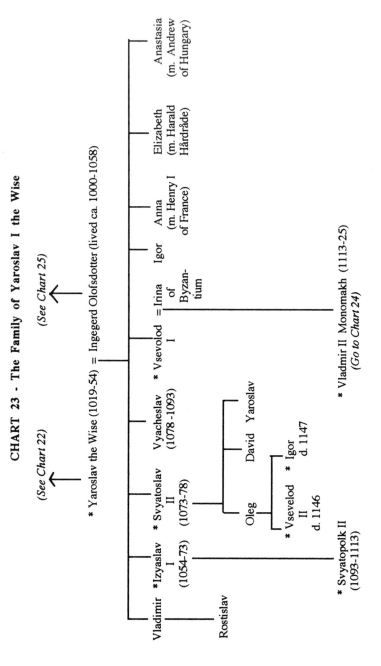

* Refers to rulers bearing the title of Grand Prince of Kiev

**CHART 24 - The Family of Vladimir II Monomakh of Kiev**

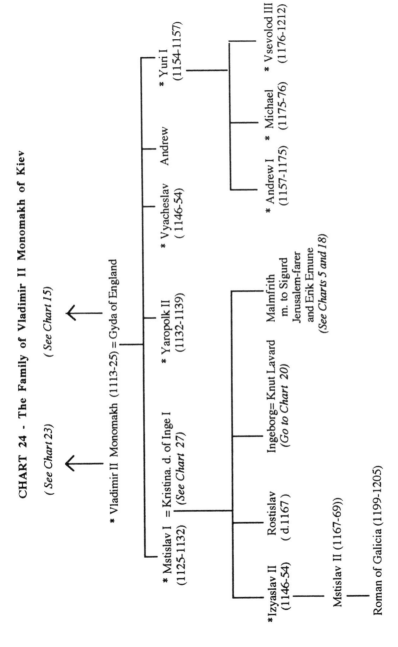

(*See Chart 23*)

(*See Chart 15*)

* Vladimir II Monomakh (1113-25) = Gyda of England

* Mstislav I  = Kristina. d. of Inge I
(1125-1132)     (*See Chart 27*)

* Yaropolk II
(1132-1139)

* Vyacheslav
( 1146-54)

Andrew

* Yuri I
(1154-1157)

* Andrew I
(1157-1175)

* Michael
(1175-76)

* Vsevolod III
(1176-1212)

*Izyaslav II
(1146-54)

Rostislav
( d.1167 )

Ingeborg= Knut Lavard
(*Go to Chart 20*)

Malmfrith
m. to Sigurd
Jerusalem-farer
and Erik Emune
(*See Charts 5 and 18*)

Mstislav II (1167-69))

Roman of Galicia (1199-1205)

* *Refers to rulers bearing the title of Grand Prince of Kiev*

# Chapter 8

## The Ivarska Dynasty of Sweden—
## from about 600 to about 1060

The history of Sweden before the year 1000 is shrouded in a great deal of mystery. In the Middle Ages, Sweden had no counterpart to Norway's Snorri or Denmark's Saxo. As a result, it is difficult to discover even the names of the Swedish rulers during the Viking period (except where they are mentioned in passing by Snorri, Saxo, Adam of Bremen, and their contemporaries). It is even harder to determine the order in which these Swedish monarchs ruled.

An inscription on the Sparlösa Stone, dated at about the year 800, mentions an Alarik, son of Erik of Uppsala, who ruled Västergötland at that time. And of course, there are the historical kings Björn and Olof who welcomed St. Ansgar to Sweden in the ninth century. More about them later on. But most of what we are told about the kings who ruled Sweden before the year 1000 is based on legend.

It was not until Renaissance times that Sweden gained some serious historians of its own. While in some cases they made a conscientious effort to record history accurately, they were much farther removed from the Middle Ages than were Snorri and Saxo, and less likely to have primary sources at their disposal.

Three early Swedish historians deserve to be mentioned. Interestingly, they were all named Olof, but being learned men, they preferred the Latinized form of the name—Olaus.

The first was Erik Olaus, who taught theology at the University of Uppsala. In 1469, he produced his *Chronica Regni Gothorum* (Chronicles of the Kings of the Goths) at the request of Sweden's Karl VIII. He drew upon the writings of Jordanes, Isidorus of Seville, Adam of Bremen, Saxo Grammaticus, and other earlier historians, and his work is still a valuable resource.

Later came Olaus Petri, who lived from 1493 to 1552. He was a clergyman, a reformer, and a Bible translator as well as a historian, and his *Chronica* is often quoted by modern writers.

The third Olaus was Olaus Magnus, who lived until 1557. His *Historia de Gentibus Septentrionalibus* was published in 1555. It is a highly patriotic and imaginative work.

Olaus Magnus' brother Johannes, also a clergyman, wrote the *Historia de Ominibus Gothorum Sueonumque Regibus* (History of All the Kings of the Goths and Svears). This work lists, in genealogical order, 109 kings who supposedly ruled Sweden up to the time of the historical Erik the Victorious. In an effort to reach back as far as possible, the work presents the first king of Sweden as "Magog, the son of Noah." (The writer apparently forgot that in the Biblical narrative Magog is Noah's grandson, not his son.)

According to Johannes Magnus, the second king of Sweden was named Sven. What a very Scandinavian name for a supposed grandson of Noah! There follow a great many Eriks, Karls, Björns, and others.

We will not follow Johannes Magnus' catalog of kings, although we will refer to it from time to time. Rather, we will begin with the legendary founder of the Ivarska dynasty.

**Ivar Vidfamne—ruled during the seventh century.**
As we noted in Chapter 1, the Ynglings allegedly ruled in Uppsala from before the time of Christ up until about 600 A. D. At that time, the last Yngling king in Sweden, Ingjald Illråde, is said to have destroyed himself and his daughter by setting fire to his palace on Lake Mälaren.

Ingjald's son was Olof Tretelgia. According to Erik Olaus, Olof Tretelgia governed Sweden for a long time, there was peace and tranquility during his reign, and he died at Uppsala and was honorably buried there.

The old Norse tales, on the other hand, state that Olof Tretelgia fled to Norway, and there became the father of the Norwegian Yngling dynasty. These stories state that in Sweden Ingjald was succeeded by Ivar, who founded a new dynasty called the Ivarska.

Johannes Magnus lists Ingjald as the 106th king of Sweden, and his son Olof Tretelgia as the 107th, but he omits Ivar. Erik Olaus, on the other hand, briefly mentions all three: Ingjald, Olof Tretelgia, and Ivar. He obviously considered them all to be historical.

We learn about Ivar primarily through the old Norse sagas. While these stories are highly imaginative, they may have a historical basis. King Ivar very likely existed, although his exploits have been greatly exaggerated by the bards.

The same holds true for Ivar's descendants up to the close of the tenth century. We will relate some of their stories, but the reader should be advised to take them with a grain of salt. After the year 1000 or so, the grain of salt may be omitted, since there are more actual historical records to help us sort out the kings of Sweden and their family relationships.

According to the old stories, Ivar's father was Halfdan Snälle. This petty king (whose name means "good-natured half-Dane") ruled over Skåne in southern Sweden. Ivar, in time, became king of Skåne himself, during the reign of the wicked Ingjald Illråde who ruled at Uppsala.

The *Ynglinga Saga* describes how Ivar raised an army against Ingjald and surrounded his great hall on Lake Mälaren. After Ingjald perished by burning down his own palace, Ivar took over the throne of Uppsala. He greatly increased his kingdom on every side and, according to the *Skjöldunga Saga,* he became the greatest Scandinavian king up to his time.

Through his marriage to the Danish princess Gyrita, Ivar acquired Jutland. In addition he is said to have subdued part of Saxony, many lands along the Baltic, and "a fifth part of England". (This term usually refers to Northumbria.) Because of all his conquests, he was called *Ivar Vidfamne,* or Ivar the Wide-Reacher.

Gyrita bore but one child to Ivar—a daughter named Oda, which means "the Rich." When she was grown, she was known as *Oda den djup Oda* or "Oda the Very Rich" since she was not only endowed with great beauty, but also was the only heir to her father's vast kingdoms. She was given in marriage to Rörek of Denmark, even though her true love was a Viking named Helge. Oda bore Rörek a son named *Harald Hildetand,* or Harald Shining-Teeth.

Ivar's family life, like that of most monarchs of his time, was marked by feuding and bloodshed. Oda's husband Rörek and her lover Helge predictably quarreled over her, with the result that Rörek killed Helge.

To avenge Helge, Ivar then killed Rörek, his son-in-law. The widowed Oda took her young son Harald and fled to the Swedish settlements in Russia, where she found refuge in the court of a petty king named Radbart. Before long, Radbart asked for her hand in marriage. A son, Randver Radbartsson, was born to this union.

Ivar, who had vanquished his daughter's first husband Rörek, now determined to punish her second husband Radbart for marrying her without asking his royal permission. While on this expedition to plunder Russia, Ivar was drowned in the Gulf of Finland.

### Harald Hildetand—ruled during the eighth century.

Upon the death of his wide-reaching grandfather Ivar, Harald Hildetand (who was only fifteen at the time) is said to have become king of both Sweden and Denmark. It is interesting to note that while the Danish historian Saxo says nothing about Ivar, both Saxo and the Norse sagas mention Ivar's grandson Harald.

We are told that Harald ruled for more than fifty years. During this time the country had peace. To prevent his men from becoming weak in peacetime, he often held contests in wielding sword, spear, and battle axe.

Harald's royal court was to be found in Lejre, a city on the Danish island of Sjaelland. He placed his younger half brother Randver as a vassal king in Uppsala. When Randver died on a Viking raid to England, his son Sigurd Ring succeeded him as tributary king of Sweden.

Peace did not remain in the kingdom, for Sigurd Ring and the other vassal kings were not happy to bow to the elderly Harald as their overlord. About 750 A. D., Harald Hildetand was killed at the Battle of Brävalla against his nephew Sigurd Ring. While many events in the lives of Sigurd Ring and Harald Hildetand are thought to be legendary, the battle of Brävalla is considered to be factual.

The old sagas shed some light on Viking funeral customs. We read that Sigurd, seeing how valiantly his aged uncle had fought, vowed to give him a proper burial. King Harald's body was carefully washed and placed in his chariot. The king's horse was taken into the funeral mound, where it was killed and harnessed to the royal chariot. Next, Sigurd Ring placed his own saddle in the mound, so that the deceased king might ride into Valhalla in style. Lastly, he called on all the warriors present at the funeral feast to bring their gifts to Harald. The men threw in bracelets, swords, and other treasures before the mound was closed. Sigurd then took over the whole kingdom.

**Sigurd Ring and Eystein-Beli—ruled during the eighth century.**

Sigurd Ring, son of Randver and nephew to Harald Hildetand, is said to have been very valiant in battle, and to have won many victories over Germans and Norwegians with his trusty sword Gram.

Sigurd Ring's queen was Ålfhild, the daughter of a petty king named Gandalf of Bohuslän. We read that their son was Ragnar Lodbrok who is said to have been as tall and strong as his ancestor Ivar Vidfamne.

In his old age, Sigurd Ring was attracted to Alfsol, the beautiful daughter of Alf, one of his vassal kings from Jutland. He asked for her hand, but her brothers Alf and Inge refused to give "so fair a maid to such a withered old man."

Furious at being rejected, Sigurd Ring vowed revenge on all Alfsol's relatives. The princess' brothers decided that it would be more honorable to end her life than to let her be carried off by Sigurd Ring, so (according to the old stories) they poisoned her.

The powerful Sigurd Ring, aided by his son Ragnar Lodbrok, overcame Alfsol's brothers in battle. It was, nevertheless, a Pyrrhic victory, for as soon as Sigurd Ring learned that Alfsol was dead, he took his own life. Ragnar then raised a great burial mound to honor his father.

After his father's death, Ragnar Lodbrok ruled over Denmark at Lejre, and placed his cousin Eystein-Beli (Harald Hildetand's son) as tributary king over Sweden in Uppsala. The legends surrounding these folk heroes are told in Chapter 5. Upon the death of Ragnar Lodbrok, his domains were divided. Sweden, we are told, went to his son Björn Järnsida.

**Björn Järnsida, Björn of Birka, and Olof of Birka—ruled in the ninth century.**

If we may trust the old sagas, Björn Ragnarsson was called *Järnsida,* or Ironside, because he wore no armor when he went to war. Amazingly, he was never wounded, so the people thought him to have sides as strong as iron, and perhaps even magical skin.

Björn Ironside is not to be confused with the King Björn who invited Christian missionaries to Sweden. But since that historical event took place in the early ninth century, we shall mention it at this point.

Ansgar, the first Christian missionary to Sweden, was sent there in 829 by Louis the Pious (a son of Karl the Great) in answer to the request of a Swedish chieftain named Björn, who ruled in Birka on Lake Mälaren.

Through Ansgar's biographer Rimbert, we learn of the missionaries' encounter with the some Viking pirates while on their way.

*The robbers took from them both ship and cargo, and they were scarce able to flee to land and escape on foot. Thus they lost even the royal gifts they should bring to the Svears, besides all they had, save that little they could snatch up when they leaped from the ships.*

Yet the missionaries would not give up. Rimbert continues:

*And so they walked a long and laborious way, crossing the seas that lay between in boats, and came duly to the harbour of the realm, that is called Birka. And here they were received with kindness by the king, whose name was Björn.*

Ansgar established a church in Birka; the king's chief minister, whose name was Hergeir, was converted; and the mission prospered for a while.

Nevertheless, the country as a whole remained pagan. Gautbert, Ansgar's successor, had to flee from Birka in 839 after a pagan uprising in which his house was destroyed and his nephew Nithard was killed.

Ansgar returned to Sweden in 855 with two companions. Olof, the new Swedish king (who doesn't seem to fit into the Ivarska genealogy), welcomed the missionaries, but would not allow them to preach without calling together a *Thing* to discuss the issue.

Much noise and shouting ensued at this assembly. Finally an old man said, "Hear me, oh King and people. If our gods can no longer help us, it is well to seek the favor of this new, mightier God."

Hearing this, Olof gave permission to build a church. In turn, the missionaries presented him with gifts. Ansgar then returned to Bremen, where he died in 865.

Meanwhile, the somewhat legendary Björn Ironside seems not to have been affected in the slightest by the missionary activity in Birka, although he is said to have been regent over Sweden, while his brother Sigurd Orm-i-Oga ruled in Denmark as the overlord.

Perhaps Björn Ironside was too busy plundering foreign shores to think much about the new religion. He is said to have made many raids upon England and to have fought great battles against King Ethelbert. He may have participated in the storming of York in 866.

Björn Ironside is also credited with making the Viking raids on the lands around the Seine River in 856 and 857. He was possibly among the Northmen whom Charles the Bald bribed with 3,000 pounds of silver in order to stop the Viking harassment at that time.

Still more amazing is the story of Björn's Mediterranean expedition in the 860s. Together with a Viking named Hastein, he launched sixty-two ships and spent four years along the coasts of Spain, North Africa, and Italy. Both Moorish and Norse chronicles tell of the terrible pirate raids which Björn and Hastein inflicted on the people. The Vikings even captured some Negroes. Amazed to see men of such dark coloring, the fair-skinned Scandinavians called them *Blåmenn,* or Blue Men.

Some two centuries later, other men of Viking descent would harry and conquer southern Italy, Sicily and much of North Africa. We refer, of course, to the Normans Robert Guiscard and his brother Roger, said by some genealogists to be direct descendants of the Norwegian Rollo who was exiled from his native land because of his piracy and who ended up carving out a duchy in France.

Björn Ironside is said to have died in 870, and we are told that he left two sons: Erik and Refil.

### Erik I Emundsson and Erik II Björnsson —ruled in the ninth century.

Snorri mentions another Swedish king who died in 870—Erik Emundsson, a contemporary of Harald the Fairhaired of Norway. For the sake of simplicity, we will call him Erik I. We learn that Erik Emundsson fought many fierce battles against the Norwegians, appropriated Norse lands, and exacted tribute from the inhabitants. He also laid claim to Finland, Estonia, and Karelia.

We are told that as part of a peace treaty made with his foe Harald the Fairhaired, Erik was given Harald's daughter Ingegerd in marriage. Erik and Ingegerd raised a son named Björn who figures prominently in the Norse/Irish sagas and genealogies as well as in the Swedish annals. Snorri tells us that Erik Emundsson died in 870, in the tenth year of Harald the Fairhaired's reign, and was succeeded by his son Björn.

Meanwhile, another Erik, the son of Björn Ironside, appears to have ruled in Sweden. Some sources give the date of this Erik Björnsson's death as 874, only four years after his father. We will call him Erik II. (There were probably many more Swedish King Eriks before him, however. Snorri lists three early Yngling Eriks—sons of Yngve, Agnar, and Agni respectively. Johannes Magnus lists six Eriks prior to Erik the Victorious—numbers 6, 37, 40, 47, 96 and 109 in his catalog.)

Erik II, we are told, had two sons: Björn Eriksson and Emund I. Emund succeeded to the throne at Uppsala, while Björn ruled at Birka.

**Emund I Eriksson, Björn Eriksson of Birka, and Erik III Refilsson — ruled in the ninth century.**
Emund I (said to be Björn Ironside's grandson) apparently made Viking raids on Finland, Estonia, and other lands along the Baltic. By this means he greatly increased his kingdom. Some sources give the date of his death as 886.

At the same time Emund I ruled at Uppsala and his brother Björn governed Birka, there was at least one other king in Sweden. We refer to Erik III Refilsson, said to have been a nephew to Erik II. Erik Refilsson is credited with being among the Vikings who besieged Paris in 886, forcing Charles the Fat to make a peace treaty on their terms.

**Erik IV Väderhatt — ruled in the ninth century.**
Now we come to a King Erik who came to be known as *Väderhatt,* or "Weather Hat." Many famous men got their surnames from what they wore — Hugh Capet and Robin Hood are just two examples.

Erik Olaus informs us that when Erik Väderhatt longed for fair weather, he offered sacrifices to idols, and at the same time turned his hat over. His prayers were heard, good weather was restored, and thus he earned his nickname. Olaus Magnus tells us that Erik Väderhatt used magic arts and "was familiar with evil spirits."

Just where Erik Väderhatt fits into the Ivarska dynasty is most unclear. For the purposes of this book, we will call him Erik IV. Johannes Magnus, however, lists him as Erik VI, the 109th king of Sweden. He tells us that Erik Väderhatt was the son of Inge, and the grandson of Olof Tretelgia. Erik Olaus shares this view, telling us that Erik Väderhatt's father was named Inge, and that his mother was a daughter of Ragnar Lodbrok.

**Björn Eriksson of Uppsala — ruled in the early tenth century.**
Snorri tells us that Björn, the son of Erik Emundsson, reigned for fifty years, from 870 to 920. Other sources give the date of his death as 910. Snorri tells us that "while Björn lived, his dominion flourished and in nowise decreased. His friends found him easy to deal with." Snorri also states that Björn Eriksson was the father of Erik the Victorious. However, the modern historian Lagerkvist tells us that Erik the Victorious was the son of Emund Eriksson. In this matter, we tend to trust Lagerkvist above Snorri.

During Björn's time, another Scandinavian — the Viking Rollo — made history by gaining Normandy from Charles the Simple.

**Olof Ring( Björnsson?)—ruled Sweden in the tenth century.**
Olof Ring probably ruled until about 930. He may have been the son of Björn Eriksson of Uppsala and the father of Erik V.

At the same time, another Swedish Olof (probably a petty chieftain unrelated to Olof Ring) and his son Gnupa sailed south, conquering the medieval trading center of Hedeby in what was then southern Denmark, and engaging in battle against Henry the Fowler of Germany.

**Erik V (Olofsson?)—ruled Sweden in the tenth century.**
The man we call Erik V is an historical person; he ruled from about 930 to 950, and was a contemporary of Denmark's Gorm the Old. We learn from accounts written in his times that he received a visit from Unni (archbishop of Hamburg/Bremen) at Uppsala in 936, shortly after Unni had made an unsuccessful visit to Gorm. Unni's missionary effort, like the previous attempts to convert the Swedes, apparently bore little fruit.

According to some writers, Erik V was a son of Olof Ring. Still other authors make him out to be a grandson of Erik Refilsson, and tell us that he was regent under his uncle Björn of Holga from 910 to 925, after which time he ruled alone at Uppsala until about 950.

Erik V may have been the father of Emund II.

**Emund II (Eriksson?)—ruled in the tenth century.**
Emund probably reigned from about 950 to 965. Lagerkvist tells us that he was the father of two kings: Olof and Erik, later surnamed Segersäll (the Victorious).

**Olof (Emundsson?)—ruled in the tenth century.**
Olof, the older brother of Erik the Victorious, was regent in Sweden from about 965 to 970. We are told that his son, Styrbjörn Starke, was still very young when Olof died, so the throne passed to Erik.

**Erik VI (Emundsson?) Segersäll—ruled from 970 to 995.**
*"Hear me, Odin! If you will grant me victory against my nephew, I will promise you my life at the end of ten years!"*

Johannes and Olaus Magnus list Erik Segersäll as Erik VII, and some European encyclopedias also number him in this way. However, since we are mostly following Lagerkvist's system, we will refer to him as Erik VI.

Erik Segersäll is an historical person, but his ancestry is not at all clear. He may have been the son of Emund Eriksson, but Snorri has a different point of view. He tells that Olof and his brother Erik the Victorious were the sons of King Björn Eriksson who died in 920, and the grandsons of the Erik Emundsson who died in 870. Still another theory is advanced by both Olaus Magnus and Erik Olaus, who tell us that Erik the Victorious was the son of Erik Väderhatt.

As in the case of Gorm the Old of Denmark, we can be more certain about Erik Segersäll's descendants than about his ancestors. Since he is celebrated in song and story, we can also say a bit more about him than about his immediate ancestors, but we must be careful to concede that Snorri and the other saga writers, although basing their tales on actual events, used a great deal of sanctified imagination.

When Erik took over the throne of Sweden at Uppsala, his nephew Styrbjörn was still very young. Styrbjörn grew up at his uncle's court, but very early showed a violent temperament. When the boy was twelve years old, he refused to come to meals at his uncle's table, and instead seated himself upon his father's grave hoping thus to win the hearts of the people.

By the time Styrbjörn was fourteen, he appeared at the *Thing* (the council of nobles) and demanded his father's kingdom with threats and shoutings. The nobles, unimpressed by the youth's violent demeanor, drove him from the assembly. His uncle, King Erik, outfitted him with sixty ships and exiled him from Sweden.

Styrbjörn proved himself to be so powerful a Viking that he was given the surname of *Starke,* which means "the strong." After establishing a stronghold in Pomerania, he spent some years in pirating, and eventually went to Harald Bluetooth, king of Denmark, hoping to secure his assistance in gaining the Swedish throne. While in Denmark, Styrbjörn married Tyra, the daughter of Harald Bluetooth. Tyra and Harald became the parents of Thorgils Sparkalägger, who in turn was the grandfather of the famous king Sven Estridsson and thus an ancestor of St. Knut and a whole race of Danish monarchs.

Meanwhile, Erik reigned in Uppsala, conquering so many kingdoms that he was given the name of *Segersäll,* which means "the Victorious."

Erik Olaus tells us that Erik the Victorious conquered Livonia, Estonia, and Karelia. He also marched his army into Skåne and occupied that land, which had been a Danish province.

Adam of Bremen relates that "Erik, the most mighty king of the Swedes, collected an army as innumerable as the sands of the sea and invaded Denmark." There he won a great naval battle against Sven Forkbeard. Sven was temporarily forced into exile (he found refuge in Scotland), and Erik ruled both Sweden and Denmark for a brief period. We are told that he remained "intensely hostile to the Christians" and was unmoved by the preaching and even the miraculous signs performed by Poppo, the German bishop who had earlier baptized Harald Bluetooth of Denmark.

Erik the Victorious was married several times. One of his wives is said to have been Sigrid *Storråda* ("great ruler"), the daughter of Skoglar Toste, a famous Viking from Västergötland. According to Snorri, she was the mother of Erik's son Olof.

About 985, according to the ancient tales, Erik fought a great battle against his still-rebellious nephew Styrbjörn on the great plain of Fyrisvall, near Uppsala.

After a whole day of bloody fighting with neither side winning, both men made sacrifices to the gods. Styrbjörn sacrificed to Thor, and we are told that a red-bearded man appeared to him and announced his forthcoming defeat. Erik, on the other hand, sacrificed to Odin, promising his own life at the end of ten years if the great god would grant him victory. A one-eyed man in a blue cloak appeared to him and sealed the bargain.

The following day Erik's forces triumphed. When Styrbjörn perished, his followers either fled or surrendered to Erik. The king ordained a great victory parade. His two-year-old son Olof was carried in arms before the triumphant troops. Because of this, he was called *Olof Skötkonung,* which means "Nurseling King" or "Lap-King." He continued to bear that name, even after he was too old to sit on anyone's lap.

Erik found it hard to get along with his wife Sigrid, due to her imperious temperament. After a while, they went their separate ways. She retired to her estates in Västergötland, where we are told that she ruled in great splendor and refused many suitors who were hungry for both her beauty and her lands. Among others, she is said to have refused Harald Gränske of Norway and King Vifavald of Russia (a petty king of whom we know nothing further). Sigrid has been called "the Haughty" and she seems to have truly earned this surname.

Erik, having disposed of Sigrid, took for a second wife Oda, the daughter of Jarl Håkan of Norway. Later, we are told, Erik married Gunnhild, a daughter of Mieszko of Poland, and a sister to Boleslav I, Poland's first king. Most historians express some uncertainty about

Erik's other wives, but Lagerkvist assures us that there is no doubt about Erik's marriage to Gunnhild.

According to the old tales, Erik fell ill and died precisely ten years after the battle of Fyrisvall. He was buried in a mound at Uppsala and his son Olof Skötkonung succeeded to the throne. His widow Gunnhild was given in marriage to his old rival, Sven Forkbeard; and Sven returned from exile and regained the Danish throne.

**Olof Eriksson Skötkonung — ruled from 995 to 1022.**
*"I am a Christian now. I can no longer preside over the sacrifices at Uppsala."*

Olof has the distinction of becoming Sweden's first Christian king. He is also famous for minting Sweden's first coins.

Like many rulers of his day, Olof kept a *frilla,* or common law wife, in addition to his official queen. (Even after the northern countries accepted Christianity, this pattern continued, as it did among the Franks in the days of Karl the Great.) A *frilla* had a higher status than that of a common servant or concubine, and her sons and daughters inherited all the privileges of royalty.

Olof's wife and *frilla* were both from the Wendish area immediately east of Denmark. This group of Slavs were called Obodrites and they lived near Mecklenburg in the Billung March. (A *mark* or *march* meant a border land.)

Olof's queen was the Wendish princess Estrid. She was born about 985 in Mecklenburg, married Olof around the year 1000, and outlived her husband, passing away about 1035. Their son was Anund Jakob, later king of Sweden; and their daughter was Ingegerd, who married Yaroslav the Wise of Russia.

Olof's *frilla,* Edla of Wendland, gave him three children: Emund, Astrid, and Holmfrid. Queen Estrid hated her stepchildren, so the king sent them away to be raised in safety. Emund was brought up in Wendland with his mother's relatives, in a totally pagan atmosphere. Princess Astrid was raised in Västergötland on the estate of a man named Egil, where she learned "pleasant manners and modest ways."

Meanwhile, Olof Skötkonung found himself drawn into a conflict against Olof Tryggvesson, King of Norway.

As we saw in Chapter 2, Snorri tells us that Olof Skötkonung's mother Sigrid had married Sven Forkbeard of Denmark, and had inspired an alliance between her new husband (Sven) and her son

(Olof Skötkonung). Jarl Erik of Norway joined these kings in fighting against Olof Tryggvesson, and the three overcame him in a great naval battle in the year 1000.

According to their previous agreement, the victors divided Norway into three parts. Olof Skötkonung received part of Trondheim and the region now called Bohüslan, which had formerly belonged to Norway. These lands Olof gave to his son-in-law Jarl Sven (a brother of his ally Jarl Erik) as a dowery for his daughter Holmfrid. Jarl Sven then became regent over the section of Norway that was handed over to the Swedish throne. Sweden thus became at this time the mightiest kingdom of the North.

After the death of the great missionary Ansgar, Christianity in Sweden had fallen into neglect for nearly a century and a half. But by the year 1000, more missionaries, especially from England, were arriving in the country.

About eight years after overcoming Olof Tryggvesson, Olof Skötkonung became a Christian and was baptized at Husaby in northern Västergötland by an Anglo-Saxon missionary named Sigfrid. Apparently Olof's queen had become a Christian previously.

Sigfrid spread Christianity through Södermanland and Småland, and founded the first Swedish bishopric at Skara. Olof Skötkonung, the first Christian king of Sweden, and his son Anund Jakob supported the Church, but their zeal was restrained by an order from a *Thing* that while they might build a church, they were not allowed to force their new religion on anyone.

After his conversion, Olof Skötkonung refused to preside over the yearly sacrifices in the heathen temple of Uppsala. This made him many enemies. He also angered his people by losing many of the lands around the Gulf of Finland which his father Erik the Victorious had gained.

In 1015 Olof the Stout (later known as St. Olof) became king of Norway. New troubles brewed between Sweden and Norway, for Olof the Stout was not happy to have Olof Skötkonung claiming part of his kingdom.

At a great *Thing* in Uppsala, an old man arose and said, "Olof Skötkonung is not like the kings of old. My grandfather could remember how Erik Emundsson conquered Finland, Estonia, and many other countries to the east. I myself accompanied Erik Segersäll on many successful Viking expeditions. But our present king is so weak that he has lost all the lands his forefathers gained. Yet he chooses to anger the Norwegians by retaining Norway under his sway. Therefore, we peasants offer you a choice, oh king: either you make peace with King Olof the Stout of Norway by giving him your daughter Ingegerd, or you meet your death at our hands."

Olof Skötkonung meekly agreed to bow to the will of the people. But when the time for the marriage came, the Swedish Olof—much like the Biblical Laban who switched Leah and Rachel—craftily substituted his illegitimate daughter Astrid for Ingegerd. Olof the Stout, seeing Astrid's beauty, agreed to the change of plans.

Ingegerd was then married to Yaroslav the Wise of Kiev. As we have seen, the daughters of Ingegerd and Yaroslav married into the royal families of Norway, France, and Hungary, and their descendants married into the later lines of Swedish kings.

It is interesting to note all the Slavic connections in Olof's life. His stepmother Gunnhild was Polish, his wives were Slavic, and he married one of his daughters to a Russian of Scandinavian descent. The Swedes had been connected through commerce with Kiev and Byzantium for centuries; yet ironically, when they converted to Christianity, it was to the Western rather than the Eastern or Byzantine branch of the Church.

Olof Skötkonung died of natural causes in early 1022. According to tradition he is buried at the Husaby church in Västergötland.

**Anund Jakob Olofsson—ruled from 1022 to 1050.**

*"Since you don't like my name Jakob, call me Anund instead,"* said the king to pacify his subjects.

At birth, Anund was called Jakob, since he was born on St. Jacob's day. This makes him the first king of Sweden to bear a Hebrew name.

When Olof Skötkonung tricked Olof the Stout into marrying Astrid instead of Ingegerd, the Swedish people grew angry with their king. A great rebellion broke out, which was quelled only when the king agreed to make his son Jakob co-regent. His pagan subjects disliked Jakob's Biblical name, so he agreed to let them call him Anund, which no doubt sounded much more patriotic to their Scandinavian ears.

Anund Jakob ruled jointly with his father until the latter's death in 1022. He made an anti-Danish alliance with his brother-in-law Olof the Stout, who was King of Norway from 1015 to 1030. Together with Olof, Anund plundered the Danish provinces of Skåne and Sjaelland in 1026, but Canute the Great of England and Denmark surprised them with a large fleet. The Swedes and Norwegians, frightened at the sight of Canute's ships, retreated to the mouth of the Helga, or Holy River, on the east coast of Skåne. There a furious battle took place.

Some sources say that Canute was defeated; others affirm that he was victorious. Apparently neither side gained a definite victory; and after the battle, the warriors concluded a peace treaty.

Canute went back to Denmark to do away with his brother-in-law, Jarl Ulf, who had been guilty of double dealing in the battle. Olof of Norway abandoned his ships and took the overland route back to Norway. Anund Jakob returned home to Sweden.

Olof the Stout, who was losing ground to Canute, later fled to Russia, where he remained until early 1030 with his wife's sister Ingegerd. He then returned home, stopping in Sweden where his wife's brother Anund supplied him with troops. However, Olof the Stout was killed on a hot summer's day in 1030 when he met a superior army at Stiklestad.

Considering the anti-Danish feeling of the eleventh century Swedes, it is interesting to note Anund Jakob's relationship to Denmark's king Sven Estridsson. Sven served Anund for twelve years in his youth and we are told that Anund gave his only daughter Jutta or Gyda (a child of his first marriage) to Sven. Although it cannot be proven, it is possible that Anund's daughter Jutta may have been the mother of Sven Estridsson's son, St. Knut of Denmark.

Adam of Bremen called Anund "the most Christian king of the Swedes" and stated that he was young in years but old in wisdom and cunning. He was called *Anund Kolbrännea* because he had the houses of evildoers burned. Like his royal father, he minted coins at Sigtuna, and these are said to have "surpassed all that were struck during the next two centuries."

King Anund lived for twenty years after the death of Olof the Stout, his ally and brother-in-law. Anund Jakob died of natural causes in 1050, when he was about forty-three years old, and was buried in Linsköping.

Anund's second wife, Gunnhild, survived him, but he left no sons to succeed him. However, he may have left descendants through his daughter Jutta. Included among these may be St. Knut of Denmark and many members of the Folkung family in Sweden.

It is interesting to note that Anund's widow Gunnhild later married Sven Estridsson of Denmark. That much-married Danish monarch thus was wed to both Anund's daughter and Anund's wife.

### Emund III Olofsson "the Old"—ruled from 1050 to 1060.

After Anund Jacob died, his half-brother Emund ruled the country alone. (He had already shared the government as co-regent during Anund's life, and had participated with Anund in the raid on Skåne, when they were repelled by Canute the Great and his brother-in-law Jarl Ulf.)

The fifteenth and sixteenth-century Swedish historians refer to Emund as *Emund Slemme,* or the Sly. More often he is called *Emund den Gamle* (the Old), presumably because he was older than Anund. However, because of being illegitimate, he was not the first to succeed to the throne.

Adam of Bremen calls him Emund the Bad, and writes that "he was born of a concubine by Olof and, although he had been baptized, took little heed of our religion."

By his first marriage, Emund had a son named Anund. Unfortunately, the youth died before 1050, probably in a battle against the Finns.

Another, more fanciful account of Anund Emundsson's death is cited by Adam of Bremen. He states that Emund sent his son Anund to a Baltic region inhabited by Amazons who despised the male sex. By poisoning the springs, the women destroyed Anund and his army.

Emund also had a daughter whose name has been lost to history.

Later, Emund was married to Astrid Nialsdotter, the widow of Jarl Ragnvald Ulfsson of Västergötland. By this union he acquired a stepson whose name was Stenkil. The youth apparently fit into the royal family so well that he was given the hand of Emund's daughter.

Emund quarreled with Adalbert, that politically powerful archbishop of Bremen, in an effort to secure the independence of the Swedish church. His efforts came to nothing, and a whole century elapsed before Sweden gained ecclesiastical independence.

Emund also had many territorial disputes with Denmark, but these were finally settled through mediation and rectification of boundaries.

Towards the end of his reign, Emund of Sweden and Sven Estridsson of Denmark agreed on the frontiers between their two realms. Skåne and Halland (in what is today southern Sweden) remained under Danish rule, and stones were set up to mark the northern and eastern borders of these areas.

Emund died in 1060. As both Anund Jakob and Emund died without surviving sons, the Svear gathered to choose a new king to rule over them.

It is interesting to note the method by which the Uppsala *Thing* elected a monarch. The new king was required to be from a royal family. When he was chosen, the nobles sat him down on a special stone in Mora Meadow near Uppsala, and charged him to govern the kingdom well, upholding the law and maintaining the peace. This ceremony was the equivalent of a coronation.

After this ceremony, the king went on a tour of his domains. This journey was called the *eriksgata*. He was guarded all the way by selected hostages until he returned to Uppsala. In this way, the new king received the allegiance of all the people.

Much later, when Christianity and its continental trappings were more generally accepted, an additional ceremony was added to the ancient Svear traditions. Upon the king's return to Uppsala, the archbishop would crown him in the cathedral and pronounce an appropriate blessing.

On this occasion, Stenkil was elected to take Emund's place. Perhaps he was chosen because he was Emund's stepson as well as his son-in-law, or perhaps because of his piety and his fairness. His line begins a new dynasty, which will be covered in the next chapter.

CHART 25 - The Family of Erik Segersäll

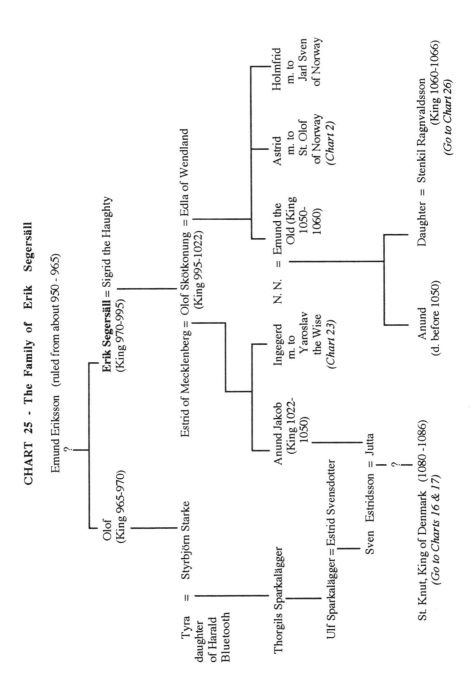

## *Chapter 9*

### The Stenkil Dynasty of Sweden
### —from 1060 to 1130

Although it is impossible to trace the ancestry of all the kings who ruled Sweden before 1000 A. D., most are assumed to be descended from Ivar the Wide-Reacher. The direct male line of these Ivarska rulers came to an end with the deaths of Anund Jakob and Emund the Old, although through Emund's daughter (Stenkil's wife) the family continued providing many future kings for Sweden.

After Emund's death, a struggle for the throne rocked the country. For a whole century, the people of Sweden endured a civil war in which rival factions and dynasties fought each other. The flame of Christianity burned low, kept alive only by small groups of believers and missionary monks who came up from the Continent to build churches in the face of incredible odds and stiff persecution.

Between 1060 and 1260, at least fourteen kings or pretenders to the throne died violent deaths. We shall attempt to trace the story of the competing dynasties, and we begin with Stenkil.

### Stenkil Ragnvaldsson—ruled from about 1060 to 1066.

*"I'm a Christian, but I won't force my subjects to accept my religion against their will."*

Stenkil was of noble ancestry. His father was the Jarl Ragnvald Ulfsson, and (according to some sources) his great-grandfather was Skoglar Toste, the father of the ill-famed Sigrid the Haughty.

Stenkil's mother, Astrid Nialsdotter, was said to be of Yngling descent. After the death of Jarl Ragnvald, she married Emund the Old, thus making Stenkil the king's stepson.

Stenkil is described as a renowned archer and as a "remarkably tall and very strong man ... bold and undaunted in fight, but also of a mild, prudent, and peaceful character." He is said to have been fair in his judgments, although at times he favored the people of Västergötland, his own land. He has also been called "a tolerant and fair-minded ruler" who did not believe in extending Christianity by force.

Adalbert, the archbishop of Bremen who had quarreled with Emund the Old, now had a strong ally in Stenkil. Adalbert sent missionaries to Sweden, where they destroyed idols and made many converts in Västergötland, but were unable to destroy the old temple at Uppsala.

Stenkil and his wife—King Emund's daughter—had at least three sons: Erik, Inge and Halsten. They may also have had a daughter who married the infamous Blot-Sven, since Inge is known as Blot-Sven's brother-in-law.

Stenkil's reign was brief; he died of natural causes in 1066, the year which is famous for William the Conqueror's invasion of England. At his death, Stenkil was called "the most Christian King."

### Erik VII and Erik VIII—ruled from about 1066 to 1067.

Upon the death of Stenkil, a civil war broke out in Sweden. It was probably caused by the difference in religion between Västergötland (which was Christian) and Uppsala (which was pagan). Two obscure rulers named Erik, pretenders to the throne, were killed in the conflict. (In Lagerkvist's list of kings, these two Eriks are called Erik VII and Erik VIII respectively.) It is said that both Eriks died together in 1067. Eventually Stenkil's young sons Erik, Halsten and Inge were acclaimed as joint kings.

### Inge I "the Elder" Stenkilsson—ruled from about 1067 to 1080.

*"These pagan people are trying to stone me! I'd better run for my life!"*

During the reign of Inge the Elder a prince called Håkan the Red seems to have ruled over at least part of Västergötland. He is mentioned by Sweden's earliest historians, and he also appears in other lists of Västergötland kings.

Although the country was divided, there was peace at this time. Olaus Magnus tells us that Håkan the Red's reign was kindly and that he never shed blood illegally. Erik Olaus tells us that Håkan ruled for thirteen years, died a peaceful death, and was duly buried.

Inge Stenkilsson governed for a time as joint ruler with his brothers Erik and Halsten Stenkilsson. These were zealous Christians. Erik died shortly after assuming the throne; Halsten died about 1070; and after that Inge (called the Elder) ruled alone.

Halsten, however, had not died without heirs. He left two sons: Filip and Inge the Younger.

Inge the Elder's queen (possibly his second wife) was the saintly Elin (Helena) of Skövde. They had a son Ragnvald, whose daughter Ingegerd later married Henrik the Hurtful, prince of Denmark. After Henrik died, Ingegerd married Harald Gille of Norway. King Inge and Elin also had three daughters: Katarina, Kristina and Margaret.

King Inge was befriended by foreigners who were eager to help Christianize the Swedes. More missionaries from the Continent began arriving in Sweden, and in 1080 Inge the Elder received a personal letter from the powerful Pope Gregory VII.

At that time Inge the Elder issued an ultimatum to the Svear of Uppland that they must convert. The Svear, in turn, demanded that Inge make pagan sacrifices at the Uppsala temple, or else relinquish the throne. As Inge persisted in his demand, the people threw stones at him and drove him away.

Adam of Breman, writing in the 1070's, describes the Uppsala temple thus:

*The shrine is adorned all over with gold and here the people worship the images of three gods. Thor, the mightiest, has his throne in the center of the hall, with Odin and Frey on either side ... Frey is depicted with an enormous phallus. But Odin is shown in armour ... while Thor with his sceptre ... seems to resemble Jupiter.*

King Inge, who refused to worship these heathen gods, was forced to flee to the safety of Västergötland where Christianity was accepted.

### Blot-Sven—ruled from about 1080 to 1083.

*"Since Inge won't make the sacrifices, I'll make them! And I'll be your new king!"*

We know that Blot-Sven was related to Inge by marriage, although the exact relationship is uncertain. Louda and McLagan's *Lines of Succession* show Inge's first wife as Maer, a sister of Blot-Sven. Other genealogical charts show Blot-Sven as married to Inge's sister (Stenkil's daughter).

When Inge was forced to flee from Uppsala, his brother-in-law Sven presented himself, offering to make the pagan sacrifices if the people would accept him as their king. Following the ancient rites, Sven immediately killed a horse and cut it up, distributing the pieces to the people so that they could feast on the sacrificial meat. The animal's blood was smeared on the heathen images as an offering to Thor, Odin and Frey. Because of this, the new king came to be known as *Blot-Sven,* meaning "Sacrifice Sven" or "Bloody Sven."

Sven ordered the death of an Anglo-Saxon missionary named Eskil, who arrived at a subsequent sacrifice and attempted to persuade the people to worship the only true God. Eskil later was honored as a martyr and a saint.

Sven went all out in trying to eradicate Christianity and restore the ancient worship. Horses, dogs, and roosters were offered to the idols at Uppsala, and the sacrifices were accompanied by dreadful wailings of the priests.

We are not told how Blot-Sven's wife, who was probably the daughter of the pious Stenkil, felt about her husband's zeal for the pagan religion. We do know, however, that they had a son named Kol Erik and a daughter named Cecilia. Kol Erik became the father of a later king—Sverker I—and Cecilia married Jedvard Bonde and became the mother of St. Erik. Although the Sverker and Erik families were destined to fight over the throne for many generations to come, they had common roots: both were descended from Blot-Sven. And through Blot-Sven's wife, both families may have descended from the Ivarska dynasty.

The Swedes have not forgotten Blot-Sven. In 1824, Ling wrote a tragedy based on the life of this ruler.

### Inge I "the Elder"—ruled again from about 1083 to 1110.

After living in exile for three years, King Inge collected a small army and stealthily took his warriors north until they reached Blot-Sven's residence. Early in the morning, while Blot-Sven and his men were still sleeping, Inge set fire to the place. Blot-Sven managed to escape the burning building, but Inge's men soon captured him and took his life. In this way, Inge did away with his brother-in-law and chief rival.

Inge regained his throne, and Christianity made great progress under his leadership. He destroyed the heathen Uppsala temple and had a church built on its site, using some of the walls and masonry that remained from the old temple. Later this church was further remodeled by St. Erik.

Nevertheless, heathen beliefs were still strongly entrenched in the masses. An anonymous priest from England wrote:

*The Svear and the Götar seem certainly, as long as everything goes well for them, in name to hold the Christian faith in honor. But when the storms of misfortune come over them, if the earth denies them her crops or heaven her rain, storms rage or fire destroys, then they condemn the worship which in name they seem to honor.*

Blot-Sven's son Kol Erik withdrew to the southeast. There he continued to preside at the heathen sacrifices of Östergötland and Småland. We will hear more about him and his descendants later.

We have already mentioned the children of Inge the Elder: Ragnvald, Katarina, Kristina and Margaret.

Ragnvald preceded his father in death. Katarina married the Danish prince Björn Haraldsson and became the mother-in-law of St. Erik. Kristina became the queen of Mstislav I, Grand Prince of Kiev in Russia. Margaret was given as a bride to King Magnus Barelegs of Norway, that ruler who enjoyed wearing short Scottish kilts.

Margaret's marriage came about in the following way: After Inge suffered some attacks from Magnus, the two kings met at a town called Kongahälle to settle their difficulties and arrange a peace treaty. With them was King Erik Ejegod of Denmark. As the three men walked out toward the plain to effect a reconciliation, the townspeople remarked on how handsome and strong they all seemed.

As a result of this "summit meeting," the three kings agreed to restore the boundaries of their countries to the former borders. Inge also promised his daughter Margaret to Magnus Barelegs, as a confirmation of the peace treaty. She therefore came to be known as *Margaret Fridkulla*, or "Peace Woman."

Magnus and Margaret apparently had no children. Magnus Barelegs died in 1103, and soon afterward Margaret was given in marriage to King Niels of Denmark. This second marriage provided Inge with a Danish grandson named Magnus Nielsson, of whom we shall hear further.

For the remainder of his life, Inge the Elder enjoyed a peaceful reign. He died of natural causes and was buried in the Varnhem churchyard. Since he left no surviving sons, he was succeeded by his nephews Filip and Inge II the Younger.

**Inge II "the Younger" Halstensson—about 1110 to 1125.**
*"It's not really my business to protect Småland from the Norwegians. That land belongs to my cousin Kol Erik. Let him protect his heathen subjects while I read my prayers."*

Inge II (called "the Younger" to distinguish him from his uncle) ruled jointly with his brother Filip Halstensson for a short time.

Filip was married to Ingegerd, a daughter of Harald Hårdråde of Norway and the widow of Olof Hunger of Denmark.

Filip died about 1118, apparently without issue. From then on, Inge reigned alone. We read the following about Inge: "He was much devoted to the Christian faith, and very mild and pious; he fasted and read prayers and masses at fixed seasons, but did not sufficiently protect his kingdom against foreign attacks."

It is said that king Eystein of Norway, while his brother Sigurd Jerusalem-farer was on a crusade, stole much of Sweden away from Inge. After Eystein died, Sigurd returned to claim Norway.

Sigurd also made Viking raids on Småland. Of course, he considered these attacks to be as much a part of his religious obligations as his pilgrimage to Jerusalem had been. He was determined to wipe out the last vestiges of pagan worship from Småland where people were still worshiping Odin and Thor in their dark forests.

Sigurd demanded that the people give him fifteen hundred head of cattle and that they accept the Christian religion by force. According to the chronicle, he ravaged the country with fire and sword, was successful in converting the Smålanders, and returned to Norway with plenty of booty. As we have already noted, the date of his crusade can be set accurately at 1122, since it is said to have occurred a year before an eclipse which astronomers have dated at 1123.

Since King Inge the Younger did nothing to protect or avenge his beleaguered subjects, he became known as a weak and worthless ruler.

Perhaps Inge felt that Småland and Östergötland were not really under his jurisdiction, since Kol Erik, the son of Blot-Sven, had taken over that land as a sort of king-priest who continued to make the heathen sacrifices. The people called him *Erik Årsäll,* or "Erik Year-Blest," because they had good crops during his reign. Snorri refers to him by this name, tells us that he came after Blot-Sven, and mentions that he "had renounced Christianity and kept up sacrifices."

However, it needs to be said that before his death even Kol Erik Årsäll came to embrace Christianity (at least nominally). Thus paganism in Småland and Östergötland finally died out. Whether or not we agree with his methods, Sigurd Jerusalem-farer gets some credit for this last phase of Sweden's Christianization.

Inge the Younger was married twice. His first wife was Ragnhild. Eric Olaus tells us that Ragnhild was a saint and that, upon her death, her relics were carefully guarded.

Inge the Younger's second wife was Ulfhild Håkansdotter, the daughter of a Norwegian Jarl named Håkan Finnsson. Yet, like his brother Filip, Inge the Younger died without issue. He was buried in Vreta Kloster, and it was rumored that he was poisoned by enemies.

With Inge's death, the direct male line of Stenkil came to an end. Nevertheless, since Stenkil's daughter may have married Blot-Sven, the descendants of the pious King Stenkil have quite possibly lived on.

After Inge the Younger's death, his widow Ulfhild was married twice more: to Niels of Denmark and also to Sverker I of Sweden.

Once again there was confusion about who should succeed to the throne of Sweden. The Götar and the Svear, Sweden's two main tribes, were often at odds. Since the kings of the Stenkil dynasty had originated in Västergötland, the Götar felt they had a right to choose the next ruler. They chose Magnus Nielsson, the son of Margaret Fridkulla and her second husband Niels of Denmark.

The Svear were enraged at this choice, and elected a noble named Ragnvald Knaphövde to rule over them.

## Ragnvald Knaphövde—ruled briefly about 1125.

Ragnvald *Knaphövde* (whose surname means "lacking in the head" or "short on intellect") went through all the proper ceremonies: He was seated on the stone near Uppsala, he heard the wise advice given to all kings, and he commenced the *Eriksgata,* the required tour of the realm. Before he had finished his tour, however, Ragnvald was slain near Falköping, at Karleby's *Thing.*

A gravestone bearing his name stands in Vreta, but historians are not convinced that his remains are actually buried in that location.

History has not been kind to the murdered Ragnvald Knaphövde. Olaus Magnus tells us that he plunged Sweden into "pernicious discord." Eric Olaus adds that Ragnvald was a giant of a man, married to a Polish princess, but that like a second Rehoboam he imprudently forsook the wise council of his elders. Some Swedish historians have gone so far as to call him a *dumskalle,* or dumb-head.

**Magnus I Nielsson—ruled from about 1125 to 1130.**
*"The Swedes have rejected me as their king! I must go to war to get Skåne back from them!"*

Magnus Nielsson was the son King Niels of Denmark and Margaret Fridkulla (a daughter of Inge the Elder). Because he was Inge's grandson, it seemed logical to the Götar to elect him as ruler over Sweden.

Magnus was married about 1127 to Rikissa, the daughter of Boleslav III of Poland and his wife Salome of Berg-Schelklingen. Magnus' queen Rikissa could claim royal ancestors from all over Europe. She was named for her great-great-grandmother Rikissa, a German princess who married Mieszko II of Poland. This first Rikissa, a niece of Otto III of Germany, could count among her ancestors not only the Saxon king Henry the Fowler, but also a Byzantine grandmother named Theophano and the early kings of Burgundy. Because Rudolf I of Burgundy had married Guille (said by the genealogist Chaume to be probably a daughter of the Carolingian king Louis II the Stammerer), the first Rikissa was in all likelihood also directly descended from Karl the Great himself.

Magnus and his queen, the later Rikissa, had a son, who eventually became Knut V, King of Denmark. Magnus was apparently more interested in Danish politics and in his continental connections than in doing a good job of governing Sweden. From Denmark, rumors came to the Götar that Magnus Nielsson had committed the dastardly act of murdering his cousin, Prince Knut Lavard. The Götar then switched their allegiance to a man named Sverker, a son of Kol Erik Årsäll and a grandson of the idol-worshiping Blot-Sven. Our next chapter will deal with him and his new dynasty.

Meanwhile, Magnus sought to retain control of Skåne, but he did not live long after the Swedes rejected him as their ruler. He was slain in the bloody battle of Fotevik in Skåne in 1134.

Some time after that date, his widow Rikissa of Poland married Volodar of Minsk. By this second marriage, she had a daughter named Sofia who later became the queen of Valdemar I of Denmark.

Rikissa's third marriage, as we shall see in our next chapter, was to Magnus Nielsson's successor, Sverker. This marriage also produced a child, and thus Rikissa, the daughter of Boleslav III, once again passed on her Polish/Bohemian/Byzantine/Saxon/Burgundian/Carolingian heritage to future rulers of Scandinavia.

**CHART 26 - The Family of King Stenkil of Sweden**

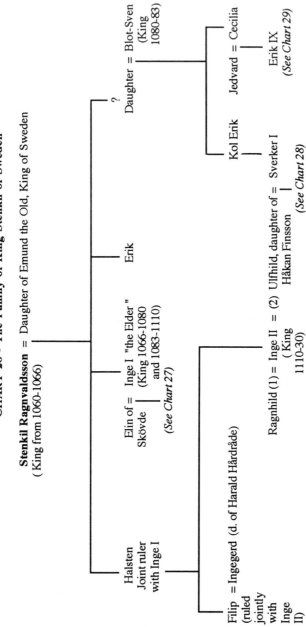

**CHART 27- The Family of King Inge Stenkilsson of Sweden**

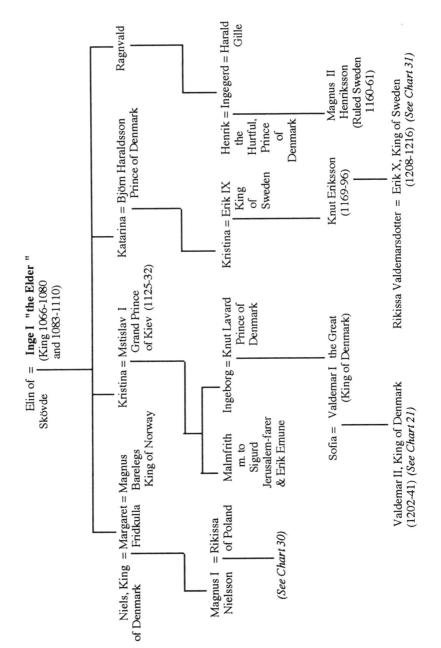

## Chapter 10

### The Sverkerska and Erikska Rival Dynasties—
### 1130 to 1250

**Sverker I "the Elder"—ruled from 1130 to 1156.**

*"Help! I'm being attacked by one of my own servants!"* Thus Sverker met his end on Christmas Eve on his way to church—a violent death, like that of Inge I and Blot-Sven before him.

Sverker, as we have seen, came to the Swedish throne during a time of great national chaos. His predecessor Ragnvald—the choice of the rival Svear tribe—had just been assassinated while on his official initiation tour. And Sverker was, in a sense, merely the second choice of the Götar, who had originally backed Magnus Nielsson.

Sverker realized that he needed to strengthen his royal position. He did this by marrying Ulfhild Håkansdotter, the widow of Inge the Younger, the last Stenkil king. (She was also the widow of Niels of Denmark.) Sverker and his queen lived in a medieval manor near Lake Vättern, and this region then took on the importance that had formerly belonged to the Lake Mälaren region where Björn had been king when Ansgar evangelized Sweden.

By his marriage to Ulfhild, Sverker had three sons: Johan, Karl and Kol. He also had a daughter Ingegerd who became prioress of the Vreta convent, as well as another daughter who was married to Knut V Magnusson of Denmark (the son of Sverker's predecessor Magnus Nielsson).

Ulfhild died in 1148 and Sverker married a second time. His new queen was Rikissa, a daughter of Boleslav III of Poland, and thus a descendant of Kasimir of Poland and Vladimir I of Russia. She was the widow of Sverker's predecessor Magnus Nielsson and also the widow of Volodar of Minsk. Her marriages and children are shown on Chart 30.

Sometimes, when widowed people remarry, a child of the bride will marry the child of the groom. This happened when Sverker's daughter married Rikissa's son Knut. Sverker and Rikissa had a son of their own named Burislev. (He was given the Scandinavian form of the Polish *Boleslav* — his maternal grandfather's name.)

It is noteworthy that Burislev's daughter, named Cecilia, later married Knut Eriksson, the son of Sverker's successor. Thus the Sverker and Erik families — foes like the Montagues and Capulets — came together in the union of their children.

Sverker suffered a great deal from Danish invasions. The Danes, who had traditionally ruled the southern part of what today is Sweden, were constantly trying to extend their borders and gain new vassals. Towards the end of his life, Sverker was unable to withstand their raids.

Sverker was also troubled by all family feuding that beset most medieval monarchs. It is said that his own son Johan led a rebellion against him.

Prince Johan, in true Viking fashion, had kidnapped both the wife and the daughter of a Danish governor in what is today southern Sweden. He carried them off to his castle, where he shamefully abused them. Because of this, he was murdered by his own subjects in 1150.

Sverker strengthened his throne by establishing good relations with the Church, which had now become a strong power. As king, he supported the reforms of Pope Gregory VII, ordered churches to be built, and granted land for monasteries to the Cistercian order. He even sent ambassadors to the pope, asking him to appoint an archbishop for Sweden, since the Swedish Christians were unhappy about being ruled by a far-away archbishop in Denmark.

In 1153 the pope gladly sent a cardinal legate, Nicholas Breakspeare of England, to settle the matter. (Later Nicholas, as Adrian IV, became the only English pope in history.)

Unfortunately, the warring Svear and Götar could not agree upon the city to be chosen for the archbishop's see. The Svear insisted it should be at Uppsala, and the Götar insisted upon Linköping. In order to avoid further civil war and still placate the unhappy Swedes, Nicholas assigned Sweden to the Norwegian archbishopric of Nidaros (Trondheim).

From this time on, the Church assumed more and more power in Sweden, and the people's voice was heard less and less. The *Things* (which had often been associated with the annual sacrifices at Uppsala) were abolished, and the bishops and priests settled matters that had formerly been taken care of by the assembly of nobles.

In 1156, before Sverker had really recovered from the murder of his son Johan, he himself was murdered. One of his attendants killed him while he was en route to midnight mass on Christmas Eve. Some historians surmise that Sverker's courtiers were unhappy with him because he would not deal with the Danes who were assaulting Sweden's coastline. It was because of this, they say, that the king was assassinated. Other writers conjecture that the crime was instigated by the Danish Prince Magnus Henriksson, a great-grandson of King Inge the Elder, who felt he was the rightful heir to the Swedish throne.

Sverker was buried in a convent at Alvastra, which had been founded by his first wife Ulfhild on property that she had donated to the church.

### Erik IX Jedvarsson (St. Erik)—ruled from 1156 to 1160.

*"I know there's an enemy outside. But let me hear the rest of the mass before I deal with him."* These were probably Erik's last words, and he has gone down in history as a saint. Let us see what led up to his death.

After Sverker's assassination, the country fell into confusion as the Svear and the Götar argued over who should succeed to the throne.

The Götar wanted to elect Karl, Sverker's son, while the Svear of Uppsala favored a noble named Erik. Erik's father, Jedvard Thordsson Bonde, was descended from the Jarl Erik Göthe, a vassal of the king of Sweden in Västergötland who was known as "the people's squire" and surnamed Göthe because he was "a prince of the Goths." Erik Göthe had married Cecilia, a daughter of St. Knut of Denmark. Through Cecilia, Erik IX was descended not only from Danish royalty but also from Alfred the Great of England and Karl the Great, king of the Franks, who were ancestors of St. Knut's wife, Adela of Flanders.

Although Erik IX was descended from Danish royalty on his father's side, his mother was Cecilia, Blot-Sven's daughter.

In the conflict which erupted after Sverker's death, the Svear won out, and Erik Jedvardsson Bonde—the descendant of both St. Knut of Denmark and Blot-Sven of Sweden—was chosen as Sweden's next king. Although at first the Götar refused to acknowledge his authority, they finally accepted him.

Erik tried to strengthen Christianity by building churches and appointing preachers. He also tried to improve the status of women by giving married women a legal right to the family property, even after a husband's death.

Under Erik, Uppsala became a bastion of Christianity. He tried to extend the faith by sponsoring a crusade against the Finns, some of whom were thought to still be pagans. This probably occurred about 1157.

In his crusade, Erik was accompanied by a singularly well prepared Englishman named Henrik, who had become bishop of Uppsala. Erik and his troops landed on the coast of southwestern Finland and went to war. Their conquest of the inhabitants was speedy, although far from permanent.

The king and his soldiers then returned home, leaving the scholarly and zealous bishop to establish and organize Finnish churches. Henrik was certainly not the first missionary to proclaim the gospel in Finland, but he is the most famous. According to some stories, the people were angry because of the financial burden he imposed on them for new church buildings. The following January, Henrik was slain with an axe by a disgruntled Finn named Lalli.

One is reminded of St. Knut, who had been murdered in Denmark nearly a century earlier for much the same reason. Like Knut of Denmark, Bishop Henrik was later canonized and the Finns made him their patron saint.

King Erik, like his bishop, was also on the way to sainthood. He was noted for his personal piety and his efforts to mortify the flesh. It is said that he fasted frequently, bathed in ice-cold water, and wore a hair shirt next to his skin. These stories, of course, may be exaggerations told by later generations who were anxious to claim him as a saint.

Erik IX was married to Kristina, a daughter of the Danish prince Björn Haraldsson. On her father's side, she was a granddaughter of Prince Harald Keisias of Denmark. On her mother's side, she was a granddaughter of Inge the Elder.

Erik IX and Kristina had two sons: Knut and Filip. (Knut later became king; Filip was destined to be the grandfather of a king—Knut the Long.) Erik IX also had two daughters. One, named Margaret, later married King Sverre of Norway. Another, named Katarina, married Nils Blaka.

As we have noted, the good King Erik met an untimely death. He was murdered at Uppsala on May 18, 1160, at the hands of the Danish prince Magnus Henriksson, who claimed the Swedish throne by virtue of his descent from Inge the Elder.

Magnus' mother Ingegerd was a first cousin to St. Erik's wife Kristina; both were grandchildren of Inge the Elder. Once again, a medieval prince was murdering his own relative.

It is said that Erik was in church on May 18, 1160, when the rival prince and his forces reached Uppsala. When he heard of the arrival of his wife's cousin, Erik replied, "Let me hear the rest of the mass." As soon as mass was over, he left the church, only to be captured and killed by the waiting Magnus.

Erik soon became known as a saint; his holy deeds were embellished in the telling by descendants who were struggling to win the throne, and by the archbishops of Uppsala, who strengthened their position by having the grave of a saint in their cathedral. Although he was never officially canonized, he was venerated for centuries as the patron saint of Sweden. (Neither St. Olof of Norway nor St. Erik of Sweden were acclaimed as saints by Rome in the way in which St. Knut of Denmark was recognized.)

With the death of St. Erik, his descendants (with Svear tribal connections) began a century of struggle with the family of Sverker (supported by the Götar). There was always uncertainty as to which family would win the throne. The Sverkers were apparently more loyal to Rome, and the descendants of Erik were more nationalistic; therefore, the Church often supported the Sverkers over Erik's family.

## Magnus II Henriksson—ruled from 1160 to 1161.

Magnus Henriksson, the murderer of St. Erik, ruled Sweden briefly. He was the son of Prince Henrik the Hurtful of Denmark, but his mother was Ingegerd, a granddaughter of Inge the Elder. Magnus made his brother Ragnvald his jarl (a title which by this time corresponded roughly to prime minister).

Magnus was connected to Sweden (through his mother), to Denmark (through his father), and also to Norway (through his wife Birgitta, a daughter of King Harald Gille of Norway).

Having gained the throne by the sword, Magnus was destined to be felled by the sword. Karl, son of the deceased Sverker, was proclaimed king of the Goths in Östergötland about 1158. Raising an army from Östergötland, he overcame and killed Magnus near Uppsala. The people, overjoyed to be rid of the man who had assassinated their saint, gladly accepted Karl as king over all of Sweden in 1161.

## Karl VII Sverkersson—ruled from 1161 to 1167.

*"Even the Pope acknowledges me as king of all Sweden's tribes!"*
Although he is called Karl VII, the monarch who could thus boast was

actually the first historically verifiable Swedish king to be named Karl.

The origin of the name *Karl* is interesting. (Related to our English *churl*, the original name was not altogether complimentary!)

The first *Karl* in Swedish mythology was said to be one of three brothers born to a divine father and a mortal mother. Karl became the ancestor of all free-born men. A short and swarthy brother became the ancestor of all *Trälls,* or bondsmen, and a third (and luckier) brother became the ancestor of all *Jarls,* or nobles. In this story we see three well-defined castes: the lowborn bondsman, the free *Karl,* and the still more privileged *Jarl.* The term *Karl* was thus applied to the middle class.

Snorri, in recording the ancient Ynglinga and Ivarska dynasties, does not mention any Karl, and certainly there is no previous Karl among the historical Swedish kings of the eleventh and twelfth centuries. We know that Sverker's son was not called the seventh in his own lifetime. It was not until the time of Johannes Magnus, who recorded six previous mythical Karls in his catalog of Swedish kings, that Karl Sverkersson began to be called the seventh. And the name stuck! (The previous Karls in Johannes Magnus' list are listed as kings number 10, 46, 93, 94 and 104.)

Karl VII was the first Swedish king to be called *Svea och Göta Konung,* or King of the Svear and the Götar. Even the pope in far-away Rome, in his correspondence, addressed Karl as *Rex Sveorum et Gothorum,* acknowledging him as ruler of both the rival tribes.

Karl engaged in various wars, winning some battles but losing one in 1164 against Novgorod.

In 1164 Sweden finally obtained an archbishopric of her own at Uppsala. The first archbishop was named Stephen, and from the time of Erik X forward, all the Swedish kings were anointed with holy oil and crowned by the archbishop in the Uppsala Cathedral.

Karl VII was married to Kristina Stigsdotter, a granddaughter of the murdered Danish Prince Knut Lavard. Their son was named Sverker after his paternal grandfather.

Karl was not destined to rule for long. Knut, the son of St. Erik, had escaped to Norway after his father's death. After only four years he returned in secret, vowing to claim the throne that he felt should be his.

On April 12, 1167, Knut surprised Karl at his palace in Visingsö and promptly murdered him. Karl's wife Kristina picked up her little son Sverker and ran for her life. After a frightful journey, she finally arrived in Denmark where she could find protection with her royal relatives.

Karl is buried in the Alvastra churchyard.

### Knut I Eriksson—ruled from 1167 to 1196.

*"King by God's grace."* This is how Knut Eriksson signed his royal letters. He believed in his divine appointment, and in his divine right to rule. The kings who followed him invariably used the same phrase and by it meant the same thing.

Knut Eriksson did not immediately reign over all of Sweden. Between 1167 and 1172, parts of Sweden were ruled by Kol and Burislev, sons of Sverker I. But this opposition to Knut was snuffed out around 1172. With both Kol and Burislev in their graves, Knut was able to take over the kingdom in its entirety by 1173.

After vanquishing most of the Sverker household, Knut made peace with the remaining members by formally adopting little Prince Sverker, whose father he had killed. Later, he let his adopted son share in the government of the nation.

Knut further strengthened his relations with the Sverkers by taking as his queen Cecilia, a niece of the king Karl Sverkersson whom he had assassinated. This probably did not seem strange to his people, who were descended from Viking marauders who often carried off the daughters or nieces of their victims.

According to some sources, Cecilia was a daughter of Sverker's son Burislev, and thus descended through his mother from the rulers of Poland. According to other sources, she was possibly the daughter of Sverker's rebellious son Johan. We tend to favor the view that she was Burislev's daughter, and we show her thus on Chart 28.

During Knut's long and important reign, the real power behind the throne was mainly wielded by Birger I Brosa, the great jarl who stood at his side as chief minister. (The office of "Jarl" in Sweden has often been compared to that of "Mayor of the Palace" in the Frankish kingdom.)

Birger strengthened Sweden's position by concluding economic treaties with other nations, and protected the country with forts, one of which developed into Stockholm. The currency system was developed, the army was strengthened, and the Church was organized.

Knut was killed at Eriksberg in Västergötland, and is buried at Varnhem. He and his wife Cecilia Burislevsdotter left four sons. One was Erik, later to become King Erik X. Three others were destined to perish in the battle of Algerås in 1205. They also had a daughter Sigrid, who was married to Magnus Broka of the Folkung family.

Because Birger Brosa (Knut's powerful jarl) and his kinfolk are the progenitors of many later kings of Sweden, we shall briefly interrupt the story of the Sverker and Erik dynasties in order to trace the Folkung family tree from which Birger sprung.

### Birger Brosa and his Family Roots

The Folkung family descended from Folke Filbyter, a somewhat legendary figure whose name may suggest booty.

Folke's sons were Ingevald, Ingemund, and Halsten. In the church-yard at Bjälbo in Östergötland, there is an ancient runic stone with Ingevald's name inscribed on it.

Ingevald's son was named for his paternal grandfather, Folke. As Folke Ingevaldsson grew, he became known as *Folke den Tjocke,* or Folke the Fat. He became jarl, or chief minister, to King Inge the Elder. His immense prestige and authority is revealed by the fact that he was married to a princess. (No commoner could have done that!) In fact, Folke the Fat was considered Sweden's most powerful man in his day.

We learn from Saxo that Folke Ingevaldsson's royal bride was Ingegerd Knutsdotter, the daughter of St. Knut, king of Denmark, and his Flemish wife Adela.

As we have previously noted, Ingegerd was not of pure Danish descent by any means. Since her grandfather was Robert le Frison, count of Flanders, she could trace her ancestry back to many kingly lines. Baldwin I of Flanders had married a daughter of Charles the Bald, so Ingegerd was descended from Karl the Great. Baldwin II of Flanders married a daughter of Alfred the Great, so Ingegerd was also a descendant of the Anglo-Saxon royal house. Another ancestor, Baldwin V, had married into the Capetian family, making her a descendant of Hugh Capet as well. And there was plenty of Bavarian and Saxon blood in her veins.

Through Ingegerd and her sister Cecilia, all these continental royal lines were brought into the Folkung family, and eventually into the Swedish monarchy. In this way, by the thirteenth century, the Swedish royal family (like so many other royal families of Europe) was directly descended from both Karl the Great and Alfred the Great.

Folke the Fat and his royal Danish bride had two sons: Bengt and Knut. They also had a daughter Inga, who was married to Asser Rig, one of the progenitors of the powerful Hvide family of Denmark.

Folke the Fat's claim to fame rests chiefly on his being the grandfather of the powerful Birger Brosa. His two sons did nothing remarkable during their lives other than the fact that one of them begat the famous Birger. It is usually assumed that Birger came from Bengt, although some historians (including Erik Olaus) speculate that he may have come from Knut.

Birger, grandson of Folke the Fat, was called *Brosa,* which means smiling. He is also called Birger I Jarl, to distinguish him from his nephew, who was Birger II Jarl. Birger Brosa had two brothers: Magnus Minnesköld *(remembrance/shield)* and Karl den Döve *(Karl the Deaf).* Both of these men were important in Swedish history, and we shall hear more of them later.

Birger Brosa, like his grandfather, married into royalty. His wife was Birgitta, the daughter of Harald Gille, king of Norway. She was a widow, having been married first (as we have noted) to Magnus Henriksson of Denmark, the man who assassinated Erik IX in 1160.

Birger and his wife Birgitta had three daughters and four sons: Filip, Knut, Folke and Magnus. Three of the sons became important jarls, so we shall give a little history about each one.

Filip Jarl Birgersson became jarl to King Sverre of Norway, as a result of a bargain his astute father made with that king. Filip was married and had a daughter, Katarina, who married Lars of Runby. Filip fell in battle about 1200.

Knut Jarl Birgersson had a daughter Cecilia who became a progenitor of the Aspenäs family line. Knut may have fallen at the battle of Lena in 1208; it is certain that he died in that year.

A third son of Birger Brosa—Folke Jarl Birgersson—fought alongside King Sverker II and died in the battle of Gestilren in 1210. Folke was survived by a son Sunne, who married Helena, daughter to King Sverker II. Sunne and Helena are to be found among the ancestors of the Swedish Svinhuvud family.

Birger Brosa's wife Birgitta, because of her Norwegian ancestry and Danish first marriage, had many contacts among the royalty of Norway and Denmark. Through her, Birger was able to have a great influence in the politics, not only of Sweden, but also of Sweden's neighbors.

As we have seen in the chapters on Norway, Birger's clout was so great that he had a say in choosing the kings of Norway.

With the powerful Birger Brosa backing him, Sverre of Norway was successful in taking the Norwegian crown away from Magnus Erlingsson.

The close ties between Sweden and Norway were further strengthened when King Knut of Sweden gave his sister Margaret in troth to Sverre in 1184. Perhaps Birger Brosa had a hand in this marriage relationship, which helped relations between these two countries.

Although there was peace with Norway during Knut's time, the Swedes continued to battle the pagans of Estonia and Livonia.

It is interesting to note that King Knut and his chief administrator were relatives. Both were descended from daughters of St. Knut of Denmark. The king could trace his ancestry to St. Knut's daughter Cecilia, and Birger Brosa could trace his family tree back to St. Knut's daughter Ingegerd.

### Sverker II Karlsson "the Younger"—ruled from 1196 to 1208.

*"I must destroy all the family of King Knut! Only thus can I keep the throne for myself."*

Although Knut I left surviving sons when he perished in 1196, after his reign the throne once again passed to a member of the Sverker family, the son of Knut's predecessor Karl. The transition was smooth because Knut—in an effort to pacify the Sverker family—had adopted young Sverker as a boy and made him co-regent. But as we shall see, Sverker showed little gratitude toward his foster father's family.

Again Birger Brosa served as the real power behind the throne, strengthening his position by marrying his daughter Ingegerd to Sverker II, the new king.

Ingegerd was Sverker II's second wife. His first wife—the mother of his children—was Benedikta Ebbesdotter. They had a daughter named Helena, who (as we have noted previously) was married to Sunne Folkesson. Later, Sunne turned against his father-in-law.

Quite possibly Sverker II and Benedikta also had a daughter named Kristina, who was married to Henry II of Rostock, and a daughter named Margaret, who was married to Wizlaw I of Rügen. There is some uncertainty about these two daughters.

Sverker II and Benedikta also had a son named Johan, who later became king of Sweden. (He should not be confused with the earlier Johan Sverkersson, that wild-oats-sowing prince who was the son of Sverker I.)

Under the firm hand of Birger Brosa, peace reigned between the lines of Sverker and Erik until Birger's death in 1202. After that, civil war broke out again. At least part of the problem was that Sverker II showered favors on the Church, exempting church lands from taxation. This made him unpopular with the nobles, who rebelled against him.

The breaking of peace between the Sverkers and the Eriks led to the battles of Algerås in 1205, Lena in 1208, and Gestilren in 1210.

Sverker II, in an effort to preserve the throne for his family, attempted to murder all of St. Erik's grandsons. He surprised Knut Eriksson's sons (his foster brothers) at Algarås in Västergötland, and managed to assassinate three of them. The eldest, who was named Erik after his grandfather, escaped to Norway.

Sverker's subjects were quite understandably enraged by his atrocities, and he was forced to flee to Denmark to the court of Valdemar II the Victorious, who helped him raise an army and a navy. By doing this, Valdemar may have hoped to add Sweden to his own dominions.

In 1208, the troops of Erik Knutsson (the surviving grandson of St. Erik) met the armies of Sverker II and Valdemar II at Lena in Västergötland. This was one of the bloodiest battles in Swedish history. As we have noted previously, Birger Brosa's son Knut probably fell in this terrible battle.

Erik Knuttson fought with all his might to avenge the deaths of his brothers. Sverker was defeated and Valdemar was forced to make peace with Erik. As part of the peace terms, Erik was given Valdemar's sister Rikissa. The Swedish throne then passed to Erik.

### Erik X Knutsson—ruled from 1208 to 1216.

*"The kings before me received the crown from the nobles. But I have been anointed and crowned by the Holy Church."*

After the battle of Lena, Erik was anointed and crowned at Uppsala, in the first known Swedish coronation by an archbishop. Pope Innocent III sanctioned the coronation and confirmed the king's right to wage crusades against Finland. Erik in turn increased the privileges of the clergy and bestowed part of the royal treasury upon convents.

Erik's reign was marked by troubled times. He led not only the battle of Lena in 1208, but also the battle of Gestilren in 1210. In both battles, he was fighting against his rival Sverker II as well as against Sverker's ally, Valdemar the Victorious of Denmark.

It was in the battle of Gestilren that Erik X's foe, the ex-king Sverker, was killed. It is said that Sverker's own son-in-law Sunne dealt him the death blow. In this battle Sunne was fighting against Sverker, while Sunne's father Folke was supporting the ex-king. Folke fell in the battle, and thus Sunne lost his father and his father-in-law all in one day. It is interesting to note that at least three of Birger Brosa's sons—Filip, Knut and Folke—met violent deaths in civil wars.

Erik's reign was marked by "crusades" against Finland, Estonia, and western Russia, in an attempt to conquer and convert the inhabitants.

As we have noted before, King Erik was promised the Danish princess Rikissa as part of a peace agreement. Their marriage provides an interesting picture of the ruggedness of the times. When Rikissa landed in Västergötland she expressed surprise that there was no carriage to take her to her bridegroom's royal court. The Swedish women who had been sent to attend her answered with asperity, "Our queens have never been too weak to ride horseback."

Erik X and his wife Rikissa Valdemarsdotter were both descended from Rikissa of Poland. Erik was the Polish princess' great-grandson, and his wife was her granddaughter, making the royal Swedish couple first cousins once removed.

Rikissa and Erik X had several daughters. Helena was married to Filip Larsson, who was killed at Herrevad Bridge in 1251. (That story is told on page 217.) Through Helena and Filip many noble Swedish families, including the Svinhuvud family, have descended. According to some genealogists, this was Helena's second marriage; she was married first of all to King Knut the Long who died in 1234. If this is true, we may well feel sorry for Helena, who lost two husbands to violent deaths.

Another daughter of Erik X—Ingeborg—was married to the famous Birger II Jarl who ruled Sweden behind the throne during the time of Erik XI. Yet another daughter—Sofia—was married to Henry III of Rostock. And a fourth daughter, Marta or Marianna, was also married and had many descendants.

Erik X died of consumption, after only eight years on the throne, and was buried at Varnhem. His only son was born posthumously. The boy was named Erik and is known either as Erik Eriksson or *Erik Läspe och Halte* meaning "the Lisping and Lame."

### Johan I Sverkersson—ruled from 1216 to 1222.

*"I know I'm very young, but at least I'm older than the son of Erik Knutsson! So I'm sure I'm better suited to the throne!"* Of course we can't look into the mind of Johan Sverkersson, but we can imagine that such thoughts may well have entered his head when he was made king.

When Erik X died, the throne was given once again to the Sverker family, even though Erik's widow wanted to claim the kingdom for the tiny son who had been born shortly after his father's death.

Johan Sverkersson ruled from 1216 to 1222. During most of this time, he was just a teenager. It is likely that he depended a great deal on his ecclesiastical advisors and on the kingdom's jarl. He increased the privileges of the clergy, and at the pope's request, he even undertook a crusade against the Estonians. In this he was aided by

Bishop Karl of Linköping (a brother to Birger II Jarl) and by Karl the Deaf (a brother to the deceased jarl, Birger Brosa). The crusade was a disaster. Johan, Karl the Deaf, and the bishop returned to Sweden in defeat.

At age 21, Johan, who never married, died childless. He passed away on March 10, 1222, at Visingsö and is buried at Alvastra.

With Johan's death, the male line of the *Sverkerska* dynasty came to an end. The family bloodline, however, continued through several female descendants of Sverker I, and thus many later monarchs could trace their ancestry to Sverker.

Throughout all these changes the office of jarl (roughly equivalent to that of prime minister) was held by a relative of Birger Brosa.

### Erik XI Eriksson "the Lame"—ruled from 1222 to 1229.
*"I may be handicapped, but I'll be the best king I can be!"*

Erik the Lisper and the Lame *(Erik Läspe och Halte)*, the posthumous son of Erik Knutsson, came to the throne in 1222, although he was still a minor (six years old). Of course, he was king only in name. The real power was in the hands of the Folkungs. Ulf Fasi (a son of Karl the Deaf) served as the kingdom's jarl.

Erik was apparently handicapped both in his speech and his gait. It was said of him that "he did somewhat lisp; and to limp also was his way."

Despite his disabilities, Erik the Lame grew up to be a strong king, beloved by the peasants and known for his fairness to all. After he became of age and was married, the Folkungs opposed Erik the Lame, fearing that he was taking too much power away from them. In 1229, they defeated him and named Knut the Long, a great-grandson of St. Erik, as king. Erik the Lame was forced to flee to Denmark.

### Knut II Holmgersson "the Long"—ruled from 1229 to 1234.
Knut's reign lasted only five years. During this time the Folkungs still exercised the primary leadership of the kingdom. Ulf Fasi, who had been Erik the Lame's jarl, continued to serve as Knut the Long's jarl.

Knut the Long's queen was named Helena. Although some historians tell us that she was a daughter of the Danish nobleman Peder Strangesens, Louda and McLagan list her as a daughter of King Erik X. Olaus Petri confirms this view. The sons of Knut the Long and his queen Helena were Holmger Knutsson and Filip Knutsson.

In 1234 Erik the Lame returned to Sweden with Danish allies and fought Knut the Long at Sparsätra. By this time, the Folkungs, like most other medieval families, were quarreling amongst themselves. Some sided with Knut, and others aided Erik the Lame, who with their help achieved the victory.

Knut the Long fell in the battle, and shortly afterward his son Holmger was put into prison to keep him from trying to get his father's throne. We believe Knut's widowed queen Helena was the same woman as the Helena who later married Filip Larsson, a noble executed at Herrevad Bridge in 1251. (That story will be told later in our narrative). Thus it seems that Helena lost both her husbands to violent deaths.

### Birger Jarl II and his Family Roots

Although Erik the Lame was once again on the throne of Sweden, the real power was still wielded by the Folkungs. Ulf Fasi, who had long served as jarl, died in 1247; and Birger Jarl replaced him

Here we will backtrack a bit to give some family background on Birger Jarl, one of medieval Sweden's most famous figures.

Birger Brosa, who died in 1202, had two brothers: Magnus Minnesköld and Karl the Deaf, who died in 1220. Karl the Deaf, as we have noted, is an ancestor of the Vasa family. Many illustrious kings, including Gustav Vasa, came from his line.

Magnus Minnesköld (brother to Birger Brosa and Karl the Deaf), lived at Bjälbo in Östergötland, and was married to Ingegerd Ylva. Their first son was born in 1210, and they named him Birger, after his uncle Birger Brosa. They perhaps never knew that he would become one of Sweden's most famous men, and the ancestor of royalty.

The other children of Magnus and Ingegerd also became famous. Their second son, named Karl after another uncle (Karl the Deaf), was made Bishop of Linköping, and helped King Johan fight in the crusade against Finland. A third son, Bengt, became a bishop as well as judge in Östergötland. A daughter of Magnus and Ingegerd, whose name was Magnhild, was married to Harved Ulf, the ancestor of Sweden's celebrated Trolle family.

Besides his children by Ingegerd, Magnus had a son named Eskil, born to a previous wife or concubine. Eskil became an important judge in Västergötland.

During the war between Erik the Lame and his second cousin Knut the Long, Birger Magnusson sided with Erik. As a reward for his service, he was given Erik's sister Ingeborg as his bride. Now he was related to the Erik family through his wife.

**Erik XI "the Lame" Eriksson—ruled again from 1234 to 1249.**
After Erik the Lame was securely settled for the second time in his kingdom, he turned to his brother-in-law and brother-at-arms—Birger Magnusson—and made him jarl. From this time on, Birger Magnusson was known as Birger Jarl. He is sometimes called Birger II Jarl, to distinguish him from his famous uncle Birger Brosa, who had also held the office of jarl. He is also known as Birger of Bjälbo.

Not only did Birger advise King Erik XI, but he also led the king's navy into war. He was successful in most of his battles against the Finns, and was even able to deal with the Danes in an iron-handed manner.

In Russia, however, Birger Jarl was less successful. In 1236, the pope persuaded the Swedes to lead a "crusade" against the Orthodox Christians of Russia. Although Birger Jarl had a large force with him, he was defeated by Alexander Nevski on the banks of the Neva River. Several of Birger Jarl's ships were sunk, and he was forced to retreat.

Erik the Lame had a wife—Katarina Sunnesdotter (a granddaughter of Sverker Karlsson)—but the couple had no sons. People began to suspect that Birger Jarl, being married to the king's sister, might have designs on the throne.

Most of the Folkungs did not want any one person to have too much power. In 1247 Birger Jarl's kinfolk turned against him, but he crushed their revolt.

When some inevitable border disputes arose between Sweden and Norway in the time of Erik the Lame, it was Birger Jarl who tried to solve them. In order to make peace, in 1251 he gave his own daughter Rikissa in marriage to Håkan, the son of King Håkan IV Håkansson of Norway. Sometime later, as we shall see, he got his son Valdemar married to the Danish princess Sofia. And after his first wife (Ingeborg) died, Birger married Matilda of Holstein, the widow of that Danish king Abel who had murdered his brother and then perished in battle.

In arranging all these marriages, Birger Jarl was not only acting as an ambassador trying to maintain good relations with other countries, but he was also trying to increase his own power by these fortuitous political alliances.

The ambitious Birger not only fulfilled the roles of ambassador, prime minister and chief justice, but he even made an attempt to assume ecclesiastical authority.

In 1248, Birger Jarl presided at a Swedish synod, and the following agreements were made between himself and a papal legate: celibacy was made binding upon Swedish clergy, ecclesiastics were forbidden to swear fealty to temporal rulers; and it was made clear that Swedish bishops should be appointed by the pope—not by the king.

In that same year, Holmger (the imprisoned son of Knut the Long) was executed; he is buried in the Sko monastery.

In 1249 Birger Jarl, moved by a plea from the pope, went with soldiers to Finland, subdued the natives, and forced those who were still pagan to accept Christianity. The historian Olaus Petri states, "Unto all who were willing to be baptized he granted both life and goods; unto the others he gave no peace."

The Swedish kings had been trying (mostly unsuccessfully) to subdue Finland for a whole century. Now, under the energetic Birger, the goal was reached, and Sweden temporarily controlled most of Finland.

On February 2, 1250, King Erik the Lame died; it was rumored that he was poisoned. He was properly buried in Varnhem, and his subjects, who perhaps loved him all the more because of his disabilities, mourned deeply. Olaus Petri gives the following tribute to him: "He was a pious and just man, and did justice upon one and all in the realm."

It is certain that Erik the Lame left no sons. According to some genealogical charts published in Sweden he did have a daughter Ingeborg, who was married to Johan I, duke of Saxony-Lauenburg. Lagerkvist, however, lists Erik the Lame as "possibly childless."

Birger Jarl—who had wielded the real power in Sweden all during the reign of Erik the Lame—was away in Finland when the king died. He hurried back, hoping to claim the throne for himself, but his thirteen-year-old son Valdemar had already been selected. Birger must not have been too unhappy with this arrangement, since as regent he was still able to wield most of the power from behind the throne.

With the death of Erik the Lisper and the Lame, the direct male line of the Erik dynasty died out. Many families of Sweden, however, are descended from Erik the Lame's sisters Helena, Ingeborg, and Marta. So the royal bloodline of the Eriks lives on to this day in countless Swedes and Swedish-Americans.

## CHART 28 - The Family of King Sverker I of Sweden

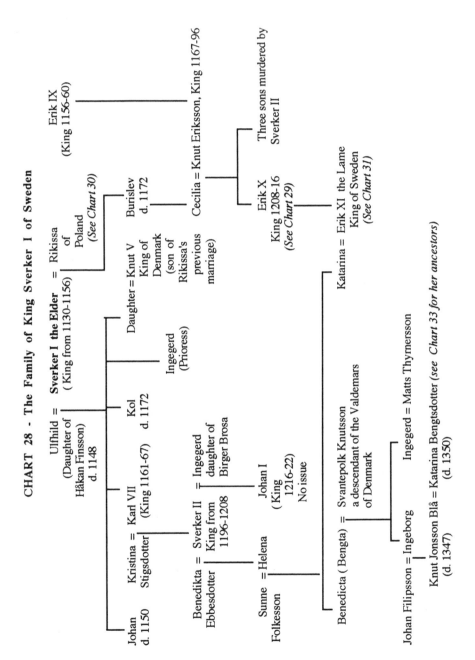

## CHART 29 - The Family of Jedvard Bonde and the Erikska Dynasty of Sweden

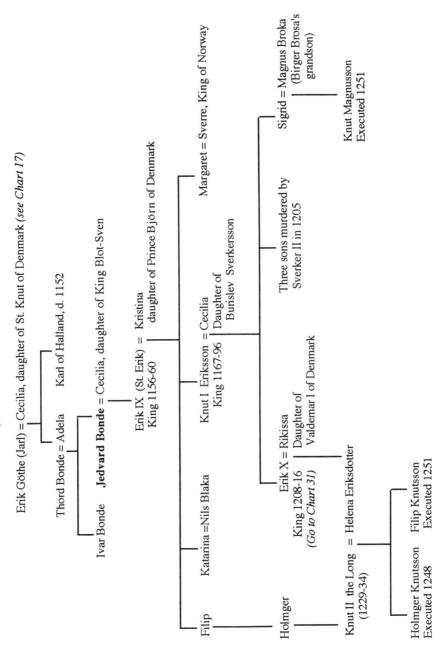

Erik Göthe (Jarl) = Cecilia, daughter of St. Knut of Denmark *(see Chart 17)*

Thord Bonde = Adela

Karl of Halland, d. 1152

Ivar Bonde

**Jedvard Bonde** = Cecilia, daughter of King Blot-Sven

Erik IX (St. Erik) = Kristina
King 1156-60    daughter of Prince Björn of Denmark

Margaret = Sverre, King of Norway

Knut I Eriksson = Cecilia
King 1167-96    Daughter of Burislev Sverkersson

Three sons murdered by Sverker II in 1205

Sigrid = Magnus Broka
(Birger Brosa's grandson)

Knut Magnusson
Executed 1251

Filip

Katarina = Nils Blaka

Holmger

Erik X = Rikissa
King 1208-16    Daughter of
*(Go to Chart 31)*    Valdemar I of Denmark

Knut II the Long = Helena Eriksdotter
(1229-34)

Holmger Knutsson
Executed 1248

Filip Knutsson
Executed 1251

# CHART 30- The Family of Rikissa Boleslavsdotter

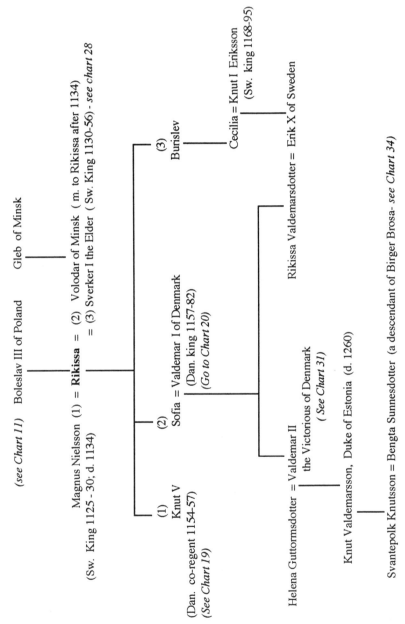

*(see Chart 11)*    Boleslav III of Poland    Gleb of Minsk

Magnus Nielsson (1) = **Rikissa** = (2)   Volodar of Minsk  ( m. to Rikissa after 1134)
(Sw. King 1125 - 30; d. 1134)                 = (3) Sverker I the Elder ( Sw. King 1130-56) - *see chart 28*

(1)                          (2)                                         (3)
Knut V                    Sofia = Valdemar I of Denmark        Burislev
(Dan. co-regent 1154-57)          (Dan. king 1157-82)
*(See Chart 19)*                  *(Go to Chart 20)*

Cecilia = Knut I Eriksson
              (Sw. king 1168-95)

Rikissa Valdemarsdotter = Erik X of Sweden

Helena Guttormsdotter = Valdemar II
                                  the Victorious of Denmark
                                  ( *See Chart 31*)

Knut Valdemarsson, Duke of Estonia  (d. 1260)

Svantepolk Knutsson = Bengta Sunnesdotter  (a descendant of Birger Brosa- *see Chart 34*)

## CHART 31 - The Family of Erik X of Sweden

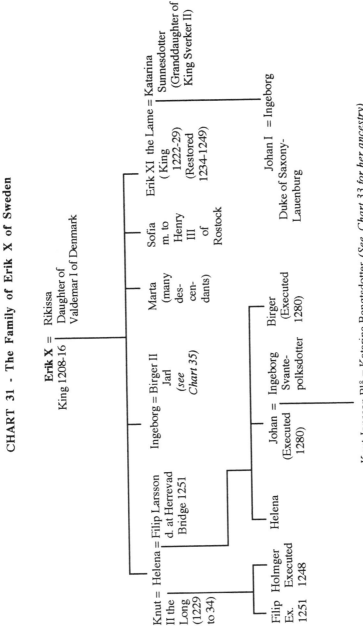

## Chapter 11

### The Folkung Dynasty of Sweden — 1250 to 1290

With the accession of Valdemar Birgersson, Sweden gained a new dynasty: the Folkungs. Of course, the Folkung kings were related to all the previous dynasties. Valdemar's grandfather was Erik X of the Erik line, and we may remember that both the competing Erik and Sverker families were descended from the same King Blot-Sven.

The Folkung family ruled Sweden for more than 100 years, from 1250 to 1364. The novelist and historian Vilhelm Moberg states:

*Murder and deeds of violence can occur exceptionally even in the best of families. But among the Folkungs they were an everyday affair. It is hardly too much to say the clan had a criminal heredity. Yes, the Folkungs were a family of criminals.*

#### Valdemar I Birgersson — ruled from 1250 to 1275.

*"Too bad I got my wife's sister into trouble. I had better make a pilgrimage to Rome to beg absolution from the pope."*

Prince Valdemar, as we have seen, was descended from both the Folkungs and the Erik family. (He was a nephew of Erik XI and a grandson of Erik X.)

Valdemar was crowned with magnificent pomp and ceremony in the Linköping Cathedral. (The Uppsala Cathedral had just burned down and had not yet been rebuilt.)

Valdemar's father, Birger Jarl, remained the real power behind the throne for many years. We may compare Birger Jarl to Mussolini of Italy, who was the *de facto* ruler, leaving the puppet "legitimate king" in the shadows.

Birger, having made one of his sons a king, strengthened his power still further by bestowing special titles on the others. His son Bengt was made a bishop, and later given the title of Duke of Finland. Another son, named Magnus, was given the title of Duke of the Svear. A fourth son, Erik, was made Duke of Småland. (It is interesting to note how the Swedish rulers by this time were bestowing the continental title of Duke upon their friends and relatives.)

Seeing how Birger was increasing his own power and that of his sons, his Folkung relatives grew envious and began to oppose him.

In 1251 a group of nobles, all members of the powerful Folkung family, revolted against the government. At the Battle of Herrevad Bridge in Västmanland, near where the Kölbeck River flows into Lake Mälaren, Birger Jarl crushed his opponents.

The forces of Birger Jarl were gathered on one side of the river, and those of the rebelling Folkungs on the other. For a while, neither army dared cross the bridge. At last, Birger Jarl sent a bishop across the bridge as an ambassador, promising the Folkung leaders full amnesty if they would come and talk to him.

As soon as the Folkungs crossed the bridge, the treacherous Birger Jarl threw his promises to the winds and ordered that the leaders be executed at once.

Birger's victims were, of course, mostly his cousins in varying degrees. One of those executed was Filip Knutsson, a son of King Knut the Long. Another was Knut Magnusson, son of Magnus Broka, and great-grandson of Birger Brosa. Still another was Filip Larsson, a son of Lars of Runby, and a great-grandson of Birger Brosa. Filip Larsson, who we believe was married to Knut the Long's widow (Helena, daughter of Erik X), left a daughter Helena and two sons: Johan and Birger.

The archbishop of Uppsala, hearing of Birger Jarl's double-dealing, imposed a heavy penance on him for perjury. The bishop who had acted as ambassador felt such remorse over his minor part in the scandal that he undertook a pilgrimage to the Holy Land, where he died.

When his son Valdemar reached the age of twenty, Birger Jarl arranged for him to be married to the Danish princess Sofia. By this marriage, he hoped to increase his son's (and his own) power.

The bride's maternal grandfather, Albrecht Duke of Brunswick, chaperoned her journey to Sweden, where she and Valdemar were married in magnificent style in Jönköping, in a new hall built precisely for the wedding.

Valdemar and his wife Sofia had five daughters and a son. Their daughter Ingeborg was married to Gerhard II, Count of Holstein. A second daughter was named Katarina, and a third girl, named Rikissa, was married to Przemyslav of Poland. A fourth daughter, Marina, was married to Rudolph of Diepholz, and a fifth girl, Margaret, became a nun. Valdemar and Sofia's only son, Erik, was married to Ingeborg Knutsdotter of the Folkung-related Aspenäs family.

Valdemar had three wives besides Sofia. None of them, as far as we know, bore him any children. His second wife was Kristina of Denmark, his third was Katarina of Gütskov, and the fourth and last was named Lucrardis. One historian has said that it was easier for Valdemar to live without a crown than without a woman.

Not to be outdone by his son, Birger himself entered into an advantageous second marriage. His new wife was Matilda (sometimes called Mechtild), the widow of Abel, king of Denmark.

While he ruled, Birger Jarl held the kingdom together with his strong hand, made peace with neighboring countries and crushed his opposition at home. Consequently, there was peace in his time.

Birger and his half brother Eskil were masterful judges. Birger was also a lawgiver who wrote statutes prohibiting the kidnapping of a bride and guaranteeing public safety. Some of his laws state:

*If one goes to the home of another and does harm to him, his household or guests, he has broken the king's oath. If a man takes a woman by force, he has broken the oath. If a man sits in ambush upon the way to business or church and slays someone or injures him in a blood feud, he has broken the oath.*

Before Birger's time, a woman received an inheritance only if there were no male heirs; if there were a man left alive in the family, she got nothing. Birger changed all this by giving daughters a half share, and sons a full share, in a family inheritance. His law stated: "A son and a daughter are the father's heirs; the son shall receive two lots and the daughter one lot." This was the law until 1845 when sister and brother received equal shares.

Birger also prohibited blood feuds between families and outlawed *järnbörd*, the old custom of trial by walking over hot plowshares to prove one's truthfulness or innocence. (In Norway, King Harald Gille had undergone this type of trial in an effort to prove his royal paternity.)

Birger Jarl established homes for students in Paris, Bologne, Prague and Leipzig, and gave scholarships to worthy students.

Birger is also credited with establishing Stockholm. When Sigtuna was destroyed, Stockholm's site plan was laid out.

Birger Jarl died at last on October 21, 1266. He was buried beside his first wife, Ingeborg, a daughter of King Erik X Knutsson. Both old and young, including the women whom Birger Jarl had sheltered and helped, bowed in deep sorrow and prayed for his soul.

Sweden's political climate changed after Birger's death, and strife broke out once again in the royal family.

Birger's son Valdemar, a womanizer, was a weak and worthless king. While married to the Princess Sofia, he had a love affair with her sister, a nun named Jutta. As a result of this affair, Jutta bore a son to Valdemar. The Lejonhuvud family (including the wife of Gustav Vasa who bore Karl IX to him) is descended from this illegitimate prince. According to one of the sixteenth-century Danish historians, Jutta also bore a second child to Valdemar—a daughter named Sofia.

In the eyes of the Church and the people, adultery with a nun was considered a far more serious offence than murder. In 1274, Valdemar made a pilgrimage to Rome, hoping to obtain forgiveness from the pope himself.

While Valdemar was away, his brothers Erik and Magnus ruled the kingdom. When Valdemar returned, the two brothers were unwilling to hand the realm back to him. The next year, with troops and revenue provided by Denmark, Erik and Magnus revolted against Valdemar. They overthrew and deposed him at Hova in Västergötland in 1275.

## Magnus III "Ladulås" Birgerssson—ruled from 1275 to 1290.

*"Peasants, lock your barns! No longer will you be required to provide sustenance for the nobles when they move from estate to estate."* This law gave Magnus his surname, *Ladulås*, or Barnlock.

After Valdemar was deposed, his brother Magnus was elected king, and his brother Erik became Duke of the Svear.

Valdemar was forced into exile. He found refuge first in Norway and later in Denmark. He returned to Sweden in 1288, but was unable to get back his crown. Instead, he was captured by his brother and lived out his remaining days as a prisoner in the castle of Nyköping where he died in 1302. Although Valdemar left a legitimate son named Erik, the lad never attempted to gain his father's throne. He probably realized that any attempt of that sort would cost him either his life, or else his liberty.

Soon after becoming king, Magnus Birgersson was married to Hedwig, a daughter of Count Gerhard I of Holstein. Through his wife's connections, Magnus invited many nobles from the Continent to his court, and in this way the ties between Sweden and the nations to the south were strengthened.

Magnus Birgersson inherited his father's strong qualities. Not for him the life of a puppet king standing in the shadows of a jarl! He would not even name a jarl to help him govern the kingdom; and after his father, no Swede ever again bore that title in the royal court.

Magnus assumed more power than any of the kings before him, forbidding the nobles and ecclesiastics to meet in councils without his approval, and issuing decrees on his own authority alone.

Magnus sought to copy the feudal customs of central Europe. He granted fiefs to his friends, and in 1280 made a law stating that anyone who served as a mounted knight to the king, the barons, or the bishops was to be free from taxes. Naturally, the more wealthy people who owned horses could discharge this duty, while the poor could not. Thus the nobility prospered more than ever.

Magnus kept a splendid court. He was basically a peaceful ruler. However, dangerous rivals to his throne still existed and he was ready to withstand any attempt at treason.

Filip Larsson had been executed in 1251. Now his sons Johan and Birger Filipsson joined a revolt against King Magnus. Their actions support the view that their mother Helena was indeed a daughter of King Erik X, for it seems they felt they had a claim to the throne through her.

In 1280, Johan and Birger were executed by royal order. Johan, however, did not die without heirs. His son Knut Jonsson Blå married Katarina Bengtsdotter, a great-granddaughter of Bengt Magnusson, the bishop of Linköping who was a brother to Birger Jarl. Knut Jonsson Blå and his wife became ancestors of the notable Svinhuvud family; and thus today many descendants of the executed Johan Filipsson are to be found both in Sweden and in America.

In all this we see the treachery of family member against family member. King Magnus was a grandnephew of Birger Brosa and thus was executing his own cousins.

Magnus and his wife Hedwig had two daughters—Ingeborg and Rikissa—as well as three sons: Birger, Erik and Valdemar.

Magnus pulled strings so that Rikissa could become an abbess. For his other children, he arranged advantageous marriages. His son Birger was married to Marta, a daughter of King Erik Glipping of Denmark. Then Birger was crowned and appointed *Rismarksken* or Earl Marshall, a new title which corresponded roughly to the old office of Jarl.

Magnus also arranged for his other sons—Erik and Valdemar—to be named dukes of different parts of his kingdom, and he gave his daughter Ingeborg as a bride to King Erik Menved of Denmark.

Magnus died in 1290 and was buried in the new Franciscan church he had founded on the island of Riddarholm to the west of Stockholm. Birger Magnusson took his father's place as king.

Much more could be said about Birger Magnusson's treachery toward his two brothers (he invited them for Christmas and then clapped them into a dungeon at Norköping Castle), about the beheading of his son Magnus, and about his own ignominious death, but we have come to 1290, where we promised to end this story.

We have attempted to show the many different royal lines which met in Sweden by this time. The brothers Valdemar and Magnus III could trace their roots to the *Erikska* family, and back from St. Erik to Blot-Sven. Through Blot-Sven's wife they were possibly descended from Stenkil, and through Stenkil's wife their roots went back to the legendary *Ivarska* line of kings.

Valdemar and Magnus III were also descended from the Polish royal family, the dukes of Bohemia, the Russian princes of Kiev, and the emperors of Byzantium.

Through their Folkung ancestors they were descended from the kings of Denmark, as well as from the early counts of Flanders, from the kings of Norway, from Hugh Capet of France, from Alfred the Great of England, and from Karl the Great, King of the Franks. Back beyond Karl the Great were (quite possibly) some rather shadowy Merovingian ancestors and the even more shadowy Visigothic kings of Spain who had given their daughters to the Merovingian kings of the Franks.

Now, long centuries later, the descendants of all these lines could be found in Sweden—no longer roving Vikings, but medieval kings full of pomp and glory, and related to all the royal families of the Continent.

## CHART 32 - The Family of Folke Filbyter

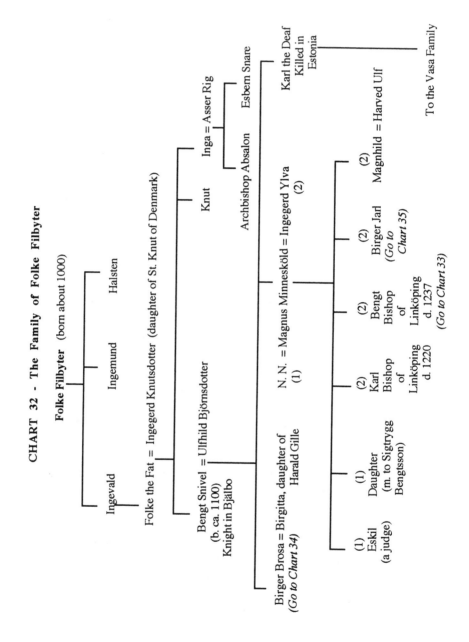

## CHART 33 - The Family of Bengt Magnusson, Bishop of Linköping

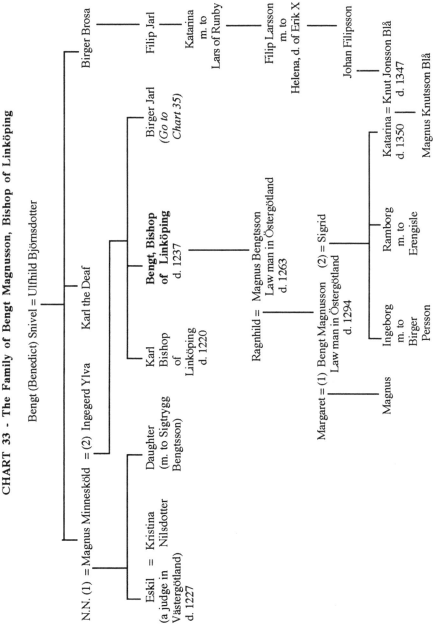

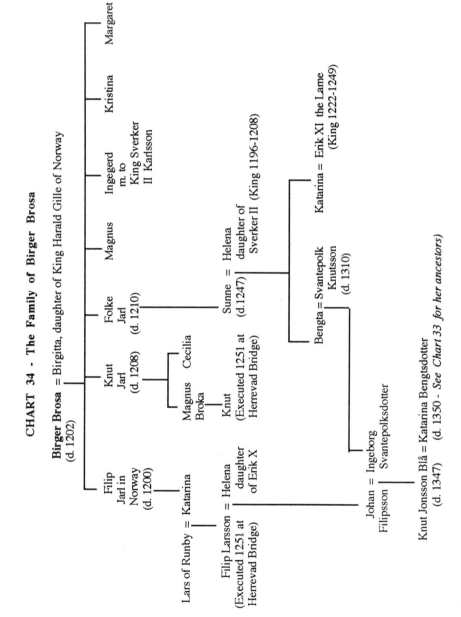

CHART 34 - The Family of Birger Brosa

Birger Brosa = Birgitta, daughter of King Harald Gille of Norway
(d. 1202)

## CHART 35 - The Family of Birger Jarl

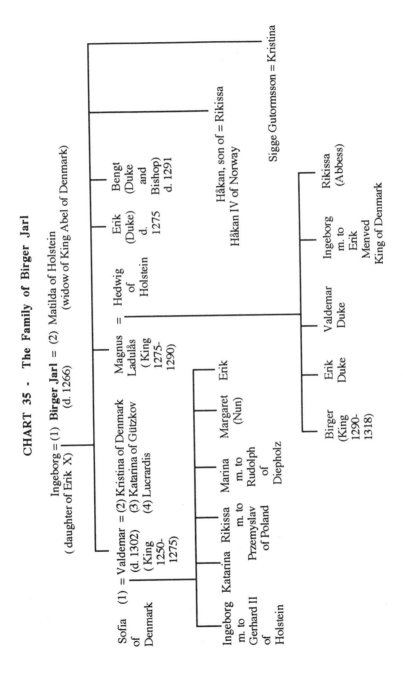

# Bibliography

Adam of Bremen, *History of the Archbishops of Hamburg-Bremen* (Translated by Francis J. Tschan). New York, Columbia University Press, 1959.

Andersson, Ingvar, *A History of Sweden*. New York, Praeger, 1956.

Asimov, Isaac. *The Shaping of England*. Boston, Houghton Mifflin, 1969.

Baum, Franz H. *Medieval Civilization in Germany*, New York, Praeger.

Brønsted, Johannes. *The Vikings* (Translated by Kalle Skov). New York, Penguin, 1965.

Brønsted, Johannes, *et. al. Kultur Historik Leksikon For Nordisk Middealder*, Copenhagen, 1959.

Bukdahl, Jørgen, *et. al. Scandinavia Past and Present*. Edvard Henriksen, Arnkrone.

Butler, Ewen. *The Horizon Concise History of Scandinavia*. American Heritage, 1973.

*Cambridge Medieval History*. Cambridge University Press, 1968.

Danstrup, John. *A History of Denmark* (Translated by Verner Lindberg). Copenhagen, 1948.

Deanesly, Margaret. *A History of Early Medieval Europe, 476 to 911*. New York, Barnes and Noble, 1956.

Dyboski, Roman. *Outlines of Polish History*. Oxford University Press.

Fryxell, Anders, *The History of Sweden*. (Edited by Mary Howitt). London, Richard Bentley, 1844.

Ganshof, François L. *La Flandre sous les Premiers Comtes*. Brussels, La Renaissance du Livre, 1949.

Gertz, M. C. (ed.). *Vitae Sanctorum Danorum*. Copenhagen, 1908-12.

Gieysztor, A. *History of Poland*. Warsaw, Polish Scientific Publishers, 1968.

Gjerset, Knut. *History of the Norwegian People*. Volume 1. New York, 1915.

Häger, Mats. *Familje Register*. Sweden (privately printed), 1994.

Halecki, O. *History of Poland*. New York, Roy Publishers, 1956.

Jägerstad, Hans. *Sverige's Historia i Årtal*. Falköping, 1964.

Jones, Gwyn. *A History of the Vikings*. Oxford University Press, 1984.

Lagerqvist, L. O. *Litet Lexicon över Sveriges Regenter*. Sweden, 1994.

Lauring, Palle. *A History of the Kingdom of Denmark* (Translated from the Danish by David Hehnen). Høst and Sons, Copenhagen, 1960.

Linklater, Eric. *The Conquest of England*. New York, Doubleday, 1966.

Lodge, Henry Cabot. *The History of Nations*. New York, Collier, 1936.

Louda, Jiri, and McLagan, Michael. *Lines of Succession: Heraldry of the Royal Families of Europe*. New York, Macmillan, 1991.

Lyon, Bryce D. *The High Middle Ages*, New York, Collier-Macmillan, 1964.

Magnus, Johannes. *Historia de Ominibus Gothorum Sueonumque Regibus*. Rome, 1555 (currently available on microfilm).

Magnus, Olaus. *Historia de Gentibus Septentrionalibus*.Rome, 1555 (currently available on microfilm).

Moberg, Vilhelm. *A History of the Swedish People*. Pantheon, 1972.

Oakley, Stewart. *A Short History of Denmark*. New York, Praeger, 1972

Oakley, Stewart. *A Short History of Sweden*. New York, Praeger, 1966.

Ohlmarks, Åke. *Stamträd över Europas Furstehus*. n. d.

Oxenstierna, Eric. *The Norsemen* (Translated and edited by Catherine Hutter). New York Graphic Society Publishers, 1965.

Pares, Bernard. *A History of Russia*. New York, Dorset, 1991.

Reddaway, W. F. *et. al. The Cambridge History of Poland*. Cambridge University Press, 1950.

Roesdahl, Else. *The Vikings* (Translated by Susan M. Margeson and Kirsten Williams). New York, Penguin, 1987.

Saxo Grammaticus, *The Nine Books of the Danish History of Saxo Grammaticus* (Translated by Oliver Elton). The Norroena Society, 1905.

Scott, Franklin D. *Scandinavia*. Harvard University Press, 1975.

Scott, Franklin D. *Sweden: The Nation's History*, University of Minnesota Press, 1977.

*Scriptores Rerum Svecicarum Medii Aevi*. Graz, Austria. 1966. (Includes the *Chronica* of Erik Olaus, *The Life of St. Ansgar* by Rimbert, and other historical documents.)

Stromberg, *History of Sweden*. New York, MacMillan, 1931.

Sturlusson, Snorri. *History of the Kings of Norway*. Translated by Lee Hollander. Austin, The University of Texas Press, 1991.

Thorndike, Lynn. *The History of Medieval Europe*. Boston, Houghton Mifflin, 1956.

Weis, Frederick Lewis. *Ancestral Roots of Sixty Colonists*. Genealogical Publishing Company, 1979.

Whitelock, Dorothy (translator), *The Anglo-Saxon Chronicle*, Rutgers University Press, 1961.

Wojciechowski, Zygmunt, *Mieszko I and the Rise of the Polish State*. Torun, 1936.

# Index to the Principal Persons Mentioned in the Narrative and/or on the Genealogical Charts